The Book of Common Prayer

Guides to Sacred Texts

What is a sacred text? The *Oxford English Dictionary* offers a definition of "sacred" as "Set apart for or dedicated to some religious purpose, and hence entitled to veneration or religious respect." The definition is necessarily vague. What does it mean to be "set apart?" What constitutes a "religious purpose?" How formal is "veneration?" Does minimal "religious respect" qualify? The sphere of meanings surrounding the word "sacred" will depend on the religion involved. For that reason "sacred texts" in this series is a term conceived broadly. All of the texts covered by this series have held special regard—they have been "set apart"—in a religion either ancient or modern. Such texts are generally accorded more serious attention than other religious documents. In some cases the texts may be believed to be the words of a deity. In other cases the texts may be part of an atheistic religion. This breadth of application indicates the rationale behind Guides to Sacred Texts.

This series offers brief, accessible introductions to sacred texts, written by experts upon them. While allowing for the individuality of each text, the series follows a basic format of introducing the text in terms of its dates of composition, traditions of authorship and assessment of those traditions, the extent of the text, and the issues raised by the text. For scripture that continues to be utilized, those issues will likely continue to generate controversy and discussion among adherents to the text. For texts from religions no longer practiced, the issues may well continue to address concerns of the present day, despite the antiquity of the scripture. These volumes are useful for introducing sacred writings from around the world to readers wanting to learn what these sacred texts are.

The Book of Common Prayer

A Guide

CHARLES HEFLING

OXFORD
UNIVERSITY PRESS

OXFORD
UNIVERSITY PRESS

Oxford University Press is a department of the University of Oxford. It furthers
the University's objective of excellence in research, scholarship, and education
by publishing worldwide. Oxford is a registered trade mark of Oxford University
Press in the UK and certain other countries.

Published in the United States of America by Oxford University Press
198 Madison Avenue, New York, NY 10016, United States of America.

Library of Congress Cataloging-in-Publication Data
Names: Hefling, Charles, 1949– author.
Title: The book of common prayer : a guide / Charles Hefling.
Description: New York , NY, United States of America: Oxford University Press, 2021. |
Series: Guides to sacred texts |
Includes bibliographical references and index.
Identifiers: LCCN 2020018761 (print) | LCCN 2020018762 (ebook) |
ISBN 9780190689681 (hardback) | ISBN 9780190689698 (paperback) |
ISBN 9780190689711 (epub) | ISBN 9780190689704 | ISBN 9780190689728
Subjects: LCSH: Church of England. Book of common prayer. |
Anglican Communion—Liturgy—Texts—History.
Classification: LCC BX5145 .H44 2020 (print) | LCC BX5145 (ebook) |
DDC 264/.03—dc23
LC record available at https://lccn.loc.gov/2020018761
LC ebook record available at https://lccn.loc.gov/2020018762

1 3 5 7 9 8 6 4 2

Paperback printed by LSC Communications, United States of America
Hardback printed by Bridgeport National Bindery, Inc., United States of America

Contents

III. CONTEXTS

Illustrations

Acknowledgments

Librarians commonly bring up the rear in the parade of an author's acknowledgments. They should come first. This book owes a very great debt to the Sherrill Library at the Episcopal Divinity School in Cambridge, now sadly dismantled, and to Aura Fluet and Anne-Marie Mulligan in particular. First-hand evidence proves beyond cavil that Anne Kenny and the staff of the Interlibrary Loan department in the O'Neill Library at Boston College are as infallible as they are indefatigable. The Beinecke Rare Books Library at Yale University routinely and cheerfully performs works of supererogation.

Were it not for Donald Kraus, its onlie begetter, and Steve Wiggins, both at Oxford University Press, this book would not have been started, let alone completed. Were it not for Cynthia Shattuck, it would never have been thought of.

Abbreviations

Brightman, *English Rite*   F. E. Brightman, *The English Rite: Being a Synopsis of the Sources and Revisions of the Book of Common Prayer.* Two volumes, continuously paginated. London: Rivingtons, 1915.

But One Use   *But One Use: An Exhibition Commemorating the 450th Anniversary of the Book of Common Prayer.* New York: St. Mark's Library, The General Theological Seminary, 1999.

Cardwell, *Conferences*   Edward Cardwell, *A History of Conferences and Other Proceedings connected with the Revision of the Book of Common Prayer from the Year 1558 to the Year 1690.* 2nd ed. Oxford: Oxford University Press, 1891.

Cardwell, *Annals*   Edward Cardwell, *Documentary Annals of the Reformed Church of England . . . from the Year 1546 to the Year 1716; with Notes Historical and Explanatory.* New ed., 2 vols. Oxford: Oxford University Press, 1844.

Griffiths, *Bibliography*   David N. Griffiths, ed., *The Bibliography of the Book of Common Prayer 1549–1999.* London: The British Library; New Castle, DE: Oak Knoll Press, 2002.

OGBCP   Charles Hefling and Cynthia Shattuck, eds., *The Oxford Guide to the Book of Common Prayer: A Worldwide Survey.* Oxford: Oxford University Press, 2006.

OHA   Rowan Strong, general ed., *The Oxford History of Anglicanism.* Five volumes.

	Oxford: Oxford University Press, 2017–2018.
OHAS	Mark D. Chapman, Sathianathan Clarke, and Martyn Percy, eds., *The Oxford Handbook of Anglican Studies*. Oxford: Oxford University Press, 2016.
OWC	Brian Cummings, ed. *The Book of Common Prayer: The Texts of 1549, 1559, and 1662*. Oxford World Classics. Oxford: Oxford University Press, 2011.
Prayer Book Dictionary	George Harford and Morley Stevenson, eds., *The Prayer Book Dictionary*. London: Pitman, 1912.
Ratcliff, *Eighty Illustrations*	Edward C. Ratcliff, *The Booke of Common Prayer of the Churche of England: Its Making and Revisions M.D.xlix.—M.D.clxi. Set Forth in Eighty Illustrations*. London: SPCK, 1949.
STC	A. W. Pollard and G. R. Redgrave, *A Short Title Catalogue of Books Printed in England, Scotland, & Ireland . . . 1475–1640*. 2nd ed. London: Bibliographical Society, 1976
Thompson, *Liturgies*	Bard Thompson, ed., *Liturgies of the Western Church*. 1961; Philadelphia: Fortress Press, 1980.
Wing	Donald Wing, *A Short-Title Catalogue of Books Printed in England, Scotland, Ireland, Wales, and British America . . . 1641–1700*. 2nd ed. New York: Modern Language Association of America, 1972.

Introduction

Sacred texts are sacred for different reasons. Some are believed to have a transcendent source; their teaching or message comes from God or the gods, through a godly oracle or an inspired prophet. The Book of Common Prayer is not one of these. It is in the first instance a practical book, sacred in that it informs sacred practice. To use it is to worship. More specifically, it is to bring about and take part in the events of corporate religious devotion that go by the name of *liturgy*.

A liturgy is something like a stage play. Both are public events, enacted by a number of individuals, who cooperate in the enactment by performing various roles that are dictated by a text. As the word *play* can mean either what is written by a playwright or what happens on stage, so *liturgy* may refer to a prescribed occurrence of a religious practice or to the writing that prescribes it. In both cases, a written text, reproduced in multiple copies, makes it possible for the same play or the same liturgy to be performed again and again by different persons in different places. The analogy is far from perfect, and it can be badly misleading, but it holds inasmuch as the Book of Common Prayer is something like the script for a play. Better, it is a collection of scripts for a repertoire of formal, corporate acts of worship.

As in a playbook, the prescriptive words in the Prayer Book are of two main kinds. Most of the text consists of speeches, meant to be uttered aloud. Some of it gives instructions. There are stage directions as it were, which assign the speeches, tell the speakers

The Book of Common Prayer. Charles Hefling, Oxford University Press (2021). © Oxford University Press.
DOI: 10.1093/oso/9780190689681.001.0001.

what they are to do, specify the costumes, props, and scenery that should be used, and so on. As when a play is staged, so also when liturgy is performed, the performance actualizes the meaning of printed words which, as printed, are only potentially meaningful. Every actual liturgy, like every production of a drama, is an interpretation of the text that prescribes it.

The speech that the Book of Common Prayer calls for is partly addressed to God and partly to the worshipers who are taking part in a liturgy. In some speeches, language is used to pray, to praise and confess, to give thanks and make requests. In others, it is used to greet and exhort, narrate and instruct, warn and affirm. The scripts order and combine these various discourses to form *services* or *offices*, terms that connote duty, an ongoing task defined and assigned by some authority. The ultimate authority for the contents of the Book of Common Prayer, on its own showing, is God, while the proximate authority is a church. The text presupposes that Christian people have an obligation to worship their God together, regularly and publicly, and that it belongs to the church, the community of Christian belief and practice in its institutional aspect, to define this duty, by regulating the form and matter of common prayer. That is what the Prayer Book does.

The particular church, or family of churches, with which the Book of Common Prayer has been identified from its inception is now known as *Anglican*. The name points to a connection with England, and it was for England's national church that the Prayer Book was originally compiled. By adopting this text, imposing it, and using it, the Church of England has in part defined itself. The Book of Common Prayer is one of its foundational texts, and it has been a primary means by which the Anglican variety of Christianity, as embodied in liturgical practice, has spread to churches all over the world.[1]

---

[1] See Appendix 2, The Anglican Communion.

In the words of that book millions of people have recognized and given voice to their joys and longings, their failures and aspirations, their grief and gratitude. By using that book they have found in their human journey from birth to burial a meaning that is more than human. One mark of a sacred text is that it may "become the author (or at least joint-author) of the stories that people tell through their lives and histories."[2] That is perhaps the most important sense in which the Book of Common Prayer has functioned as a sacred text.

Overview

Liturgical worship in general, and the services of the Book of Common Prayer in particular, are less familiar now than perhaps they used to be. There was a time when Prayer Book phrases were threads in the fabric of a widely shared cultural heritage. But times change. This book does not assume any acquaintance with the text it expounds.

Except when notice is given to the contrary, the text expounded here will be the one that can most appropriately be called *the* Book of Common Prayer. There have been, and are now, a number of other texts with the same title—ancestors, descendants, and cousins, so to say, of the English liturgy published in 1662, which is commonly regarded as the Prayer Book par excellence and will be so regarded in this guide. It is still in print and still, for the Church of England, authoritative.

Of the various liturgies for which this "classical" Prayer Book provides a script, some have taken place more frequently than others. By way of introducing all of them, the first chapter here will describe one service in some detail. Taking the whole history of the Book of Common Prayer into account, this service is the one that

---

[2] John Bowker, *The Message and the Book: Sacred Texts of the World's Religions* (New Haven, CT: Yale University Press, 2011), 3.

has been conducted more often, and experienced by more people, on more occasions, than any other. In that sense it may claim to be the typical event of Anglican worship. The chapter that describes it will explain, along the way, some of the most important specialized terms used thereafter.

The next three chapters examine the other texts in the Prayer Book—its less frequently performed offices, its self-presentation, and the rules that structure its intimate, complex relation to Christianity's most sacred text, the Bible.

Chapter five is concerned with origins, in a particular sense. In 1549, when the Book of Common Prayer was first issued, it was at once a product and an instrument of the upheaval in western Christianity known as the Reformation. Especially relevant in that regard is one of its liturgical texts, the order for celebrating the Lord's Supper or Holy Communion. The Prayer Book has always been a contested document, but its Communion service more than any other has been a site of contestation. The form this service takes in the definitive Prayer Book of 1662 differs from the original text, which was revised substantially after a three-year tryout. Because the revisions are important for understanding the purpose and meaning of the whole liturgy, chapter five offers an account of what was revised and why.

The next five chapters, six through ten, trace a narrative arc with 1662 at its midpoint. Chapters six and seven are concerned with the events of the previous hundred years, during which time the Book of Common Prayer was imposed, assimilated, attacked, defended, exported, and for a while abolished. Chapter eight tells how in 1662 the book was at length established, in two senses: the text was issued in what turned out to be, in England, its final form; and it was (re)incorporated into the law of the land by an Act of Parliament which from then on defined its wording and governed its use. The two chapters that follow survey the Prayer Book's fortunes since 1662. Chapter nine gives special attention to a line of development outside the Church of England which made its way to the modified Book of Common

Prayer adopted in the United States. Chapter ten recounts the gradual displacement of the classical text as the norm of Anglican liturgy.

Two concluding chapters consider the Prayer Book text in two specialized contexts, visual and aural—as it has been seen, embodied in print, and as it has been heard, set to music. In different ways, how the words look on the page and how they sound when they are voiced both have a bearing on how they mean what they have meant and how they have been received and appropriated.

Books about the Book of Common Prayer are many, and each, in its own way, is selective. This one is too. Many things that could be said are left, regrettably, unsaid here. Three may be mentioned. The Prayer Book did not generate the practice it regulates; its services have roots in a long, rich tradition of Christian liturgy. It is not only a religious book; its text is commonly acclaimed as a monument and treasure of English prose. And its influence has not been limited to Anglican churches, or to its classical form; the Book of Common Prayer has given rise to a profusion of translations, adaptations, remakes, and substitutes that could perhaps be regarded as its functional equivalents. All these topics are well worth exploring, and can be explored elsewhere.[3] Here, there is only so much space.

Conventions and Terminology

The Book of Common Prayer is in several ways an in-house document. It presumes that users, particularly those who organize its services and preside at them, know what sort of thing happens in

---

[3] Starting points: Francis Procter and Walter Howard Frere, *A New History of the Book of Common Prayer* (London: Macmillan and Co., 1951), ch. 1; Stella Brook, *The Language of the Book of Common Prayer* (Oxford: Oxford University Press, 1965); and *OGBCP*, 229–444.

Christian liturgy and that they have some familiarity with a special vocabulary. Terms that are essential for understanding the text will be explained here as they come up, especially in the first chapter. *Service* and *office* have been mentioned. A few others should be explained in advance.

The full title of the Book of Common Prayer uses the words *rites* and *ceremonies*, apparently with the same meaning. Professional liturgists, however, prefer to use *rites* for stated forms of corporate religious practice, as distinct from *ceremonies*, which are meaningful but nonverbal actions. This book will observe the distinction, though not very rigorously. Here, a rite is a service of worship as prescribed or the form of words that prescribes it; a ritual consists of ceremonial activity as performed; and a ritualist is someone for whom ceremonies are a high priority.

Rubric is a convenient name for printed liturgical instructions, which may be single words or extended paragraphs. They usually stipulate and organize what is to be said or sung, but no one ever sings or says them. The Prayer Book itself almost never uses the term *rubric*, and it is somewhat misleading, inasmuch as it implies that the print it refers to is red (in Latin, *ruber*). That is rarely the case, but there is always some kind of typographical differentiation between these directions and texts meant to be uttered.

The word *edition* is used here as bibliographers use it. An edition is the whole number of copies printed from the same setting of a text in type, corrections excepted. By extension, *edition* may also refer to the (correct) sequence of words printed in those copies. Either way, what is meant in this book by an edition of the Book of Common Prayer must be clearly distinguished from what is meant by a *version*. Different editions print the same words differently: different versions print different words. From time to time, the text of the Prayer Book has been revised significantly; the original form and the successive revisions are here termed versions. Any one version may exist, and usually does, in a number of editions that vary in physical dimensions, number of pages, layout, typography, and so on, while the wording remains constant. The entries in the standard bibliography of the Book of Common Prayer are editions in that sense, listed chronologically by year of publication.[4] Versions as well as editions are sometimes identified by year, but the context will always make it clear which is which. Four of the most important versions discussed in this book are listed in Table 4.1.[5] The version of 1662, as stated earlier, is the primary point of reference throughout this book. Hundreds of editions, some more accurate than others, have been published. Because there have also been certain changes, mostly small but not insignificant, Prayer Books that currently print the 1662 version are not exactly the same as when it was first printed. Two copies of the first edition have been used here as benchmarks. The same first-edition text is readily available in an Oxford World Classics edition, which for scholarly purposes could hardly be bettered. While it is not necessary to refer to that edition, or any other, while reading this book, readers may find it helpful to do so, especially in the first five chapters. The World Classics page numbers will be referred to parenthetically with the abbreviation owc.[6] Together with the whole 1662 Prayer Book, that volume includes partial transcriptions of two earlier versions, one of them the original. Both will be cited in the same way.

In quotations from the Book of Common Prayer and elsewhere, spelling and orthography have usually been modernized, as they are in most editions that are currently available. Titles of books and pamphlets appear in their original form. The exception is the title of the Prayer Book itself, which began as The Booke of the Common

---

[4] David N. Griffiths, *The Bibliography of the Book of Common Prayer 1549–1999* (London: The British Library; New Castle, DE: Oak Knoll Press, 2002). Bibliographers employ further refinements, which do not affect the discussion in this book.

[5] These and other versions, together with a wealth of other texts connected with the Book of Common Prayer, are available online at the website maintained by Charles Wohlers at http://justus.anglican.org/resources/bcp/.

[6] Brian Cummings, ed., *The Book of Common Prayer: The Texts of 1549, 1559, and 1662* (Oxford: Oxford University Press, 2011). No standard method of citing the Prayer Book text exists, although attempts to provide one have been made. In 1662 the pages were not numbered.

Prayer, and has been The Boke of Common Prayer and The Booke of Common Praier. The two words *kalendar* and *Mattins* keep their old spelling. Mattins, otherwise known as Morning Prayer, is not the medieval liturgy called Matins, and the kalendar in the Book of Common Prayer is not the ordinary secular calendar, although in both cases there is a close relation. *Holyday* is so spelled for the sake of preserving the connotation of holiness that *holiday* has lost.

PART I

CONTENTS

One

Divine Service

The Book of Common Prayer contains a dozen liturgical texts. Each of them prescribes not only what will be said and done in a particular act of worship, but also when and why it is meant to happen. Some services take place ad hoc, if and when specific circumstances call for them. These "occasional" services, which chapter three will discuss, do not vary. The Prayer Book's marriage rite, for example, is the same at every wedding. By contrast, the "regular" services discussed in the present chapter are expected to take place at stated intervals, irrespective of contingent events; and unlike the occasional offices they do vary. Although they are performed repeatedly, every so often, the repetitions are not exactly the same. Each of these services has a formal structure that remains constant, but the Prayer Book text that prescribes its contents also calls for variations in some of what is said or sung. Different words are uttered, different speeches spoken, at different times.

The name used in the Prayer Book to refer to the regular, nonidentically recurring worship it prescribes is *Divine Service*. In its basic form, Divine Service is literally an everyday event. The two offices of Morning Prayer and Evening Prayer, also called Mattins and Evensong, are to be recited daily throughout the year. This twice-a-day recitation is a duty for members of the clergy, who are expected to give other people the opportunity to pray together with them, especially on Sunday, the day par excellence for common, public prayer.

On Sunday morning, Divine Service takes an extended form, which this chapter will describe in some detail. Following

The Book of Common Prayer. Charles Hefling, Oxford University Press (2021). © Oxford University Press.
DOI: 10.1093/oso/9780190689681.001.0001.

Morning Prayer, two further offices are said: the Litany or General Supplication, and at least the first part of the Lord's Supper or Holy Communion. This liturgical sequence—Morning Prayer, Litany, Communion—has sometimes been called the "long service."[1] It can be regarded as the normal Prayer Book liturgy, in the sense that it is the event of public worship which has taken place most often since the Prayer Book began to be used. Since Divine Service as prescribed for Sunday includes nearly all the liturgical elements that occur in other services as well, the description that follows will serve to introduce much of the specialized vocabulary used throughout this book.

Constants and Variables

Divine Service, as it is ordinarily performed, is audible discourse. It consists of speech and, usually, of almost nothing else. Prescribed words are uttered, either by the priest or minister who presides,[2] or by others who are present, or by all together. At a few points the rubrics call for kneeling or standing, but with the exception of these symbolic postures the carrier of meaning throughout Morning Prayer, the Litany, and the first part of Holy Communion is language.

The uttered words in which Divine Service consists function in different ways. Many of the speeches prescribed in the text are prayers, verbal expressions of praise, thanks, confession, or request, addressed to God. There are also exhortations,

---

[1] The rubrics require all three offices to be said, in the order stated. They do not explicitly require them to be said consecutively, without pausing, but that has been the most common practice.

[2] The words *minister* and *priest* are often used interchangeably in the Prayer Book. There is a difference, however, which chapter three will explain in connection with the Ordination services.

greetings, dialogues, and the like. Divine Service is thus a sequence of distinct and various components, rather than a continuous declamation. Table 1.1 lists these different components in the order prescribed for Morning Prayer, the first and longest of the offices on Sunday. Many of the generic labels in the table appear in the Prayer Book itself, but some are imported, as are the descriptions of the three sections, which the text does not explicitly distinguish.

Table 1.1 Components of Morning Prayer

---

1 Preparation: penitence (owc 239–241)
    sentence(s) from scripture and address
    confession of sin, pronouncement of absolution
    Lord's Prayer

2 Praise and edification (owc 241–247)
    versicles (*preces*)
    Psalm 95, *Venite, exultemus Domino*
    Psalms of the day
    first lesson (from the Old Testament)
    canticle (*Te Deum laudamus* or *Benedicite, omnia opera*)
    second lesson (from the New Testament)
    canticle (*Benedictus* or Psalm 100, *Jubilate Deo*)
    Apostles' Creed

3 Prayer (owc 247–248)
    salutation, response, and Lesser Litany
    Lord's Prayer
    versicles (suffrages)
    collect of the day; two constant collects

A number of the items listed, the *confession* and the *versicles* for example, are constant; their wording is exactly the same whenever Morning Prayer is said. Other components differ specifically from one performance to another. There is always a *canticle* after the first *lesson*, for example, but it may be either of the two alternatives listed in the table. Both of these canticles are printed in the Prayer Book at the assigned place in the script. The lessons themselves are not. Each of them differs from day to day, and the minister must read them both from a copy of the Bible. Likewise, the *Psalms of the day*, as the name implies, are different on different days. The Prayer Book does include these texts, but not within the script for Morning Prayer. They must be recited from another section of the book.

Unlike the script for a stage play, then, the script that prescribes the contents of Morning Prayer is incomplete. The same is true of Evening Prayer and Holy Communion. There are blanks, as it were, that have to be filled in by inserting other texts into the text of the service as printed. The whole service must be reassembled every day, on the same general plan but with different particular parts. The variables vary, however, according to stated protocols, and nothing is subject to change without notice. It follows that a concrete description of what takes place at a particular service of Morning Prayer must apply the appropriate rules so as to specify the components which are called for but not specified—the Psalms and lessons, that is, as well as one of the prayers, the *collect of the day*.

The rules for ordering Divine Service will be examined in chapter two. At the moment, it will be enough to say that variation in the content of the regular offices is governed chiefly by the date on which they are said. For purposes of illustration, therefore, this chapter will assume a particular date, which will be September 5, 1762. Almost any other date would do as well, but the one chosen here is not chosen arbitrarily. The day was Sunday. In the morning, Divine Service would therefore include the Litany and Holy Communion as well as Morning Prayer. The year 1762 was the midpoint, roughly speaking, of the Prayer Book's active history. There was one Prayer Book, one version of the text, which was used not only in Great Britain and Ireland but in North America and elsewhere as well. On September 5, this "classical" text had been in use for just a hundred years.[3]

On that morning, there is reason to believe that Divine Service was conducted in perhaps as many as ten thousand places. There is also reason to suppose that the way it was conducted at, say, a parish church in Virginia and at an English cathedral would have differed in very many respects. Nevertheless it would have been the same service in so far as it complied with the prescriptions of the same script, and it is with those prescriptions that the present chapter will be concerned. The intention is not to reconstruct a historical event, so much as to describe a typical or representative Prayer Book liturgy.

Divine Service: Mattins

Like several other Prayer Book rites, Mattins or Morning Prayer begins with a set address, spoken by the minister, that puts those who are present in mind of what they are present for. They have met together, he says, to pray and to listen; "to render thanks" to God "for the great benefits, that we have received at his hands, to set forth his most worthy praise, to hear his most holy word, and to ask those things, which are requisite, and necessary, as well for the body as the soul" (OWC 240). All of this will happen in the ensuing service.

---

[3] Officially, this version of the Prayer Book came into use on Sunday, August 24, 1662. Owing to the transition from the "old style" to the "new style," Gregorian calendar, the centennial of that day fell on September 4, 1762, which was Saturday. The first American version of the Book of Common Prayer was not adopted until 1789.

Preparation: Penitence

First, however, minister and people kneel and recite aloud, in unison, a formal expression of remorse, contrition, and repentance known as the General Confession. Before the address begins, the first speech heard at Morning Prayer is a sentence from the Bible, one of several listed at the beginning of the service. Each of these brief quotations refers to penitence in some way, and the address expands it: "Scripture moveth us," the minister avers, "to acknowledge and confess our manifold sins and wickedness" and to ask for God's pardon. With that acknowledgment common prayer begins.

The General Confession at Morning and Evening Prayer

Almighty, and most merciful Father; We have erred, and strayed from thy ways like lost sheep. We have followed too much the devices, and desires of our own hearts. We have offended against thy holy laws. We have left undone those things which we ought to have done; And we have done those things which we ought not to have done; And there is no health in us. But thou, O Lord, have mercy upon us, miserable offenders. Spare thou them, O God, which confess their faults. Restore thou them, that are penitent; According to thy promises declared unto mankind in Christ Jesu our Lord. And grant, O most merciful Father, for his sake; That we may hereafter live a godly, righteous, and sober life, To the glory of thy holy Name. Amen.

The General Confession having been said, a rubric instructs the priest to stand and pronounce the absolution or remission of sins. He declares that God "pardoneth and absolveth all them that truly repent." The people answer "Amen," a word that means roughly "yes, so it is; may it be so." Then they join the minister in reciting the Lord's Prayer, which the New Testament reports that Jesus Christ taught to his followers: "Our Father, which art in heaven . . ."

Praise and Edification

After the penitential opening, the central section of the service begins with a prayer *for* prayer, a request that prayer may happen, which takes the form of a short dialogue:

PRIEST: O Lord, open thou our lips.
ANSWER: And our mouth shall show forth thy praise.

In liturgical parlance, these two lines are a *versicle* and its *response*. In this case, the priest speaks in the plural, on behalf of everyone, and the response completes the request, which is that God will enable their speech so that they can praise him aloud. After another versicle and response, priest and people do what they have asked to made capable of doing: they give voice to their praise. The dialogue continues with a *doxology*, an acclamation that lauds and glorifies. Here it is the so-called Lesser Doxology, an ancient form that praises the three who in Christian teaching are one God:

PRIEST: Glory be to the Father, and to the Son : and to the Holy Ghost;
ANSWER: As it was in the beginning, is now, and ever shall be :
    world without end. Amen.

This text is also referred to, as are many others in the Prayer Book, by its *incipit*, the opening words in Latin; in this case, *Gloria Patri*.

The Lesser Doxology introduces a series of longer speeches that alternate, as Table 1.1 shows, between poetic discourse and edifying or instructive prose. First there are Psalms, then two lessons, each of which is followed by a canticle, a "little song."

Psalms

The Psalms are 150 prose-poems collected in one of the books that make up what the Christian Bible calls the Old Testament. Individual Psalms range widely in length, style, and mood. There are poignant laments and fierce curses, entreaty and thanksgiving, narrative and lyric, remorse and jubilation. An English translation of the whole collection is included in the Book of Common Prayer, which refers to it as the *Psalter*. From the Psalter at least two Psalms, usually more, are recited at Morning Prayer. The first one does not vary; it is always Psalm 95, *Venite, exultemus Domino*, "O come, let us sing unto the Lord," or *Venite* for short.[4] With its invitation to "show ourselves glad in him with Psalms," the *Venite* is an apt lead-in to the other Psalms that are recited immediately afterward.

These *Psalms of the day* are the first variable component in Morning Prayer. For the day of the Morning Prayer service described here, the Prayer Book appoints the Psalms numbered 24, 25, and 26 (owc 484–486). Every Psalm is made up of *verses*, few or many, each of which is usually one sentence. The three appointed Psalms begin, respectively, with the following verses. Notice that two of them are themselves prayers addressed to God.

> The earth is the Lord's, and all that therein is :
>   the compass of the world, and they that dwell therein.
>
> Unto thee, O Lord, will I lift up my soul, my God, I have put my trust in thee :
>   O let me not be confounded, neither let mine enemies triumph over me.
>
> Be thou my judge, O Lord, for I have walked innocently :
>   my trust hath been also in the Lord, therefore shall I not fall.

[4] Exception: on Easter Day the *Venite* is replaced by specially appointed New Testament texts.

Notice also that each of these verses has a binary form: the second half in some way complements the first. It is the same with nearly every verse in every Psalm. This characteristic of biblical poetry has an important bearing on the way in which the Psalms have been recited. The Prayer Book Psalter marks the division with a colon, or in some editions with an asterisk. After the last verse of every Psalm, including the *Venite*, the rubrics order the *Gloria Patri* to be added.

Lessons (Chapters)

Like the Psalms of the day, each of the two lessons at Morning Prayer varies according to rules that chapter two will discuss. The rubrics sometimes refer to these lessons as chapters, and with a few exceptions each does consist of an entire chapter of a biblical book.[5] Unlike the Psalms, the Morning Prayer lessons are not transcribed in the Prayer Book; as mentioned earlier, the minister reads them directly from a Bible, announcing each according to a set formula.

At the representative service described here, the announcement of the first lesson would be, "Here beginneth the nineteenth chapter of the Second Book of the Kings." This chapter narrates an episode in the reign of Hezekiah, a virtuous king of ancient Judah, which ends with the angel of the Lord God smiting an army of invaders in response to the king's prayer. Reading this chapter aloud takes ten minutes, more or less. The New Testament lesson, the sixth chapter of the Gospel according to Matthew, is somewhat shorter—six or seven minutes—and somewhat different. Its context is the long discourse traditionally called Jesus' Sermon on the Mount, which in the part of it reported in Matthew 6 includes several of his most

---

[5] Note that this statement applies to the prescriptions that were operative until the nineteenth century, when somewhat shorter lessons began to be appointed.

noted teachings about prayer, almsgiving, fasting, and indifference to worldly concerns.

The Psalms and lessons are the core of the first office in Divine Service. In light of their contents on this Sunday, it might be asked what they have to do with each other. Nothing, evidently—or, if there happens to be a connection, it happens fortuitously. On most Sundays, the lessons and Psalms follow three independent schedules. As chapter two will explain, there are certain days of the year on which all the assigned Bible readings are intentionally coordinated, but September 5, 1762 was not one of those days.

Canticles

Following each lesson at Morning Prayer a song or prose-poem is recited. In each case this may be either of the two alternatives listed in Table 1.1. One of the four texts provided is an ancient hymn, *Te Deum laudamus*, "We praise thee, O God." One is Psalm 100, *Jubilate Deo*, "O be joyful in the Lord." One is a poetic passage from one of the New Testament gospels: *Benedictus*, "Blessed be the Lord God of Israel." One is a Psalm-like section of one of the Apocrypha or intertestamental books: *Benedicite*, "O all ye works of the Lord, bless ye the Lord." The Prayer Book calls only the last of these texts a *canticle*, but the word is commonly used for all of them. As their opening words show, the canticles are all doxological, each a variation on the theme of praise.

The *Te Deum* does not come from the Bible, though parts of it do; otherwise, the whole central portion of Morning Prayer is a mosaic of biblical extracts. In that regard the liturgy has been called, fairly enough, a "scripture delivery mechanism."[6] The designated

---

[6] For the phrase, see Alec Ryrie, *Being Protestant in Reformation Britain* (Oxford: Oxford University Press, 2013), 322; he cites Catharine Davies, *A Religion of the Word* (Manchester: Manchester University Press, 2002), 137. It should be said that the biblical status of the *Benedicite* has not gone unquestioned.

Psalms, chapters, and canticles are presented audibly, without exposition or commentary, exactly as they are printed in the Bible or transcribed from the Bible in the Prayer Book. If the Prayer Book itself is a sacred text, much of its sacredness accrues to it from the text which for Christians mediates God's own word. To hear that word is a stated purpose of Morning Prayer, announced in the opening address, and most of the service is given, one way or another, to "scripture delivery."

That being said, it should also be observed that the scripture which Morning Prayer delivers it delivers packaged. The deliveries, whatever they may be, are uttered and heard in a context that selects, moderates, organizes, orients, and interprets them. The liturgy situates the appointed lessons and Psalms within a movement that begins with assurance of pardon and continues with reiterated gratitude, awe, and joy. The unvarying context of the variable texts is doxology: "Glory be," "Let us heartily rejoice," "We praise thee, O God," "Blessed be the Lord," "O be joyful."[7]

The Apostles' Creed

In and with the doxology there is a good deal of theology in Morning Prayer, if theology is understood broadly as talk about God, about divine characteristics and deeds, about what God may be expected to do and what God expects of human beings. But there is only one explicitly doctrinal component, which is positioned so as to follow the biblical passages as a kind of anchor. This formal statement of basic Christian teaching is known as the *Apostles' Creed*. Like the General Confession and the Lord's Prayer, the Creed is recited by everyone, minister and people, in unison. Unlike those texts, it is

---

[7] See further David Bagchi, "'The Scripture Moveth Us in Sundry Places': Framing Biblical Emotions in the *Book of Common Prayer* and the *Homilies*," in *The Renaissance of Emotion: Understanding Affect in Shakespeare and His Contemporaries*, ed. Richard Meek and Erin Sullivan (Manchester: Manchester University Press, 2015), 45–64, esp. 52–54.

phrased in the first person singular: "*I* believe. . . ." The beliefs it articulates are set out in three paragraphs, corresponding to the Christian doctrine of God's triple identity as Father, Son, and Holy Ghost. The second paragraph, which is the longest, is a series of clauses, derived from the New Testament, that specify who Jesus Christ, the Son of God, was and is. In the third paragraph, the affirmation "I believe in the Holy Ghost" is extended to include belief in the church, forgiveness, and embodied life after death.

The Apostles' Creed is almost but not quite invariable. On thirteen days of the year, three of which are always Sunday, its place at Morning Prayer is taken by a much longer and more technically phrased formula, *Quicunque vult,* "Whosoever will be saved" (owc 257–259). This "confession of our Christian faith" is "commonly called the Creed of Saint Athanasius," although it is not so much a creed as a theological manifesto or a doctrinal ode, and is not likely to have been written by its namesake. The day of the morning service discussed here was not a day on which the Athanasian Creed would have been recited, so nothing will be said about it now, but it will come up again in later chapters.

Prayers and Collects

The last section of Morning Prayer begins with a salutation, "The Lord be with you," spoken by the minister, to which the answer is "And with thy spirit." After the bidding, "Let us pray," scripted prayers begin with the so-called *Lesser Litany,* which consists of three short appeals, alternating between minister and people: "Lord, have mercy upon us. *Christ, have mercy upon us.* Lord, have mercy upon us." The Lord's Prayer is said, for the second time. Six versicles, usually known as *suffrages,* follow, each with its response. Like other versicles, they are short prayers, mainly extracted from the Psalms, which ask God to show mercy, grant salvation, save his people and make them joyful, endue his ministers with righteousness, save the king or queen, "give peace in our time," "make clean our hearts within us."

Each of the three prayers which these suffrages lead to is a *collect*. There are nearly a hundred collects in the Book of Common Prayer, each of them a single sentence that very often exemplifies this pattern:

> (1) O God, who . . .
> (2) grant that . . .
> (3) so that . . .
> (4) through Jesus Christ.

A typical collect (1) addresses God as characterized by some divine attribute or deed, which is commonly expressed in a relative clause. It then (2) asks for some benevolent act on God's part, often one that is related to the address, and (3) states the resulting benefit, the end to which the prayer aspires. Finally, every collect (4) concludes with a formulaic acknowledgment that God grants prayers on account of his Son Jesus Christ.

Two of the three collects recited at Morning Prayer never vary, but the first one, the *collect of the day*, does. The Prayer Book orders this collect to be "the same that is appointed at the Holy Communion." In 1762, the Sunday that fell on September 5 was the Thirteenth Sunday after Trinity. This designation will be explained in chapter two, together with the rules that assign the following collect to the Sunday so designated:

> [1] Almighty and merciful God, of whose only gift it cometh, that thy faithful people do unto thee true and laudable service: [2] Grant, we beseech thee, that we may so faithfully serve thee in this life, [3] that we fail not finally to attain thy heavenly promises, [4] through the merits of Jesus Christ our Lord. *Amen.*

This is a fair specimen of the collect form. It is also a theological statement: its address, request, and aspiration are all informed by Christian doctrine. The benefit for which it prays is that those who pray will succeed, as God has promised, in reaching heaven (3). Their success depends on faithfully serving God here and now (2); but genuine, praiseworthy service is itself God's gift (1), given for Christ's sake (4). In other words, God alone gives the means to the end he promises. Thus, like many of the Prayer Book collects, this one is a prayer for God to be God. It asks God to be and do what only God is and does.

In both of the two fixed or constant collects that follow the collect of the day, the operative word is *defend*. They are prayers for protection—from the assaults of enemies, from falling into sin, and from any kind of danger. Positively, the third collect goes on to ask "that all our doings may be ordered by thy governance, to do always that [which] is righteous" in God's sight (owc 248). With that aspiration Morning Prayer concludes on Sundays, as it does also on Wednesdays and Fridays. Instead of five further prayers that are said on the other days of the week, Divine Service goes on to a long prayer or set of prayers called the (Greater) *Litany* or General Supplication.

Divine Service Continued: The Litany

Formally, a litany is a series of requests, phrased so that each is completed by the same repeated response. Compared with Morning Prayer, the Prayer Book's Litany is easy to describe; there are no variable components that depend on the day or the date. The priest announces the object of each short prayer, and the response asks God to grant it. For example:

> From lightning and tempest; from plague, pestilence, and
> famine; from battle and murder, and from sudden death,
>   *Good Lord, deliver us.*

From all sedition, privy conspiracy, and rebellion; from all false doctrine, heresy, and schism; from hardness of heart and contempt of thy Word and Commandment,
   Good Lord, deliver us.

And so on, through eight *deprecations* that enumerate banes and perils from which priest and people pray to be rescued. The Litany continues with another, longer, positive series of *supplications* in this form:

That it may please thee to strengthen such as do stand, and to comfort and help the weak-hearted, and to raise up them that fall, and finally to beat down Satan under our feet,
   We beseech thee to hear us, good Lord. . . .
That it may please thee to give and preserve to our use the kindly fruits of the earth, so that in due time we may enjoy them,
   We beseech thee to hear us, good Lord.

Most of the Litany is made up of these responsorial, back-and-forth prayers. Following the supplications there are versicles, the (third) Lord's Prayer, and several longer prayers that are not distributed between different voices but said by the priest alone.

Divine Service Concluded: Holy Communion

The Litany is a liturgical office in its own right, though in practice it can be thought of as an extension of Morning Prayer. On Sundays and holydays, it also leads to what has been called the Second Service or Latter Service, for which the proper name is the Lord's Supper or Holy Communion.

   The whole Communion office, as set out in the Book of Common Prayer, culminates in a ceremonial distribution of bread and wine. To receive and consume these is to "communicate" or "take communion"; those who do so are "communicants." The rubrics, however, permit abbreviation: the service must take place every Sunday, but it may stop before it reaches the ritualized meal.[8] In that case, paradoxically, it is a Communion service with no communion. Until fairly recently, however, the Lord's Supper was "celebrated" in full only rarely, perhaps three or four times a year, and the normal (though not normative) way of meeting the Prayer Book's requirement has been to conduct only the first part of the service, which liturgists refer to as *ante-Communion*. Since that is how ordinary churches, if not cathedrals, were wont to do things in 1762, the following account, which describes only ante-Communion, can claim historical warrant. The omission of the second part of the service will be made good later.

The Collect for Purity at Holy Communion

Almighty God, unto whom all hearts be open, all desires known, and from whom no secrets are hid; Cleanse the thoughts of our hearts by the inspiration of thy holy Spirit, that we may perfectly love thee, and worthily magnify thy holy Name, through Christ our Lord. *Amen.*

Abbreviated or not, Holy Communion begins with the (fourth) Lord's Prayer and a prayer of preparation known as the *collect for purity*, said by the priest "standing at the north side of the Table." In a church building "oriented" in the traditional way, his position would be to the left of people facing forward and therefore eastward. The table he stands at is one of the few physical furnishings that the Book of Common Prayer mentions explicitly. Whether it

---

[8] And it must stop, if no one who is present intends to take communion. The priest may not continue on his own.

should be called an *altar*, as it frequently was and is, has been a controversial question. The word does not appear in the 1662 Prayer Book. However it is named, the rubrics imply that, except when he preaches the sermon, the priest will remain there, standing or kneeling, throughout ante-Communion, which for that reason has informally been called "table prayers."

Having said the two opening prayers, the priest turns from the table to face the people and "rehearse" the Ten Commandments. According to the book of Exodus, from which the Prayer Book takes them, these laws were spoken by God himself. Most of them are prohibitions; they forbid having any other God, making and worshiping material images, committing blasphemy, murder,[9] adultery, theft, or false witness, and coveting what belongs to another. One commandment enjoins honoring parents and another reverence for the sabbath or seventh day. After each of the ten is rehearsed, the people, who have been kneeling since the service began, respond with a short prayer: "Lord have mercy upon us and incline our hearts to keep this law." Two collects follow. One is a prayer for the king; the other, the same collect of the day that was said earlier at Morning Prayer.

Like Morning Prayer, the Communion office includes two readings from the Bible, both of which are variable. The first of these comes from one of the New Testament books called epistles,[10] the second from one of the four gospels. The rubrics refer to them simply as *the epistle* and *the gospel*. Both are printed out, together with the preceding collect of the day, as a set; these sets are collected in a long section of the Prayer Book—a hundred pages or so (owc 271–388)—that comes between the Litany and the Communion rite. As a rule, the liturgical epistle and gospel are excerpts, shorter

[9] The wording in the 1662 Book of Common Prayer and its predecessors is "Thou shalt do no murder," not the perhaps more familiar "Thou shalt not kill."

[10] Very occasionally there is instead a reading "for the epistle," taken from elsewhere in the Bible.

than the whole chapters read earlier at Morning Prayer.[11] There are no canticles at Holy Communion; collect, epistle, and gospel are read consecutively. Since the priest can read them in order from a Prayer Book, he need not have a Bible at the table where he stands.

The collect for the day, the Thirteenth Sunday after Trinity, has been quoted already. The epistle for that day is a passage from one of the letters of Paul the Apostle, which deals with the status of the "old" Law, as Paul speaks of it, now that Christ has come (Galatians 3:16–22). The liturgical gospel includes Jesus' well-known parable of the "good Samaritan" who rescued a traveler mugged by thieves, thereby demonstrating what it is to be a neighbor in the true sense (Luke 10:23–37). While the gospel is being read, the people stand to show respect—one of the few nonverbal, ceremonial expressions in Divine Service—and they remain standing while the Nicene Creed, a doctrinal formulary much like the Apostle's Creed though somewhat longer, is recited.

To this point, ante-Communion is in many ways a reprise of liturgical elements that have figured earlier in Morning Prayer: a penitential opening, collects, formally announced readings from scripture, creed. That may explain the unofficial name Second Service. Next, however, the Prayer Book calls for a *sermon*. Here, and nowhere else in the regular offices, what is said is whatever the minister chooses to say. His sermon may be long or short, original or borrowed.[12] It would be a fair guess that many congregations in 1762 would hear a substantial discourse, lasting maybe

---

[11] Notable exceptions: the very long liturgical gospels for certain days in the week before Easter.

[12] The Prayer Book provides for a sort of authorized borrowing. The minister may read one of the "Homilies . . . set forth by authority" (owc 393) in two sixteenth-century collections entitled *Certain Sermons or Homilies*, usually called the Books of Homilies. They were already somewhat old-fashioned in 1662, and by 1762 they were seldom if ever preached, although they retained a certain authority as doctrinal statements and were studied as such.

three-quarters of an hour, but sermons have always been as diverse as the preachers who preach them.

Having preached, probably from a pulpit, the priest is instructed to return to the table for what the Prayer Book terms the *offertory*. Church officials collect "in a decent basin" the people's donations of money, alms for the poor, and other "devotions" or gifts. Meanwhile sentences from scripture that commend generosity are read. The long prayer that comes next begins by asking God to "accept our alms and oblations," meaning by implication the collected gifts; and it continues with petitions on behalf of the king, whose name is printed, the bishops and other clergy, the present congregation, and "all them who in this transitory life are in trouble, sorrow, need, sickness, or any other adversity" (owc 395). The well-being of these persons, all of them alive, is what is meant by "the whole state of Christ's church militant here in earth" in the bidding that precedes the prayer.

At the conclusion of the prayer for the church, the second part of Holy Communion begins, if the service is to be celebrated in full. If not—as on the Sunday described here—the priest turns over several pages, to the end of the script, and says one or more of the general collects appointed for use when there is no communion. He then brings the Second Service to a close with a prescribed blessing or benediction.

The Benediction at Holy Communion

The peace of God which passeth all understanding, keep your hearts and minds in the knowledge and love of God, and of his son Jesus Christ our Lord: And the blessing of God Almighty, the Father, the Son, and the holy Ghost, be amongst you, and remain with you always. *Amen.*

Evening Prayer

Evensong, to use its popular name, is as much a daily obligation as Morning Prayer. Formally, these two offices are almost exactly alike. The penitential opening is the same, word for word, and with one exception each of the generic items listed in Table 1.1 has a counterpart at Evening Prayer. Specifically, the collect of the day would be the same as the one said earlier at Morning Prayer (and again at Communion),[13] but the other variable components, the Psalms and chapters, would not. Three further differences should be mentioned.

First, Evening Prayer has no constant invitational Psalm to match the *Venite* at Morning Prayer. The variable Psalms of the day, as appointed for the particular evening, are recited immediately after the versicles that begin with "O Lord, open thou our lips."

Nunc dimittis
or the Song of Simeon, the canticle after the second lesson at Evening Prayer

---

Lord, now lettest thou thy servant depart in peace :
   according to thy word.
For mine eyes have seen : thy salvation,
Which thou has prepared : before the face of all people;
To be a light to lighten the Gentiles :
   and to be the glory of thy people Israel.
Glory be to the Father, and to the Son : and to the Holy Ghost;
As it was in the beginning, is now, and ever shall be :
   world without end. Amen.

---

[13] Exception: on Saturday, and also on the day before any holyday "that hath a vigil or eve," as some though not all holydays have, the collect for the following day is to be read at Evening Prayer (OWC 271).

Second, Evening Prayer has its own canticles. After each lesson, as at Morning Prayer, either of two alternatives may be recited. One alternative, in both cases, is a Psalm; but the canticles for which Evensong is best known are the other two: *Magnificat* after the first lesson, *Nunc dimittis* after the second. Both come from the beginning of one of the gospels, both are phrased in the first person, and both are connected with the birth of Christ.

The *Magnificat*, called the Song of the blessed Virgin Mary in one rubric, praises God, who has "regarded the lowliness of his handmaiden," for having "scattered the proud in the imagination of their hearts," "exalted the humble and meek," and "filled the hungry with good things." *Nunc dimittis*, the Song of Simeon, might be described as a grateful valediction, sung in response to the arrival of salvation in the person of Christ, whom God has sent "to be a light to lighten the Gentiles, and to be the glory of thy people Israel." As chapter twelve will point out, musical settings of "*Mag* and *Nunc*" have done much to make Evensong perhaps the most widely known and highly regarded service in the Book of Common Prayer. But whether sung or said, these two canticles both stand in the first rank of religious poetry.

Third, the two constant collects that follow the variable collect of the day are not the same as those at Morning Prayer, although they are similar in that they both pray for defense—in the second collect, from the fear of enemies; in the third, from the perils and dangers of the night. Each of these collects contains one of the Prayer Book's memorable phrases: "that peace which the world cannot give" and, picking up a word from the *Nunc dimittis*, "lighten our darkness."

The Collect for Aid against All Perils
the third collect at Evening Prayer

Lighten our darkness, we beseech thee, O Lord, and by thy great mercy defend us from all perils and dangers of this night, for the love of thy only Son, our Savior Jesus Christ. *Amen.*

Dramatis Personae

Divine Service lends itself to description in words, since words are what it consists of. Almost nothing that the Prayer Book prescribes needs to be visualized. Nor are the words unpredictable, apart from the sermon. They are meant to be uttered just as they appear on the pages of either the Prayer Book or the Bible. What this chapter has left a little vague is exactly who utters them and how.

The vagueness has been deliberate. The Prayer Book itself is not always unambiguous when it comes to the assignment of speaking parts. Obviously the voice of the officiating clergyman is the voice heard most of the time—the only voice, if there happens to be no congregation. Although the expectation is that laypeople will be given the opportunity to pray with the minister, the rubrics do not expressly demand much vocal participation on their part. They are to say "Amen" after every prayer; together with the minister, they are to recite the General Confession, the Lord's Prayer, and the Apostles' Creed at Morning and Evening Prayer. In the Communion service they are to respond to each of the Ten Commandments and (probably) to say the Nicene Creed.

Beyond these explicit requirements, the audible contribution of the congregation at large is left to custom, circumstance, and individual willingness. There are other places where the printed words are undoubtedly meant to be said by someone besides the minister, but the rubrics do not assign them to anyone else in particular. When *Answer* appears before the response to a versicle, some sort of dialogue is obviously called for. Obviously too, the Litany is meant to be said by alternate voices. In principle, words that respond to the minister might be spoken by everyone else. In practice, at least one person would be ready, willing, and able to speak them: the clerk. The rubrics mention this personage only rarely, but as a rule there has been at least one clerk in every parish church, whom the minister could rely upon to be equipped with a copy of the Book of Common Prayer and able to find his way around it. By 1762, many members of the congregation might have had their own Prayer Books; editions for personal use were readily available, and more and more people were able to read them. If they and others joined the clerk in making the responses, so much the better; if not, he could and often did act as their spokesman in a literal sense.

Much the same is true of the Psalms and canticles. For anything the rubrics say explicitly, the minister might read the Psalms by himself. Elsewhere in the Prayer Book, however, there are indications that the Psalms were, and were meant to be, recited responsively, "one verse by the priest, and another by the clerk and the people."[14] By analogy, the same method might be used for reciting the canticles. If the people could not (or did not) speak their lines, the priest and the clerk might have to perform a duet. That seems to have been what happened quite often.

Who utters the words in Divine Service depends in part on how they are uttered. The assumption throughout this chapter has been that the printed text is made audible by saying the words as they would be said in ordinary speech, if perhaps more distinctly and loudly. But there are several parts of the liturgy which, according to the rubrics, are to be "sung or said." In Divine Service, the option of singing is explicit with regard to the *Venite*, the evening Psalms, *Te Deum*, the Litany, and the Nicene Creed; probably it extends to

---

[14] The evidence in the Prayer Book itself appears in two of the State Services (OWC 656, 662), which were not added until 1662. But there is solid evidence, which will be discussed in a later chapter, that clerks, if not everyone, had been reciting the Psalms with the minister since the first Prayer Book was issued.

all the Psalms and canticles. No doubt all these texts have been said more often than sung; but as chapter twelve will outline, there has been a more or less continuous tradition of singing them in some fashion.

If parts of Divine Service are in fact sung, the Prayer Book does not rule out their being sung by trained singers. Like the clerk, a choir may function as a representative congregation, singing on behalf of everyone else. Only once, however, does the text allude to choristers as such, and when it does, the role it assigns to them is unrelated to the prescribed words of the liturgy. After the third collect at both Morning and Evening Prayer a famous rubric orders that "in quires and places where they sing, here followeth the anthem." *Quire* is the same word as *choir*; it means the part of the church where a choral ensemble sings as well as the musicians who sing there. An *anthem*, however, in this connection, is a musical setting of a religious text that may be one of the texts in the service itself, but usually is not. The rubric makes room for such an extra, but there are no instructions that tell how the room may be furnished.

Apart from the anthem rubric, the Book of Common Prayer makes no allowance for extra-liturgical music, vocal or instrumental. Hymns, in the modern sense, are never mentioned.[15] On the other hand, musical embellishment is not ruled out either. If the church could afford it, an organ may have been played at the service this chapter has described; in 1762 there may have been a parish orchestra, such as the one Thomas Hardy portrays in *Under the Greenwood Tree*; and in all likelihood rhymed paraphrases of biblical Psalms were sung before and after Divine Service, and perhaps between the offices as well. Music, in and for the Prayer Book offices, is a large topic, best left for later, but it should be pointed out

---

[15] Certain texts such as the *Te Deum* are referred to as hymns, using the word in an older, wider sense; and there are rhymed stanzaic hymns in two of the Ordination services, although they are not so named.

here that while Divine Service is always a verbal event, its discursive character may be, and frequently has been, modified by the manner in which the words on the page are vocalized and accompanied. Their meaning may thus take on a nonverbal dimension that goes beyond what a verbal analysis of the text—such as the present chapter—can convey.

Two

Preambles: Time and the Prayer Book

At the front of the Book of Common Prayer, before the first liturgical text begins, there are fifty pages or so of what would now be
called prelims.[1] They include prefaces, which might be expected,
and transcripts of legislation, which might not. There is also a kind
of user's manual, which this chapter will investigate. Nothing in any
of these pages is ever said or sung. They are apt to be overlooked,
and small-size, personal-use Prayer Books often leave them out. Yet
they all bear, in different ways, on the content and constitution of
the services of worship they precede.

The *raison d'être* of the various tables, rules, directions,
definitions, and schedules in an unabridged Prayer Book was indicated in chapter one. Every Prayer Book liturgy is scripted,
but not every script comes ready-made. There may be "some as-
sembly required." At Morning Prayer, Evening Prayer, and Holy
Communion, the text as printed must be filled out with other texts,
which are printed elsewhere and which vary from one performance
to another according to a systematic scheme. The directives at the
beginning of the Prayer Book define this scheme and tell how to
deploy it in order to determine what is to be read at Divine Service.

From a practical standpoint, the apparatus for ordering the regular offices need not concern anyone except ministers who conduct
public worship and individuals who recite Morning and Evening
Prayer privately. But it is none the less meaningful for that. The

---

[1] In England, the numbering of pages in the Book of Common Prayer has never been
standardized; until lately it was rare for them to be numbered at all. In the first edition of
1662, Morning Prayer begins on the fifty-fifth unnumbered page; in the Oxford World
Classics edition, the prelims are pages 186 through 238.

The Book of Common Prayer. Charles Hefling, Oxford University Press (2021). © Oxford University Press.
DOI: 10.1093/oso/9780190689681.001.0001.

rules and tables have a part to play in making the Book of Common Prayer the sacred text it is. For one thing, they regulate the workings of its "scripture delivery mechanism," and define its relationship to the Bible. For another, they inform common prayer as a practice, an ongoing spiritual exercise. Divine Service is not a discrete, one-off event: it is a constitutive moment in a dynamic pattern, a continuous process that has been called the sanctification of time. For both reasons, the Prayer Book's regulations for ordering its services are well worth examination.

Sundays and Holydays

The specific contents of Divine Service differ from day to day for different reasons. On any given day certain components may be different from the day before simply because it is a new day. Or they may be different because the day is also a holyday. In the Book of Common Prayer every day is regarded as time that is to be sanctified by prayer, morning and evening, but some days are regarded as sacred or holy in themselves. These days, formally designated as holy by Christian tradition or church authority, are made actually holy inasmuch as they are observed or kept by persons who acknowledge their status and act accordingly. One way of enacting the holiness of holydays, so that they become what they are, is common prayer. One thing, therefore, that determines the contents of Divine Service on a given day is whether that day is a holyday.

Holydays, in the classical Book of Common Prayer, are either feasts or days of fasting and abstinence. Literal feasting and fasting have been nearly universal ways of expressing and owning the exceptionally joyous or exceptionally somber character of exceptional days. The Prayer Book, however, has no explicit directives in that regard; nor does it prescribe any of the special ceremonies which in some Christian traditions are attached to certain feasts and fasts. It does include one special office, appointed for use on the first day of the penitential season of Lent; but although that day is named Ash Wednesday, ashes play no part in the liturgy. Penitence is evoked and expressed in words, not visible, tactile symbols. Similarly, all the other Prayer Book holydays are differentiated from ordinary days by what is audibly said or sung in Divine Service, but not otherwise.

On most ordinary days, finding the appointed Psalms and chapters at Morning and Evening Prayer is a fairly straightforward matter of consulting a list of dates, which will be discussed in a moment. Included in this list as well are a number of feasts that are kept on the same date every year. The most familiar example is Christmas Day, the birthday of Jesus Christ, which is always December 25. Several other feasts that commemorate events reported in the New Testament narrative are likewise observed on fixed dates, as are the feasts kept in honor of individuals who figure prominently in that narrative—saints, as the Prayer Book uses the word.

Not all holydays, however, fall on dates that never vary. Every Sunday of the year is a feast, distinguished as such from other days of the week by the celebration of Holy Communion. Every Sunday also has a unique ecclesiastical designation. The fact that a certain day is Sunday can be known in any number of ways, but to know which particular Sunday it is, and which texts will therefore be read in the services, some of the rules at the beginning of the Prayer Book must be applied.

The service described in chapter one, for example, took place on a Sunday, and in particular on the Thirteenth Sunday after Trinity. In 1762 it so happened that the day was also the fifth day of September. It need not happen so, however, and usually does not. This specific Sunday is designated by its place in the sequence of what is known as the Christian or ecclesiastical or church year. For most Sundays, this one included, that place is reckoned in relation to Easter Day, the greatest Christian feast. Easter, however, is a "moveable feast," observed on a date that varies from year to year. It may fall as early as March 22 or as late as April 25, but never on the same date in successive years. As the date of Easter moves from one year to the next, the dates of most Sundays in the church year, including the Thirteenth Sunday after Trinity, move in tandem with it. The same is true of certain other observances that are not feasts: in relation to the civil calendar, they are moveable.

The date of Easter can always be determined in advance, and determining what it is in any given year is always necessary in order to know how the other Sundays and moveable holydays in the ecclesiastical series will line up with the ordinary series of dates in that year. That is why the Prayer Book's preliminaries include several items that bear on finding when Easter will occur. Those tables and rules will be discussed at the end of this chapter. More directly relevant to specifying the variable components of Divine Service is the list of dates mentioned three paragraphs back, which the Book of Common Prayer refers to as its *kalendar*.

The Kalendar Pages

The kalendar in the Book of Common Prayer is not a complete roster of the ecclesiastical year. If it were, it would be valid for a certain year only. Like a secular calendar, and partly for the same reasons, it would become obsolete at the beginning of the next year, in which, among other differences, the Sundays would not have the same dates. What the Prayer Book therefore provides instead is a set of generic lists, one for each month, which can be used in any year. These twelve pages can best be understood by inspecting one of them.

Figure 2.1 shows the first page of the kalendar printed in the first edition of 1662. There are thirty-one lines, one for each day of January. Since these dates are not grouped in weeks or given weekday names, the list can represent any January, no matter which of the dates are Sundays and therefore feasts. The other kalendar

The Kalendar.

JANUARY hath xxxj. Days.

The Moon hath xxx.

					MORNING Prayer		EVENING Prayer	
					1 Lesson.	2 Lesson.	1 Lesson.	2 Lesson.
2	1	A	Kalend.	Circumcision of our Lord				
	2	b	4. No.		Gen. 1.	Matth. 1.	Gen. 2.	Rom. 1.
10	3	c	3. No.		3.	2.	4.	2.
	4	d	Pr. No.		5.	3.	6.	3.
19	5	e	Nonæ		7.	4.	8.	4.
8	6	f	8 Id.	Epiphany of our Lord.				
	7	g	7 Id.		9.	5.	12.	5.
16	8	A	6 Id.	Lucian, Priest and Martyr.	13.	6.	14.	6.
5	9	b	5 Id.		15.	7.	16.	7.
	10	c	4 Id.		17.	8.	18.	8.
13	11	d	3 Id.		19.	9.	20.	9.
2	12	e	Pr. Id.		21.	10.	22.	10.
	13	f	Idus.	Hilary, Bishop & Confess.	23.	11.	24.	11.
10	14	g	19 Kl.Febr.		25.	12.	26.	12.
	15	A	18 Kl.		27.	13.	28.	13.
18	16	b	17 Kl.		29.	14.	30.	14.
7	17	c	16 Kl.		31.	15.	32.	15.
	18	d	15 Kl.	Prisca,Rom.Virg.& Mart.	33.	16.	34.	16.
15	19	e	14 Kl.		35.	17.	37.	1 Cor.1.
4	20	f	13 Kl.	Fabian B. of Rome, & M.	38.	18.	39.	2.
	21	g	12 Kl.	Agnes Rom.Virg.& Mart.	40.	19.	41.	3.
12	22	A	11 Kl.	Vincent Span. Deac.& M.	42.	20.	43.	4.
1	23	b	10 Kl.		44.	21.	45.	5.
	24	c	9 Kl.		46.	22.	47.	6.
9	25	d	8 Kl.	Conversion of S. Paul.				
	26	e	7 Kl.		48.	23.	49.	7.
17	27	f	6 Kl.		50.	24.	Exod.1.	8.
6	28	g	5 Kl.		Exod.2.	25.	3.	9.
	29	A	4 Kl.		4.	26.	5.	10.
13	30	b	3 Kl.	K. Charles Martyr.	* 6.	27.	7.	11.
3	31	c	Prid. Kl.		8.	28.	9.	12.

Note, that * Exodus vj. is to be read only to Verf. 14.

FEBRUARY.

Figure 2.1 Kalendar Page for January
First edition of the 1662 Book of Common Prayer.
Courtesy of the Beinecke Rare Books Library, Yale University.

pages are similar; taken together, they have a place for every day of any year.

In their origins, these twelve pages are older than almost anything else in the Prayer Book. Their layout is inherited from ancient Roman calendars by way of medieval manuals of devotion and Books of Hours.[2] This venerable history has left a trace in the Prayer Book kalendar, where the fourth column of each page seriates days according to the old Roman method. After the *Kalends*, the first day of the month, the count runs backward from *Nonæ*, the Nones (fifth line), then backward from *Idus*, the Ides (eight lines below), and finally backward from the Kalends of the following month. The twenty-third line, for example, is labeled 10 Kl., meaning the tenth day (inclusive) before the Kalends of February.[3] Roman reckoning by backward count was a little old-fashioned in 1662, though it was by no means extinct. Liturgical books had always used this system, as did earlier versions of the Book of Common Prayer. Editions that omit the fourth column of the kalendar, as some do, are breaking a deliberate link with a very long tradition.

The second column gives the more familiar forward count from one to thirty-one. The somewhat mysterious first and third columns, which bear on Easter calculations, can be postponed for the moment. The fifth column, like the corresponding columns in ancient and medieval kalendars, sets the names of annual events next to their respective dates. Since 1662 only ecclesiastical

---

[2] See the ancient January page illustrated in Michele Renée Salzman, *On Roman Time: The Codex-Calendar of 354 and the Rhythms of Urban Life in Late Antiquity* (Berkeley: University of California Press, 1990), Figure 24; and the many illustrations in Roger S. Wieck, *The Medieval Calendar: Locating Time in the Middle Ages* (New York: The Morgan Library and Museum, 2017). A kalendar page from a missal printed in 1500 is reproduced in Ratcliff, *Eighty Illustrations*, plate 2.

[3] For the whole Roman system of reckoning, see E. G. Richards, *Mapping Time: The Calendar and its History* (Oxford: Oxford University Press, 1998), 210–213 with Table 16.2 there.

observances have been listed. Earlier Prayer Books related those observances to the natural cycles of the stars and the seasons by including references to the Zodiac such as *Sol in Aquario* on the January page. Listed as well were the equinoxes and, curiously, the beginning and end of the Dog Days.[4]

The four columns on the right have no ancient or medieval precedent. As the headings indicate, they list the first and second lessons that are to be read at Morning and Evening Prayer, day by day, according to the dates in the second or the fourth column. The list merits scrutiny.

The numerals in these four columns are citations that refer to the numbered chapters into which books of the Bible were, and are, conventionally divided. Four chapters are appointed for each day. (The blanks will be explained presently.) During most of January, the first lesson at both Morning and Evening Prayer is a chapter from Genesis (*Gen.*), the first book in the Old Testament. Genesis has fifty chapters, which are read in order, two each day, through the morning of January 27. That evening, the reading of Exodus, the second Old Testament book, begins; it continues on the morning of January 28; and so on.

The second lessons are read in two concurrent series. In the morning, the first half of the New Testament, which begins with the four gospels and continues with the book of Acts, is read chapter by chapter and book by book, starting with the gospel of Matthew (*Matth.*). The second half of the New Testament contains the epistles. The first of these, the epistle to the Romans (*Rom.*), is read at Evening Prayer through January 18; First Corinthians (*1 Cor.*), the next epistle in biblical order, follows on the next evening; and so on. The two series of New Testament chapters finish together in May. Both series then start over, with Matthew and Romans; at the end of August they begin for a third time and continue through December.

[4] See further David Siegenthaler, "Zodiac and Prayer Book," *Journal of Theological Studies* N.S. 26.2 (1975): 427–434.

The Old Testament chapters do not repeat; it takes a whole year to read them all.

Collect for the Second Sunday in Advent ("Bible Sunday")

Blessed Lord, who hast caused all holy Scriptures to be written for our learning; Grant that we may in such wise hear them, read, mark, learn, and inwardly digest them, that by patience and comfort of thy holy word, we may embrace, and ever hold fast the blessed hope of everlasting life, which thou hast given us in our Savior Jesus Christ. *Amen.*

This simple method of working through scripture "in course," reading each consecutive chapter of each consecutive book, presupposes the Bible's internal order and accepts its chapter-divisions as they stand, despite some notable inequalities. On September 27, for example, the first lesson at Morning Prayer has only six verses, while on March 7 it has more than sixty.[5] Course-reading does however serve one of the stated purposes of the Book of Common Prayer, in so far as it provides a scheme for regular and (mostly) uninterrupted engagement with the biblical text. Nor is it as artificial a scheme as it might appear to be. There are exceptions and adaptations built in, particularly where the first lessons are concerned.

For one thing, quite a number of Old Testament chapters are not scheduled for reading at all. In January the omissions are not extensive—three chapters of Genesis, which consist almost entirely of genealogies that would be as tedious to read as to listen

---

[5] The chapters are Malachi 4 and Deuteronomy 28, respectively.

to.[6] Later in the year, parts of Numbers are left out. So are First and Second Chronicles, perhaps because they repeat what has been read from other books. Few chapters are assigned from the perplexing book of Ezekiel, very few from Leviticus with its intricate ritual regulations, and none at all from the amorous poetry of the Song of Solomon. Another exception is that the book of Isaiah is not read in its place in the biblical canon of books; the kalendar postpones it, as prophecy of Christ's coming, to the weeks before Christmas. A third exception is that on Sundays and holydays, when attendance at Divine Service is obligatory, a special provision set out in one of the preliminary tables overrules the kalendar and a special first lesson—sometimes a second lesson as well—must be read in place of the chapter assigned to the day of the month.

It should also be noted that among the first lessons are about a hundred chapters from the books called the Apocrypha, a collection of ancient texts that usually come between the Old Testament and the New in Bibles that include them. Not all Bibles do. Whether any of these writings should be counted as holy scripture and read as such in public worship has been a disputed question. Lessons from them are in any case scheduled, beginning in late September.

Such is the "scripture delivery mechanism" of the Book of Common Prayer, as it operates on the lessons at Mattins and Evensong.[7] It is quite a comprehensive scheme. At the same time, it also controls, selects, and prioritizes. The Holy Bible may be equally holy throughout, but to judge by the allocation of its chapters, not everything it contains is equally urgent, equally edifying, equally suitable for public worship. In the course of a year, all of the New Testament—except the difficult, visionary book of Revelation—is read three times at Divine Service, while the Old Testament is read

---

[6] The omitted chapters are 10, 11, and 36. But the part of Genesis 11 that includes the well-known story of the Tower of Babel is the first lesson at Morning Prayer on Monday in Whitsun Week, which is a feast, so it is not omitted altogether.

[7] Or as it originally operated, rather. As chapter one has mentioned, revised lectionaries have since been substituted, with shorter lessons, designed to improve the "mechanism" on principles that are beyond the scope of this book.

once, and not all of it at that. Here is not the place to analyze the hermeneutical judgments that may inform the kalendar's table of lessons, but it can be mentioned that the omission of parts of the Old Testament and the inclusion of chapters from the Apocrypha seem to imply an understanding of biblical authority that has not been found acceptable by all.

The Psalms in Course

When it comes to the Psalms of the day, nothing is omitted. Although it has been argued again and again that for liturgical purposes the Psalms should be abridged, so as to rid Divine Service of ideas and sentiments that are out of place in Christian worship, the rubrics of the Prayer Book order the whole Psalter to be recited from beginning to end, once every month.

The method for reciting it is so straightforward that no separate column in the kalendar is necessary. The Prayer Book Psalter divides the 150 Psalms into sixty portions. Headings and labels assign two of these portions to each of thirty numbered days. The portions are more or less equal, measured by the time it takes to recite them, but because individual Psalms vary greatly in length, a given portion may consist of just one long Psalm or as many as six short ones. Psalm 119, the longest by far, is subdivided. The first of the sixty portions is recited at Morning Prayer on the first day of every month, the next portion at Evening Prayer on the same day, the one after that on the morning of the second day of the month, and so forth, through the thirtieth day. At the service described in chapter one, for example, the three Psalms recited at Morning Prayer are the portion for the fifth morning of every month.

The obvious convenience of this method makes up for the fact that preserving the biblical order sometimes puts into a morning portion a Psalm that would be more suitable for the end of the day and vice versa. In months that have thirty-one days, the last two portions are repeated, morning and evening; in February, the series is cut short at the twenty-eighth or twenty-ninth day as the case may be. Otherwise, no Psalm is left behind; each of them is read in course as often as the others, and none of the imprecation and vengefulness that color several of them is censored. The thirty-day cycle is suspended only on Christmas, Easter, and four other holydays, when specially appointed or "proper" Psalms supersede the portions that would otherwise be recited.

Immoveable Feasts

Other things being equal, the lessons at Mattins and Evensong depend on the date, and the kalendar tells what they are. But other things may not be equal. On Sundays, the first lessons are not read in course but instead as appointed in a separate table, organized not by date but according to the ecclesiastical year, which will be explained presently. Nor are other things equal on other feasts, when course reading is suspended entirely and chapters appropriate to the day are read.

Of the twenty-nine days that the Prayer Book lists as feasts in addition to the Sundays of the year (OWC 234–235), a few are moveable. The others, as was mentioned earlier, are assigned to fixed dates, three of which fall in January. They appear in the fifth column of the kalendar page on the lines for January 1, 6, and 25. Following a custom inherited from medieval scribes, Prayer Books sometimes use red ink to print the names of feasts. The edition illustrated in Figure 2.1 does so, although black-and-white reproduction makes the difference hard to see. These "red-letter days" are to be distinguished from the other, minor commemorations listed in the same column, which have no liturgical consequences and which by custom are printed differently—in black, if the feasts are red. Lucian, Hilary, Prisca, and the others whose names appear in the

January kalendar are saintly individuals but not, as the Prayer Book uses the word, saints. January 30 is an anomaly: a red-letter day, printed as such, but not a feast. It is kept, rather, as a "solemn day" in memory of King Charles the Martyr, with a service of its own that will be discussed later.

The three red-letter feasts in January honor the Circumcision of Christ, his Epiphany, and the Conversion of St. Paul. To each of these days, and to each of the other designated holydays throughout the year, the Prayer Book assigns special chapters which, like the Old Testament lessons on Sundays, are listed among the preliminaries in a separate table. Although the kalendar could have included them, it has blank lines on those three dates. Each major holyday also has its own special epistle and gospel, since the expectation is that Divine Service will include, as it does on Sundays, at least ante-Communion if not a full celebration. It is these "proper" readings from scripture, together with a proper collect, and in a few cases proper Psalms, that differentiate the regular services and make holydays, liturgically speaking, holy. Something should therefore be said about the propriety of these proper texts, and it can best be said with an example.

Feast-Day Propers: The Epiphany

When a feast is kept in honor of an event reported in the New Testament, one of the variable Bible readings, usually the liturgical gospel at Holy Communion, will be the narrative that reports it. That is so on January 6, the feast of the Epiphany. The appointed gospel is the well-known story of certain wise men who traveled from somewhere in "the east," guided by a marvelous star, to pay homage to the baby Jesus. The collect (owc 282), which is said at each of the three regular offices on Epiphany, makes reference to that event:

> O God, who by the leading of a star didst manifest thy only be-
> gotten Son to the Gentiles: Mercifully grant, that we which know
> thee now by faith, may after this life have the fruition of thy glo-
> rious godhead, through Jesus Christ our Lord. *Amen.*

This prayer, which in its original form is far older than the Prayer
Book, states succinctly the significance that Christian tradition
has ascribed to the sages from the east: as foreigners, they were
Gentiles, not Jews, and their visit was therefore the first occasion
on which Christ was made known to the rest of the world as well as
to his own people. Hence the Prayer Book's alternative name for the
feast, The Manifestation of Christ to the Gentiles.

The other biblical readings at Divine Service on Epiphany elaborate and comment on this theme; that is what makes them "proper."
The second lessons at Morning and Evening Prayer both narrate
further epiphanies or manifestations of Christ. His identity was
made known at his baptism, when a heavenly voice announced that
he was God's Son; his authority was displayed when he performed
his first miracle, changing water into wine.[8] The first lessons on
Epiphany, each of them a chapter from the book of the prophet
Isaiah, contain passages that have long been construed as presages
or foreshadows of Christ's manifestation. One of these lessons
mentions kings bringing gold and frankincense, which according
to the gospel reading were two of the gifts that the wise men
brought to Jesus. The other Old Testament chapter mentions an un-
named servant of the Lord, given as a light to foreigners. At Holy
Communion, the epistle comes from a letter written by St. Paul,
whose conversion to Christianity is celebrated later in the month,
and who is known as the apostle or messenger to the Gentiles. In
the assigned excerpt he writes about himself in that role.

---

[8] These lessons are Luke 3:1–23 and John 2:1–12. Both passages were associated with
Epiphany long before the Prayer Book.

These six lections are also read at Morning or Evening Prayer on other days, in the ordinary course set out in the kalendar; but on the feast of the Epiphany, each is lifted from its context and constellated with the other readings around the story of the wise men and the star. Together, the texts suggest and invite a symbolic, poetic, theological, and (in one sense of the word) mystical understanding of that story as it bears on the meaning of Christ. Such an invitation may not have much in common with modern, academic hermeneutics and biblical exegesis, which privilege the meaning of scriptural texts in their original settings. The Prayer Book, in its allocation of proper readings for many of the major holydays, exemplifies an older, more eclectic, and more imaginative tradition of biblical interpretation. The juxtaposition of the appointed texts, within acts of corporate worship, sets up a context of verbal, emblematic, figurative parallels, resonances, and associations that allows the readings to be grasped as parts of a whole, as commentary on each other, as variations on a theme, which at Divine Service on the Epiphany is the theme of God's Son disclosed to the world. The feast commemorates an event, but not an event confined to only one temporal moment or one spatial location. The Prayer Book does not demand that the readings be understood in this way, or any other way for that matter. It does imply, performatively, that there are more ways than one to "read, mark, learn, and inwardly digest" scripture.

Moveable Holydays and the Date of Easter

On the feast of the Epiphany, as on other immoveable feasts, the proper lessons at Morning and Evening Prayer do not cancel or replace chapters that would otherwise be read; they only cut into the queue. The kalendar makes room for them, and the sequence of course-reading resumes the next day. What the kalendar does not and cannot do is take account of holydays that fall on different dates in different years—Sundays and other moveable holydays.

Table 2.1 The Sundays of the Christian Year
according to the Book of Common Prayer

Christmas sequence

    Sundays in Advent (*four Sundays*)

        CHRISTMAS DAY, *December 25*

    Sunday(s) after Christmas

        The Epiphany, *January 6*

    Sunday(s) after the Epiphany

Easter sequence

    Septuagesima, the Third Sunday before Lent

    Sexagesima, the Second Sunday before Lent

    Quinquagesima, the next Sunday before Lent

        Ash Wednesday, the first day of Lent

    Sundays in Lent (*five Sundays; the first is Quadragesima*)

    The Sunday next before Easter

    EASTER DAY

    Sundays after Easter (*five Sundays*)

        Ascension Day

    The Sunday after Ascension Day (*sixth Sunday after Easter*)

    Whitsunday

    Trinity Sunday

    Sundays after Trinity

Sundays as Moveable Feasts

The ecclesiastical year has the same fifty-two or fifty-three Sundays as the concurrent civil year. A few of these Sundays are counted and designated in relation to Christmas Day, a fixed date; but most of them belong to an ordered arrangement within which they are seriated before and after the moveable feast of Easter. The whole church year thus combines two unequal series or sequences, as summarized in Table 2.1, which follows the order of the Sunday collects, epistles, and gospels in the Book of Common Prayer.[9]

What this table calls the Christmas sequence is straightforward. There are always four Sundays in the Advent season that begins the liturgical year and precedes Christmas; after Christmas there is at least one Sunday before January 6, the Epiphany, and sometimes two; after Epiphany there is at least one Sunday, which is so designated, and there may be as many as six. The number of Sundays after Epiphany depends on when the moveable Sunday with the odd name Septuagesima falls in a given year.

On Septuagesima the Easter sequence, as the table calls it, begins. This part of the church year continues through the seasons and individual Sundays listed in the table, all of which occur, always in the same order, every year. Only the last and longest season varies, because the whole sequence is moveable. All the Sundays between Trinity Sunday and the beginning of a new yearly cycle on the first Sunday of Advent are Sundays after Trinity. There are at least twenty-two and never more than twenty-seven, but their number is different every year, depending on when Easter is observed. The earlier the date of Easter, the more will be the Sundays after Trinity and the fewer the Sundays after Epiphany. In years when Easter is late, it is the other way around.

For the visually minded, or as a remedy for information overload, a graphic presentation of the church year may be helpful. Figure 2.2 shows the one included in what must be the only Prayer Book with moving parts. This edition, published in 1717, is something of a tour de force, and more will be said about it in chapter eleven. Near the beginning it provides the "circular table" shown in the illustration, which takes the form of a *volvelle*, a kind of sliding chart. The inner circle is separately printed, cut out, and threaded

---

[9] As in Table 1.1, the headings have been added. The Prayer Book does not refer to "sequences." Nor does it divide the ecclesiastical year in two on the First Sunday after Trinity, as some commentaries do.

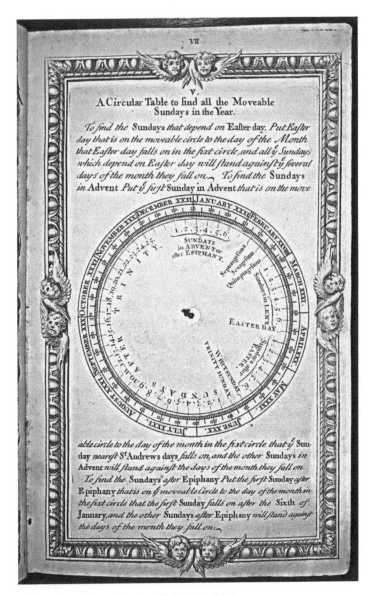

Figure 2.2 A Prayer Book with Moving Parts

An edition entirely engraved by John Sturt, 1717.

through the page so that it rotates. The outer, stationary ring is a 365-day calendar with dates but not the days of the week. On the moveable wheel, turned as shown in the illustration, the Sundays governed by the date of Easter begin about where one o'clock would be, and they extend clockwise to about the eleven o'clock position. For present purposes, the segment in between, at the top of the wheel, can be disregarded.

Following the printed instructions, Easter Day on the rotating circle has been aligned with April 11, the date of Easter in 1762. Clockwise from this this are the six Sundays after Easter (the sixth is also named the Sunday after Ascension), then Whitsunday, Trinity Sunday, and finally the numbered Sundays after Trinity, all as in Table 2.1. Notice that the Thirteenth Sunday after Trinity points to September 5, the date of the service described in chapter one. Notice also that with this setting of the *volvelle*, Septuagesima falls on February 7; counting backward, there are four Sundays after Epiphany. The Prayer Book provides for a fifth and a sixth Sunday, but those services would be omitted for the year.

The mobile diagram in the illustration has its limitations, but its circular arrangement does make it easy to see how the whole ec-clesiastical sequence from Septuagesima through the Sundays after Trinity shifts back and forth in relation to the ordinary cycle of 365 days. In the previous year, for instance, Easter Day fell on March 22. The inner wheel would be rotated counterclockwise so as to eliminate all but one Sunday after Epiphany, while the Thirteenth Sunday after Trinity would move back to the middle of August.

The Date of Easter Day

Figure 2.2 shows very graphically why mapping the ecclesias-tical year onto a secular calendar depends almost entirely on knowing when Easter will be observed. In the first edition of the 1662 Prayer Book, the relevant dates through 1700 are listed in a

Table of Moveable Feasts, also called the *almanack*, together with the corresponding dates of Septuagesima, Whitsunday, and other observances that depend on Easter (OWC 236–237). From time to time later editions have updated the almanack, usually for the next forty years or so. For most practical purposes nothing more is needed in order to assign dates to all the Sundays listed in Table 2.1 and to the other moveable holydays. For those dates, once they are known, the proper epistle, gospel, and (in some cases) Psalms and lessons can then be found. In addition to its almanack, however, the Book of Common Prayer provides instructions for finding the date of Easter in any year, whether the almanack includes it or not. Because the whole scheme of the Christian year depends, in a sense, on these instructions, the rest of this section will explain them. Because they are a bit technical, some readers may choose to pass over the explanation and go on to the end of the chapter.

Easter is observed on different dates because of the way it is defined. According to the Prayer Book's statement of the definition, Easter Day is "always the first Sunday after the first full moon which happens next after the one and twentieth day of March." Easter, by definition, must be observed in Spring, which is deemed to begin on March 21, no matter what the exact moment of the vernal equinox may be. Easter must also be observed on a Sunday, again by definition. Which particular Sunday this will be depends on the date of a full moon, where by "full moon" is meant the "ecclesiastical" full moon, a notional event determined by an artificial scheme. Like the beginning of Spring, the phases of the moon, as this scheme dates them, may not coincide exactly with astronomical data, although they keep more or less closely in step with what can be observed in the sky. Because every full moon, in this sense, can be predicted, it is possible to know in advance the date of the Sunday in Spring on which Easter will fall.

Unfortunately, at that point the 1662 Prayer Book's definition is faulty. It implies that if an ecclesiastical full moon happens on March 21, the first day of Spring itself, it is not the Paschal or Easter moon, which in turn implies that if the next day is Sunday it cannot be Easter. In fact it can. Easter fell on March 22 in 1668, which ironically is the date correctly listed in the 1662 almanack. What the definition ought to have said, and what it was eventually amended to say, is that the full moon of Easter is not the one "next after" March 21 but the one "*on or* next after." The mistake is trivial, but worth noticing because it was seized upon as an excuse for withholding the formal assent which members of the clergy were required by law to give to the contents of the Book of Common Prayer. Some fastidious ministers, ill-disposed to the book in general, insisted that because its Easter rules were false, assenting to it would be lying.[10]

Correctly defined, the date of Easter depends on one fixed date and on two recurring cycles, the days of the week and the phases of the moon. Each of these cycles can be computed in advance, starting in either case from the number of the year, reckoned as a "year of our Lord." Simple arithmetic yields, for any given year, two determining factors. One of these, known as the *Golden Number*, pertains to the lunar cycle; the other, the *Sunday Letter* or *Dominical Letter*, pertains to the seven-day cycle of the week. The arithmetic was explained in early Prayer Books, and editions available today explain it. The edition published in 1662 inexplicably does not, although it does list the Golden Number and Sunday Letter for each of the years covered in its almanack.

As inspection of the almanack shows, and as might be expected, both the seven Sunday Letters and the nineteen Golden Numbers are themselves cyclical. The Golden Number increases by one every year. In most years, the Sunday Letter moves backward one place. The letter was F for 1661, E for 1662, D for 1663. But in leap

---

[10] The most notable objector was Richard Baxter, of whom more later; see *The Nonconformists Plea for Peace: or An Account of their Judgment* (London, 1679), 160. The controversy had yet to subside when Robert Watts wrote *The Rule for Finding Easter in the Book of Common-Prayer, Explain'd and Vindicated against . . . the Misrepresentations of Mr. Baxter, Mr. Calamy, and other Dissenters* (2nd ed., London, 1714).

years, according to a statement added to some early Prayer Books, "the Sunday Letter leapeth." It moves back at the beginning of the year, as usual, and then "leaps" back again after the extra day in February.[11] A leap year thus has two letters, for example CB in 1664. Consequently the letter for 1665 is A, for 1666 it is G, and so on. The seven Sunday Letters register the fact that there are seven ways for the days of the week to align with calendar dates. The Golden Letters register the fact that there are nineteen ways for lunar months of 29½ days to align with the 365¼ days of the solar year. Every nineteenth year, in other words, all the dates on which a lunar month begins with a new moon, in the computational sense, are the same. Each year of this cycle is assigned a Golden Number. Some early Prayer Books repeat the plausible but probably mistaken idea that these numbers are called golden because scribes wrote them in gold. It was more likely the other way around—the name came first.

Because a given year belongs to both a seven-year cycle and a nineteen-year cycle, it may have any of the 133 possible combinations of a Sunday Letter and a Golden Number. Each of these pairs of letter and number corresponds to a date on which Easter may fall. Once the letter and the number are known, that date can be found in several ways, two of which appear in the Prayer Book's preliminary pages. One way involves nothing more than counting lines on the kalendar pages. Alternatively, there is a table on the last preliminary page, entitled To Find Easter for Ever (owc 238).

Each kalendar page, as mentioned earlier, has two columns that bear on finding the date of Easter. The numbers in the first column are Golden Numbers; the letters in the third column are Sunday

---

[11] This bit of folk-etymology was removed in 1662. The ambiguity of "the extra day in February" is deliberate. Before 1662, the Prayer Book ordered this day to be added after February 23. The lessons for that day were to be repeated; the kalendar for the month had twenty-eight lines. The 1662 version gives no instructions, although there are twenty-nine lines in the kalendar.

letters. The letters are simply a device to make counting easier. They appear in order, A through G, over and over throughout the year, beginning on January 1. In any year, every date with the Sunday Letter for that year will be a Sunday. Suppose that the Sunday Letter for a certain year is E. Figure 2.1 shows that the first Sunday of the year will be January 5. Every seventh day after that—every date in the second or the fourth column aligned with an E in the third column—will likewise be Sunday. If the year is a leap year, the letter will shift back one place after the extra day in February, and the Sundays from then on will fall on dates aligned with D. One of the dates in Spring that have the relevant Sunday Letter will be Easter Day. To know which one, the Golden Number is necessary.

All nineteen Golden Numbers—the wrong ones, in a few instances[12]—appear in the first column. Any date that has a Golden Number is a date on which a (computational) lunar month begins with a new moon. Suppose that the Golden Number for a certain year is 5. On the January kalendar page, the number 5 appears (correctly) in the line for January 9. A new moon, as computed, falls on that date every nineteen years, when the Golden Number is 5. Counting down fourteen places (inclusively) gives the date on which the same moon will be full. The dates of ecclesiastical full moons in any other month of the same year can be found in the same way, beginning with the same Golden Number, wherever it appears in the first column of the kalendar page for the month. One of these full moons—the first one that falls on or after March 21— will be the Easter moon in that year. Easter will therefore fall on the next date which has the Sunday letter for the year, as listed in the third column of the kalendar. If the date of the full moon is a Sunday, the next Sunday is Easter.

---

[12] The Golden Numbers for January 1, 3, and 30 should be 3, 11, and 14 respectively. See Frederic F. Grensted, "Calendar," *Prayer Book Dictionary* 116–122 at 117 col. 2. All three were correct when Golden Numbers were introduced into the Prayer Book kalendar in 1552; see *The First and Second Prayer Books of Edward VI* (New York: Everyman, 1910), 335. Eventually they were corrected.

The table To Find Easter for Ever is simply a compilation of these calculations, arranged in a seven-by-nineteen grid with a column for each Sunday Letter, a row for each Golden Number, and a date at each of the 133 intersections. Since Easter, correctly defined, may fall on March 22 at the earliest, or April 25 at the latest, there are only thirty-five possible dates. Some dates, therefore, appear more than once in this table. Five different pairs of number and letter indicate that Easter will be April 19, which in the (very) long run is the date on which it most frequently falls. It rarely falls on the earliest or the latest date, each of which appears in the table at only one intersection.

The title of the table, however, turned out to be too optimistic. In 1750 it was invalidated by an Act of Parliament that amputated eleven days from the civil calendar, so that in England and its colonies the date of the day after September 2, 1752, was September 14. This drastic surgery brought the dates from then on into conformity with the calendar decreed by Pope Gregory XIII, which had long been used in other countries, although the pope was never mentioned. The "new style" calendar, which is still in use, did not change the definition of Easter, but it did, and does, require regularly scheduled maintenance to prevent the defects of the old system from returning. At the end of every century, these adjustments may (but do not always) change the arithmetic for calculating Sunday Letters, or the placement of Golden Numbers in the kalendar.

The "Gregorian" date of Easter still corresponds to a combination of a Golden Number and a Sunday Letter. A seven-by-nineteen table of combinations can still be constructed, and an unabridged 1662 Prayer Book available today will still have one; but it will come with an expiration date. The first such table drawn up after the "new style" was adopted in 1752 could be used through 1899; the current one is due to expire at the end of 2199. In case anyone needs them, there are instructions for making the calculations that will apply in any later century, into the far distant future. The date of Easter is as predictable as it ever was, but there cannot be a table to find it forever.

Conclusion: Prayer Book Time

The rules that regulate the Prayer Book's regular offices derive in part from the regularity of the natural world, which many religions have seen as a manifestation of divine constancy. "The heavens declare the glory of God," as a well-known Psalm says, "and the firmament showeth his handiwork." One way for earthly worship to declare this glory has been to align itself with the cycles of day and night, the phases of the moon, the position of the stars. Not all Christian traditions have ordered their collective prayer in keeping with the orderly cosmos, but the Book of Common Prayer inherits a tradition that does.

It was suggested in the introduction that Prayer Book liturgy forms and informs the stories people tell through their lives and histories. One way in which it fulfills that function is by telling a story of its own, the vast and many-faceted story that defines the Christian God. It tells that story over and over, year by year, mediating its meaning and values through the regulated pattern of variations in Divine Service. In relation to this "sanctification of time," even the pragmatic users' manual in the Prayer Book is a sacred text.

Three
Occasional Services

In the course of a year, if its own rubrics are followed, the Book of Common Prayer will be used to conduct nearly a thousand regular services. Morning and Evening Prayer will be recited every day. On Sundays, Wednesdays, and Fridays the Litany will be added; on Sundays, Holy Communion will follow, with or without a full celebration of the Lord's Supper. The Communion office will also be said on feasts and certain other holydays. All these are instances of public prayer, Divine Service performed as a matter of duty, scheduled and varied according to the rules that were discussed in chapter two.

Many of the scripts in the Prayer Book, however, prescribe liturgies that do not recur at prescribed intervals. These "occasional services" take place from time to time, as need arises. They sanctify those times, those particular moments and episodes, rather than time as duration measured in cycles. For the time of a wedding, the Prayer Book provides the Form of Solemnization of Matrimony; for the time of a funeral, the Order for the Burial of the Dead. There are scripts for the initiation rite of Baptism, for a rite of passage called Confirmation, for visiting the sick, giving thanks after childbirth, and commissioning members of the clergy.

Ordination

On the last of these, the Ordination services, all the other Prayer Book liturgies depend, in so far as they must be performed by a clergyman. Ordination produces the church's authorized ministers,

The Book of Common Prayer. Charles Hefling, Oxford University Press (2021). © Oxford University Press.
DOI: 10.1093/oso/9780190689681.001.0001.

whose functions include presiding over liturgical worship. Three Ordination rites are incorporated at the end of the Book of Common Prayer under the (sub)title of The Form and Manner of Making, Ordaining, and Consecrating of Bishops, Priests, and Deacons—the Ordinal, for short. Each of these services inducts a member or members of the church into one of the three ranks or orders of ministry that the preface of the Ordinal says the church has maintained from the first.

The three orders are cumulative and hierarchical. Deacons are probationary priests, as it were. After a year, a deacon can expect to be ordained a second time and thereby promoted from the diaconate to the priesthood.[1] By a third ordination, usually termed consecration, a priest may be promoted to the episcopate, the order of bishops. But bishops, like admirals, are few. For that reason, and because deacons are not deacons for long, most members of the clergy have been priests. That may be why the Prayer Book rubrics sometimes appear to use the words *priest* and *minister* interchangeably, although deacons and bishops too are ministers, "clerks in holy orders."

Their ministries, however, are not the same. One difference is that the minister who presides at any of the three Ordination rites must be a bishop. When the order of priesthood is conferred, for example, the deacons who are being ordained kneel before the bishop, who together with the priests who are present lays his hands on each candidate's head, as he alone recites a solemn formula that begins, "Receive the Holy Ghost for the office and work of a priest in the church of God, now committed unto thee by the imposition of our hands." And it is the bishop who then delivers a Bible to each new priest, saying, "Take thou authority to preach the word of God, and to administer the holy sacraments" (owc 642).

---

[1] There have always been deacons who did not enter the priesthood. Lewis Carroll is perhaps the most famous example.

The meaning of these ceremonies, in themselves, is fairly evident. An aspirant is being set apart, inducted into a new identity and role, endowed and entrusted with authority, and equipped with the instrument by which he will carry out new responsibilities. According to the preface of the Ordinal, the laying-on of hands is not only symbolic but essential; without it, none of the Ordination services would be what it is or do what it does. But "public prayer" is necessary as well, and the visible "stage business" goes on within a discursive context that explains and particularizes what it means.

The whole service takes place "in the face of the church," on a Sunday or a feast, when a congregation can be expected to witness what is done. At an ordination of deacons or priests, the bishop issues a formal call for the disclosure of any crime or impediment that would disqualify any candidate. If someone raises an objection, the service stops. If not, it goes on to a scripted interrogation, in which those who are being ordained avow publicly their willingness to fulfill the responsibilities of the office they are about to take on. There is always a sermon in which the preacher is expected to expound the nature and necessity of the ministerial order that is to be conferred. The special ordination ceremonies are woven into Holy Communion, at which a special collect, epistle, and gospel, chosen for their relevance to the occasion, replace the ones that would otherwise be used.

Two features of the Ordinal that set it off from the rest of the Prayer Book should be mentioned. One is a hymn, the only hymn, in the modern sense, that is ever called for. When a bishop is consecrated or a priest is ordained, alternate verses of "Come Holy Ghost," a rhymed paraphrase of the ancient text *Veni Creator Spiritus*, are sung (or said) by the bishop and the congregation, invoking the divine Spirit that the candidate is to receive at the laying-on of hands. The other exceptional element is silence. Just before this hymn, at the ordination of a priest, "there shall be silence kept for a space" so that members of the congregation may pray on their own (owc 639). In practice, no doubt, opportunity for silent prayer has been introduced into many Prayer Book services, but this is the only rubric that requires it.

Solemnization of Matrimony

Like the ordination services, the Solemnization of Matrimony is an inauguration. The liturgy both expresses and accomplishes a transition; it signifies, and by so doing effects, an entry into a new pattern of life characterized by new relationships, privileges, and responsibilities. Like holy orders, holy matrimony is a sanctified state of being, instituted by God according to the Prayer Book, and the service that solemnizes its inception resembles an ordination in some ways. At the beginning of both rites, after a prescribed address that states the nature and importance of the new status that certain persons are about to enter, there is a formal call for objections, in case some circumstance exists that would prevent their entry. In both rites the individuals concerned openly affirm their willingness and determination to accept the stated expectations that their new roles will entail. In both, a physical token that makes a symbolic reference to what has been promised—in Matrimony, a ring; at an Ordination, a book—is ritually given and received.

The marriage service is brief. The minister's prescribed address reminds those who are present of the purpose for which they have gathered, and goes on to define marriage by its origins, its meaning, and its ends, which are three: procreation of children, avoidance of fornication, and mutual society, help, and comfort. This is the point at which the service might have to be cut short, if an obstacle to lawful wedlock is alleged, as happens in a memorable chapter of Charlotte Brontë's *Jane Eyre*. To avoid last-minute revelations, the rubrics instruct the minister to "publish the banns of marriage" on three previous Sundays or holydays, by announcing the names of the bride and bridegroom and calling for disclosure of any objection to their proposed union.

Film and folklore notwithstanding, no one says "I do" at a Prayer Book wedding. When the priest goes on to ask the bridegroom if he will have the bride to his wedded wife, and the bride if she will have him to her wedded husband, the prescribed answer is "I will." After the woman has been silently "given" by her father (or a friend) to be married to the man, she and he do what they have both declared their willingness to do. Each, taking the other's hand, uses personal names and first-person verbs to announce a fact: "I (*name*) take thee (*name*) to my wedded husband" or "my wedded wife." Similarly, when the bridegroom gives the bride a ring he makes the declarative statement that "With this ring I thee wed."

By so doing, husband and wife have "given and pledged their troth," their truth, their being true, "either to other." That is how the Prayer Book puts it. A philosophy of language might put it in terms of "speech-acts" or "performative utterances." The uttered propositions "I take" and "I wed" are sayings that do what they say. The fact expressed in such an avowal *is* a fact when, and because, it is expressed. To voice the words honestly is to make them true; it brings about the condition or the state of affairs they refer to. A woman who takes a man to her wedded husband commits herself to being what she has thereby become, and to becoming what she has made herself be—her husband's wife; and vice versa. This deliberate act of self-constitution on the part of two individuals is the event that the service of Matrimony solemnizes.

Baptism

According to its full title, the Book of Common Prayer provides for the "administration of the sacraments." According to its Catechism, a pedagogical text that will be discussed shortly, a *sacrament* is "an outward and visible sign of an inward and spiritual grace . . . ordained by Christ himself" (OWC 429). There are two sacraments, so defined: the Lord's Supper and Baptism. As Holy

Communion is a ritualized meal, Baptism is a ritualized bath. The "outward and visible sign" is water, used in a symbolic washing. Both Holy Communion and Baptism, according to the Catechism, are "generally necessary to salvation." Why Baptism is necessary is explained in the address with which the office begins. "All men," the minister says, "are conceived and born in sin, and . . . none can enter into the kingdom of God, except he be regenerate and born anew of water and of the holy Ghost" (owc 408). As there is no exemption from the general necessity of regeneration or new birth, so too there is no time in any particular human life before which baptism is unnecessary. That is part of what is meant by the theological term *original sin*. New parents must therefore be warned against putting off their child's baptism for more than a few days after birth. As a rule, the service would be conducted in church, at Divine Service on the next Sunday or holyday. However, if a newborn appears unlikely to live, the rule may be suspended and another, shortened rite, Private Baptism, may be used to administer the sacrament at home instead.

For "such as are of riper years"—adults and older children— there is a third baptismal office, suitably modified. Normally, however, the service will be Public Baptism of Infants, conducted after the lessons at Mattins or Evensong. As at a marriage or an ordination, consent to the proceedings is declared at the outset in a series of formal questions and answers. In the service of Matrimony the minister asks, "Wilt thou have this man" or "this woman?" In Baptism the question is, "Wilt thou be baptized?" An infant who is brought for baptism cannot understand this ritual interrogation, much less take a deliberate part in it, so the responses are spoken by proxies. Addressing these "godmothers" and "godfathers" as individuals, the priest asks:

> Dost thou, in the name of this child, renounce the devil and all his works, the vain pomp and glory of the world, with all covetous desires of the same, and the carnal desires of

the flesh, so that thou wilt not follow nor be led by them?
Answer: I renounce them all.

To this renunciation a positive affirmation is added. The minister recites the Apostles' Creed in the form of a question: "Dost thou believe in God the Father Almighty" and so on. In response to two further questions, the godparents affirm willingness to be baptized in the faith that the creed defines, and to keep God's holy will and commandments.

Christening, as the act of baptism is sometimes called, follows. The rubrics assume that the church will have a font, a permanent ceremonial basin for the water that will be used (see Figure 11.7 for an example). After praying that God will sanctify this water, the priest directs the godparents to "name this child," whom he addresses by name and dips "discreetly and warily" in the font, saying "I baptize thee in the Name of the Father, and of the Son, and of the Holy Ghost." He then makes the sign of the cross on the child's forehead, to signify that she or he "shall not be ashamed to confess the faith of Christ crucified" (owc 412).

With that, the Prayer Book says, the child has been initiated, "received into Christ's holy church, and . . . made a lively member of the same" (owc 408). The liturgy has various ways of expressing what the initiation is and does. Baptism is cleansing, a washing away of sin. It is rescue, passing through the waves of the troublesome world, secure in the ark of Christ's church. It is death and resurrection, the dying of carnal affections and burying of "the old Adam," followed by rising in triumph over the devil, the world, and the flesh (owc 409, 411). These images all refer to the "inward and spiritual grace" which the Catechism says is received by means of the "outward and visible sign" of water. As to how a baptized baby receives this benefit, there can be and has been disagreement.

The wording of the Prayer Book's baptismal rite has raised, among others, questions about the relation of the sacramental sign to the gift or grace it signifies—whether the two coincide, whether they always coincide, and whether they coincide then and there, at the moment when the sacrament is administered. The text appears to say they do. As soon as the infant has been signed with the cross, the priest introduces the Lord's Prayer with the words, "Seeing now, dearly beloved brethren, that this child is regenerate . . ." They have been contentious words. On the face of it, the implication is that an infant comes to the font unregenerate, "conceived and born in sin," and leaves it regenerated, born again. Yet there is nothing to show that a change has taken place; and it can happen that a person who is regenerate by the criterion of having been baptized is manifestly unregenerate by the criterion of virtuous and godly living.

Perhaps, then, the statement that "this child is regenerate" is an expression of hope, a charitable hypothesis, spoken by anticipation and meaning that there is reason to expect that a child who is sacramentally adopted into the church will, in time, fulfill the promises made on his or her behalf. Or perhaps—what may come to the same thing—to say "this child is regenerate" is to speak of an incipient, preliminary regeneration that has still to be completed. On the other hand, at the end of the service stands the categorical assertion that "it is certain by God's word that children which are baptized, dying before they commit actual sin, are undoubtedly saved" (OWC 414). While that might appear to settle the matter, not everyone has thought so.

Here the point is not to analyze the disagreements, let alone resolve them: it is to draw attention to the fact that they can and do arise. The Book of Common Prayer is among other things a doctrinal text, a repository of Christian teaching, which has been appealed to again and again as an authority in controversies about right belief. Liturgy inevitably expresses theological teaching, which in the case of the Prayer Book has been taken very seriously. That is not the least important sense in which it has been a sacred text. For the same reason, it has also been a contested text, and both of its sacramental rites, the Lord's Supper and Baptism, have been sites of contestation from the first.

Thanksgiving of Women after Childbirth (Churching)

Baptism, public or if necessary private, is not the only Prayer Book office concerned with the birth of children. There is another, "commonly called the Churching of Women," which it will be appropriate to consider here.

When an infant is christened using the Book of Common Prayer, the godparents are vocal participants, but parents are not mentioned at all. Their presence at the service is neither required nor discouraged. They do not act as godparents.[2] The child's mother, however, is expected to come to the church later, when she is well enough, for her Churching. The Thanksgiving of Women after Childbirth, to use its proper name, is a tiny service. After one sentence addressed to the mother, who kneels "decently appareled . . . in some convenient place, as hath been accustomed," the priest recites a Psalm that speaks of deliverance from the snares of death and of paying vows to the Lord, or another Psalm that celebrates children and the fruit of the womb as a heritage and gift from God.

Without going into the historical antecedents of this office, it can be mentioned—and may be obvious—that Churching represents the survival, in attenuated form, of a purification rite. It was so named in the original Book of Common Prayer (owc 91). The idea that a woman who has given birth is unfit to come to church until she has been ritually purified can still, perhaps, be read into the service, but the text as it stands carries no such implication.

---

[2] Not, that is, until very recently, when certain alterations of the rubrics were made. They appear in the Everyman edition (1999) at 267 and the Penguin edition (2012) at 277.

Catechism and Confirmation

At the end of the office for the Public Baptism of Infants, the priest delivers a charge to the godparents. They are told they must call upon their godchild to hear sermons and to memorize three of the texts that are regularly said in Divine Service: the Apostles' Creed, the Lord's Prayer, and the Ten Commandments (owc 413). In addition, baptized children are expected to learn the Church Catechism, which is the next item in the Book of Common Prayer after the three baptismal rites.

A catechism is a stylized dialogue between a teacher and a learner or catechumen, usually in the form of questions with set answers, said by rote. As catechisms go, the one in the Prayer Book is short and simple. The first of its five sections opens with questions that establish a connection with the learner's baptism: "What is your name?" and "Who gave you this name?" Then the catechumen repeats the three required formularies and recites a brief exposition of what each of them teaches. One of these replies includes a phrase worth mentioning as evidence that Shakespeare was brought up on the Book of Common Prayer. When Hamlet calls his hands "these pickers and stealers," the allusion is unmistakable; according to the Catechism, it is a duty toward neighbors "to keep my hands from picking and stealing."

Although the Catechism is not itself a liturgical office, the rubrics require instruction and examination in its contents to take place at Evening Prayer, after the second lesson; and they require parents, masters, and dames of schools to send their children, servants, and apprentices to church at the appointed time to be catechized. When these learners can say the Catechism by heart, they may be confirmed; once they have been confirmed, they may receive the sacrament of Holy Communion.

Confirmation is thus a further rite of passage for those who have "come to years of discretion" and can "with their own mouth and consent openly before the church ratify and confirm" what was promised on their behalf at their baptism. The rite is brief; there is neither lesson nor sermon nor Psalm. Immediately after the usual scripted address, the officiating minister—always a bishop—asks those who are to be confirmed whether they do, in the presence of God, acknowledge themselves to be bound by the baptismal vow that was taken in their name. When they have answered audibly "I do," he prays that God, who at their baptism regenerated them, will now strengthen them with the Holy Ghost. Then, as at Ordination, the bishop lays his hand on their heads, one by one, while he says a short prayer that begins, "Defend, O Lord, this thy child" or, when adults are confirmed, "this thy servant." After the Lord's Prayer, a prayer for the newly confirmed, and another more general prayer, the bishop's blessing brings the service to a close.

The Visitation of the Sick, and the Burial of the Dead

Although its placement immediately before the Burial office might suggest otherwise, the Order for the Visitation of the Sick is not meant to be used only when someone is *in extremis*. Nevertheless the tone of the service is grim. It takes for granted a conception of divine providence in which illness is not only intentional on God's part but in some sense punitive. Bodily affliction is divinely inflicted. As "fatherly chastisement," it may have been sent to test the patience and display the faith of the afflicted, or to correct and amend some offense. In any case it should move those who have fallen sick not only to imitate Christ in his suffering, but also to examine, accuse, and condemn themselves for their own faults.

Accordingly, after a very long exhortation that dwells on these themes, the minister who visits an invalid at home asks for a profession of belief in the articles of the Apostles' Creed, using much the same interrogative form as in Baptism. Then—very unusually—the rubrics tell him what sort of thing he is to say, without giving him the exact words in which to say it. He is to urge the sick person to forgive, reform, settle worldly affairs, give to the poor, and finally to make a special confession of sins. This is the only occasion for private, individual, "auricular" confession that is mentioned explicitly in the Prayer Book. It has its own formula of absolution, which has always been controversial.

In pronouncing absolution at Morning and Evening Prayer, the priest says, "Almighty God . . . pardoneth and absolveth all them that truly repent." In the Visitation office he says, "*I* absolve thee from all thy sins." The usual, public formula is evidently a declarative statement about what God does, whereas the speech prescribed for Visitation appears to be a speech-act, a performative utterance in which the priest himself does what he says, by saying it. In both cases the full wording makes it clear that absolution rests on delegated authority and power; at issue is what this power consists in.

When a priest is ordained, the bishop declares at the laying-on of hands, "whose sins thou dost forgive, they are forgiven; and whose sins thou dost retain, they are retained" (owc 642). This declaration can be understood as an affirmation of sacerdotal mediation: absolution depends ultimately on God but proximately and necessarily on the priest. However, as with regeneration as the effect of Baptism, forgiveness as the effect of absolution can be disputed on various grounds. The most common objection to what the Visitation office seems to imply has been that no human agency can affect the individual believer's direct, unmediated access to divine mercy. Remission of sins depends solely on God; although the priest may pronounce it, he cannot dispense or control it.

Whatever absolution may be or do, it is to take place as part of Visitation only if the invalid humbly and heartily desires it. After that, the rest of the office consists of a Psalm and prayers, which may be abbreviated if preparations have been made to celebrate Holy Communion. For this special celebration in a sick person's house, a very brief epistle and gospel are appointed, but nearly everything in the service is the same as it would be in church. There must be a congregation, so that three or at least two other communicants can receive the sacrament together with the priest and the invalid. It is still a service of *common* prayer.

The Visitation office provides a solemn prayer for use "at the point of departure," which commends the soul of the dying person into the hands of its faithful Creator and merciful Savior. Once that soul has departed, the Prayer Book presumes that the corpse left behind will be buried in the ground, there to await the resurrection of the body that the Apostles' Creed affirms. With that affirmation the Order for the Burial of the Dead begins: "I am the resurrection and the life, saith the Lord," the first of the burial sentences, is said or sung by the priest and clerks at the entrance to the churchyard, the boundary of sacred ground, as they meet the procession that brings the mortal remains of the deceased, for the last time, into the church.

The Burial Sentences

I am the resurrection and the life, saith the Lord: he that believeth in me, though he were dead, yet shall he live. And whosoever liveth and believeth in me, shall never die.

I know that my Redeemer liveth, and that he shall stand at the latter day upon the earth. And though after my skin worms destroy this body, yet in my flesh shall I see God: whom I shall see for myself, and mine eyes shall behold, and not another.

We brought nothing into this world, and it is certain we can carry nothing out. The Lord gave, and the Lord hath taken away; blessed be the Name of the Lord.

The service in the church consists of a lengthy lesson, preceded by two Psalms that emphasize the fleetingness of earthly life. They include these verses:

Behold, thou hast made my days as it were a span long :
  and mine age is even as nothing in respect of thee,
  and verily every man living is altogether vanity.

The days of our age are threescore years and ten, and though
men be so strong that they come to fourscore years :
  yet is their strength then but labor and sorrow;
  so soon passeth it away and we are gone.

The rest of the service takes place at the grave. An anthem reiterates
the impermanence of all things human and prays for deliverance
from the bitter pains of eternal death. Interment begins with a
ritual casting of earth onto the body, as the priest commits it to the
ground, "earth to earth, ashes to ashes, dust to dust, in sure and certain hope of the resurrection."

The prayers in the Burial service request no benefits for the
person whose body is buried. None of them is a prayer *for* the deceased. Nor is there any commendation, such as the one in the
Visitation office. To judge by what the prescribed prayers say, the
congregation may hope that "this our sister" or "this our brother" is
at rest with God in joy, but they do not pray for it; what they pray is
that they will themselves receive perfect consummation and bliss,
together with all who love and fear God, at the general resurrection on the last day. Chapter five will have more to say about this
emphasis, or lack of emphasis, in the Prayer Book's funeral rite. It
is deliberate.

Other Liturgies and Texts

Toward the back of the Book of Common Prayer are several liturgical texts that are neither regular, public offices like Morning
and Evening Prayer, nor occasional services that concern specific individuals, as Baptism and Matrimony do. The first of
these liturgies, which is printed after the Churching service, is

A Commination, or Denouncing of God's Anger and Judgments against Sinners. Between the Psalter and the Ordinal there are Forms of Prayer for Use at Sea; at the very end of the book are three liturgies for "solemn days," usually called the State Services.[3]

The only day on which Commination is mandatory is Ash Wednesday, the beginning of the somber season of Lent that leads to Easter. This anomalous liturgy, mentioned in chapter two, includes Psalm 51, the most poignant of the penitential Psalms. But before this Psalm is said, the service lives up to its full name. At the beginning is a litany of divine curses upon wrongdoers, each of which the congregation affirms with an *Amen.* Then comes a fire-and-brimstone compilation of biblical excerpts that denounce (that is, declare) God's wrath and the peril of disregarding it. The quotations and allusions in this fearsome speech are neither expounded nor applied: they roll out relentlessly and, considered as rhetoric, to good effect. Considered as theology, or perhaps psychology, they imply that before there can be repentance, as expressed in the Psalm, there must be contrition, regret, sorrow; and that genuine contrition is the result of being made personally cognizant and convinced of sin, with which God is justly angry.

The State Services and what has been called the Sea Service are comparative newcomers, added to the Book of Common Prayer in 1662. What needs to be said about them can best be postponed for the moment.

Since 1662 many editions of the Prayer Book have included certain nonliturgical texts, of which the most important is the collection of short doctrinal statements formally entitled the Articles of Religion. The Thirty-nine Articles, as they are almost always

---

[3] The status of the three State Services as official Prayer Book contents has been disputed. They were taken out in the nineteenth century, and present-day editions do not include them. The somewhat similar Accession Day service, which they usually do include, was not in the 1662 version when it was first issued. See A. P. Percival, *The Original Services for the State Holidays, with Documents Relating to the Same* (London: J. Leslie, 1838).

called, are very important as one of the foundational documents of Anglican Christianity, and it is often assumed that because they share this status with the Book of Common Prayer, they also belong to its official contents. In fact they do not. One of the Articles endorses the Ordinal, however, and several of them bear on common prayer inasmuch as they are concerned with the nature of the sacraments, the qualifications of ministers, the language of public worship, and the authority of the church in regard to rites and ceremonies.

The Table of Kindred and Affinity likewise has, or had, an official status. It is a list of relatives with whom marriage is forbidden "in scripture and our laws," drawn up in the sixteenth century and inserted into the Prayer Book. Since then, changes in both civil and ecclesiastical regulations have rendered it obsolete.

Four

Preambles: "But One Use"

There cannot be many sacred texts that begin with some twenty pages of statutes enacted by a national legislature. The Prayer Book does. The first item in its table of contents is "The Acts for the Uniformity of Common Prayer." While the two documents so named may bear only indirectly on the form and contents of the liturgical rites that this book has introduced, it would be a mistake to ignore them. Together with the three prefatory essays that follow, the legislation transcribed at the beginning of the Prayer Book belongs to its self-presentation, the text's internal account of its own status, purpose, and ancestry. The account is official and, as might be expected, not altogether impartial. It does however afford a preliminary context for understanding why the Book of Common Prayer is the book it is and how it came to contain what it does. The present chapter's brief survey of what the book says about itself in these preliminary pages will thus serve as a point of entry for the more extensive account of its origins and reception that begins in chapter five.

Genealogy

The Act of Uniformity with which the 1662 Prayer Book opens was passed in 1559 by the first Queen Elizabeth's first Parliament in the first year of her reign. The Act which follows it, and which authorizes the whole book and governs its use, deliberately mirrors its predecessor, especially at the beginning.

The Book of Common Prayer. Charles Hefling, Oxford University Press (2021). © Oxford University Press.
DOI: 10.1093/oso/9780190689681.001.0001.

Each Act of Uniformity opens, in the usual way, with a "whereas" section that rehearses the circumstances in which the provisions that follow were framed and explains the reasons for framing them. The Elizabethan Act reports that at one time there was a most excellent liturgy, the Book of Common Prayer. Regrettably, the use of that book was discontinued. Now the Act restores it, with certain small amendments, which are stated briefly. The opening of the 1662 Act of Uniformity tells a similar story. "During the time of the late unhappy troubles," which are not particularized, the liturgy that Queen Elizabeth restored in 1559 was done away with. Now it is restored to use again, and again there are revisions. These are not particularized either, but the next item in the contents, the Preface, which was composed for the restored book in 1662, mentions several improvements: rubrics have been clarified, language is updated, a new translation of scripture has been made use of, and new services for special occasions are included. Anyone who wants to know the details is invited to compare the former text with the revision.

These reports, as far as they go, are accurate. In 1552, during the reign of Elizabeth's brother King Edward VI, Parliament did, as stated in the Elizabethan Act, establish "one uniform order of Common Service, and Prayer." The next year Edward died and his successor Queen Mary, his and Elizabeth's sister, abolished this liturgy. Six years later, the Uniformity Act of 1559 repealed the abolition and reinstated the liturgy, which the Act of 1662 reinstated again. Thus, on its own showing, the Book of Common Prayer is a twice-restored and twice-revised recension of a text that goes back more than a century to the reign of Edward VI.

This official genealogy is summarized in Table 4.1, which lists the three successive versions of the Prayer Book—1552, 1559, and 1662—to which the Acts of Uniformity refer, together with the corresponding sovereigns and legislation. Allowing for the revisions,

Table 4.1 Versions of the Book of Common Prayer 1549–1662

versions of the Prayer Book	reigning sovereign	legislation	effective date
The Original Book of Common Prayer			
1549	Edward VI reigned 1547–1553	*First Act of Uniformity* 2 & 3 Edward VI c. 1 January 21, 1549	Whitsunday June 9, 1549
The Classical Book of Common Prayer			
1552	Edward VI	*Second Act of Uniformity* 5 & 6 Edward VI c. 1 April 14, 1552	All Saints Day November 1, 1552
	Mary I reigned 1553–1558	*First Statute of Repeal* 1 Mary statute 2 c. 2 November 8, 1553	December 20, 1553
1559	Elizabeth I reigned 1558–1603	*Third Act of Uniformity* 1 Elizabeth I c. 2 May 8, 1559	Feast of St. John the Baptist June 24, 1559
		Ordinance for the Taking Away of the Book of Common Prayer January 3, 1645	March 13, 1645
1662	Charles II reigned 1649/ 1660–1685	*Fourth Act of Uniformity* 14 Charles II c. 4 May 19, 1662	Feast of St. Bartholomew August 24, 1662

these texts are similar enough to warrant the umbrella term "classical" used in the table.

The table also takes account of the fact, which is nowhere mentioned in either of the Acts or in the Preface, that the classical Prayer Book had a more remote ancestor. In 1549, three years before King Edward's "uniform order," an earlier Act of Uniformity authorized a text with the same title—the first Book of Common Prayer. This earlier liturgy has much of the same content as the classical versions, but there are significant differences as well. How the original Prayer Book of 1549 bears on the later versions will be examined at some length in the next chapter; for now, its existence will simply be registered at the beginning of the table.

Authorization

The 1662 Act of Uniformity that is included in the Prayer Book includes the book that includes it. Each of these texts contains, in a sense, the other. The Act refers repeatedly to a long title:

> The Book of Common Prayer,
> and Administration of the Sacraments,
> and other Rites and Ceremonies of the Church,
> according to the use of the Church of England,
> together with the Psalter, or Psalms of David,
> Pointed as they are to be sung or said in Churches;
> and the Form and Manner
> of Making, Ordaining, and Consecrating
> of Bishops, Priests, and Deacons;

and lest there be any doubt as to exactly what text this name refers to, a full manuscript is, or was, "annexed and joined" by strings to the original engrossment of the Act that refers to it. At some point the two documents were separated and the Book Annexed, as it is called, was mislaid for a while, but both are extant. Furthermore, the Act requires a number of printed copies of this manuscript, carefully vetted and certified, to be preserved for future reference. These too still exist. Legally speaking, the textual constitution of the

1662 Book of Common Prayer is as definite and unambiguous as it could well be.

To all and everything contained and prescribed in the text thus defined, the Act requires "unfeigned assent and consent" on the part of every minister of the Church of England. This blanket acceptance of the Prayer Book must be declared openly, in a stated form, following a solemn, public reading of Morning and Evening Prayer as the book prescribes them (owc 196). The feast of St. Bartholomew, August 24, is set as the deadline for the clergy to make their declarations, and for every church and chapel in England and Wales to purchase a copy of the restored liturgy. Until that date, Queen Elizabeth's Prayer Book is to be used; from then on, the version named in the Act and none other. Also as from that date, any minister who has not been ordained by a bishop, in such a way as to meet the requirements set out in the revised Ordinal, is barred from holding an ecclesiastical post or carrying out an ecclesiastical ministry.

These and the many other provisions of the 1662 Act of Uniformity are important, not because they are all now in force but because for a very long time they were. The Book of Common Prayer is more than "a schedule attached to an Act of Parliament," but it is that too; and the fact that in England, Wales, Ireland, and elsewhere its contents and its use have been regulated by civil law is not incidental to its meaning, its reception, and its influence. Whether that fact makes the Prayer Book any less sacred a text depends on how religious and civil authority, church and state, the sacred and the secular, are or ought to be related. That question will come up again and again.

What is not in question is that the history of the Book of Common Prayer has had a political dimension—not in spite of its religious meaning but because of it. On the one hand, in 1662 it could be maintained, as it is in the Act of Uniformity, that "nothing conduceth more to the settling of the peace of this nation . . . than an universal agreement in the Public Worship of almighty God"

(OWC 195), where by agreement is meant not subjective consensus but objective uniformity. Conversely, on the other hand, it is partly because this uniformity was a legal obligation that the Book of Common Prayer came to be familiar, customary, and even venerable, for it meant that the same prescribed services were attended by a great many people on a great many Sundays and holydays and at a great many weddings and christenings and funerals.

To that extent, the Act of Uniformity was not unsuccessful, which is not to say that the Book of Common Prayer meets or has met everyone's religious needs or theological requirements. It has not. It has, however, for better or worse, been the one authorized liturgy of what has been in principle if never in fact a national church. In that regard the statutory liturgy has enjoyed the considerable advantage of expressing a set of religious attitudes and convictions that are congruent with and supportive of certain kinds of patriotism, national memory, and civic loyalty. In turn, this aspect of its meaning has had a profound effect on the dissemination and acceptance of the Book of Common Prayer in places beyond the boundaries of the church "by law established" in England.

As for the immediate occasion of (re)establishing the book itself, the 1662 Act of Uniformity and the Preface that follows it are both reticent. The Preface refers to "late unhappy confusions," which it says are "too well known to the world, and we are not willing to remember" (OWC 209). Use of the Prayer Book had been abrogated—illegally abrogated, according to the Preface, for mischievous purposes that are best forgotten. Ironically, it was to ensure that these unhappy confusions would *not* be forgotten that two special forms of Divine Service were annexed to the revived liturgy. One of these, as chapter two has mentioned, commemorates the execution of King Charles I, which had brought an end to England's monarchy in 1649. In this annual liturgy the late king is honored fulsomely as a Christian martyr—canonized as a saint in all but name—while his executioners are referred to in scathing terms. The other new form of prayer celebrates the end of the Great Rebellion, as the unhappy confusions came to be called, and the restoration of monarchy in the person of King Charles II, the martyr's son. When the prayers in this service offer effusive thanks for the return of "the public and free profession of thy true religion and worship" (OWC 664), it would not be far-fetched to surmise that God is being thanked for the restoration of religion consonant with the Book of Common Prayer.

If so, not everyone was prepared to be thankful. The Preface admits as much. When it became evident that the use of the liturgy that had been interrupted for years would soon be resumed, the same opposition that had engineered the interruption flared up again. Various objections were raised, nearly all of them old ones, as the Preface observes, and many of them as old as the Prayer Book itself. What these arguments amounted to, who made them, and why, will need to be examined, for two reasons. One is that the rejection of the Book of Common Prayer belongs to the history of its reception. The same qualities that moved many sincere and earnest people to jettison its rites as ungodly made it, for many others, a sacred text. Another, more specific reason is that a number of the alterations that were judged to be expedient when the liturgy was restored in 1662 had been proposed at a colloquy convened for the purpose of relieving the "tender consciences" of those who were so repulsed by the religion of the Elizabethan Prayer Book that they could not bear to practice it.

Origins and Purpose

Beginning as it does with the Acts of Uniformity and with a newly written Preface, the Prayer Book begins *in medias res*. Those texts are concerned with revival and revision, amendment and restoration; not with how and why there came to be a Book of Common Prayer in the first place. What little the book has to say about its own origins is said in two short tracts or essays, both of which were written for the original version of 1549 and retained ever since. One of these essays, originally the preface, was renamed "Concerning the Service of the Church" in 1662 when the new Preface was added. The other essay, entitled in full "Of Ceremonies, Why some be abolished, and some retained," was printed in 1549 as a sort of appendix, then moved to the front of the book. Both essays are anonymous, but no one doubts who wrote them. The author was the archbishop of Canterbury, Thomas Cranmer, who by reason of his office was the highest-ranking member of the Church of England's clergy.

The archbishop's theme in "Concerning the Service" is recovery from decay. He commends the new Prayer Book as "an order for prayer, and for the reading of the holy scripture, much agreeable to the mind and purpose of the old Fathers" (owc 213). In their time, the springtime of the church, common prayer stirred the clergy to godliness and equipped them to exhort others. The more their knowledge of God increased, the more their people were "inflamed with the love of his true religion." That above all is what the service of the church is for: to edify. But everything human is corruptible, even the godly and decent practice of the old fathers of the church. Over time, common prayer came to be bloated with liturgical add-ons—stories, legends, vain repetitions, invitatories, anthems, responds, verses. What had once been the continuous reading of the Bible was constantly interrupted; sorting out the intricate rules for ordering what should be read took more time than it took to read what the rules ordered; and even when the order had been sorted out, what was read was read in Latin, which people could hear but for the most part could not inwardly digest.

Nothing that Cranmer says in "Concerning the Service" had not been said by others. In fact he seems to have cribbed much of his argument in the essay, which turns out to be more of a preface to Mattins and Evensong than a preface to the whole Prayer Book.[1] By

---

[1] Cranmer's sources are set out in parallel columns in Brightman, *English Rite*, I: 34–38. For an interpretation of the use he made of them, see Stella Brook, *The Language of the Book of Common Prayer* (Oxford: Oxford University Press, 1965), 179–181.

comparison with the late medieval rites that they displaced, those two offices are indeed simpler; they are said in English; the kalendar they follow does prescribe continuous reading of nearly the whole Bible, which, as Cranmer observes, is the only book other than the Book of Common Prayer that is necessary for conducting Divine Service. The small library of liturgical volumes that every church once had to own is now surplus to requirements.[2]

An emphasis on simplicity for the sake of edification is evident as well in the essay "Of Ceremonies." Here, perhaps because nothing is said in "Concerning the Service" about "administration of the sacraments and other rites and ceremonies of the church," Cranmer explains why these too needed to be purged. The explanation is still very general, though. Cranmer limits himself to humanly devised ceremonies, which as such are subject to change, but does not mention any ceremony in particular. To keep such ceremonies or leave them out is a small matter, he says, but like the accumulated verbal embellishments in Divine Service, they are too many. Some ceremonies, of course, there must be, for the sake of common order and discipline. And there are ceremonies that edify: they declare Christ's benefits and are "apt to stir up the dull mind of man to the remembrance of his duty to God." These should be retained, the implication being that the Prayer Book retains them, whatever they are. On the other hand, many ceremonies are dark and dumb, meaningless in much the same way that prayers are meaningless when they are said in Latin. Moreover, ceremonies can be abused, as Cranmer says they have been, partly owing to ignorant superstition—a term he does not define—but also inasmuch as ceremonies have become a commodity, marketed by avaricious ministers for their own profit.

---

[2] Brightman, *English Rite*, I: 36. A sentence about eliminating the need for costly liturgical books had become irrelevant by 1662 and was omitted from "Concerning the Service." The books are described in Kenneth Stevenson, "Worship by the Book," *OGBCP*, 9–20.

All things considered, the Prayer Book strikes a balance, in the archbishop's judgment, between newfangleness, which he says should always be eschewed, and incurable addiction to every punctilio of ceremonial custom. In virtue of this judicious moderation, the new book is better suited to the purposes of common prayer than the old books were. Using it will glorify God, it will edify the people, and—not incidentally—it will unify England and England's church. One of the complaints in "Of Ceremonies" is that worship has been too diverse. In different places, services are conducted according to different "uses," different sets of liturgical customs. With the arrival of the Book of Common Prayer, Cranmer announces, that will change: "from henceforth all the whole realm shall have but one use" (OWC 213).

Fused in that portentous announcement are two ideals. Liturgy is to be comprehensive, common to everyone throughout "all the *whole* realm," and at the same time uniform, conducted everywhere according to "but *one* use." Public worship will be at once universal and invariant, at once all-inclusive and self-identical. Whether this twofold ideal is practicable—whether liturgical uniformity is compatible with institutional comprehensiveness—would be put to the test again and again in the next hundred years. The events of those turbulent years will need to be investigated, but it may already be evident that in 1662 the Act of Uniformity was, among other things, an emphatic reassertion of "but one use" for "all the whole realm."

The impression that Cranmer's two essays are apt to give is that the making of the Book of Common Prayer was mostly a matter of decontamination. They suggest that once everything superfluous and everything superstitious has been scoured away, what is left will be liturgy as it was for the old fathers, which is to say liturgy as it ought to be. In 1549 such an appeal to antiquity was neither new nor, as far as it goes, particularly controversial. Cranmer does not adduce much evidence for the actual practices of the ancient church, but a short preface is not the place for that. What his essays do not acknowledge, although it is true and could not be more important, is that the book for which he wrote them was put together and promulgated not only with a view to the past as normative in itself, but also in the light of definite, positive, contemporary teaching about what it is right to believe and how it is right to worship.

For not only is the Book of Common Prayer a collection of scripts for performing church services; at the same time, as the last chapter pointed out, it is also an expression of theological doctrine, of beliefs and convictions about God, about the human condition, and about how God and humankind are and ought to be related. The same is true of many another liturgical text. What needs to be emphasized here is that the particular convictions which inform the Book of Common Prayer are not simply derived from the church as it was thought to have been long ago, before corruption and decay set in. They exemplify the thought and practice of the early modern movement in western Christianity that came to be known as the Reformation. In that movement Thomas Cranmer played a leading role, and of that movement the liturgy he wrote his two essays to commend was at once a product, a vehicle, and an engine.

In order to situate the original Prayer Book in this context, and more particularly to explain what is arguably its most consequential service, something should be said about the Reformation, about its chief doctrine, about the tradition of worship it overturned, and about what it put in its place. A very brief and very selective review of these topics at the beginning of the next chapter will lead back to the text of the Book of Common Prayer as it was in 1549 when Cranmer wrote his essays, and to the one Prayer Book liturgy that has yet to be examined.

PART II
CONTINUITIES

Five

Beginnings

Since 1662 the Book of Common Prayer has presented itself as an old book newly refurbished and restored to active use. It does not mention the still older book from which much of its content is derived. That older book, the original Book of Common Prayer, is similar but not the same; the text which superseded it in 1552, and which has remained largely unchanged ever since, differs from it at many points, sometimes widely. This chapter will be concerned with some of the differences between the classical versions of the Prayer Book and their predecessor. Those differences are important for two closely related reasons.

In the first place, it was not only the phrasing of the 1549 Book of Common Prayer that changed in 1552. The changes affected its theology and its religious meaning as well. In so far as those changes were deliberate, the difference between the original words and what replaced them is evidence for why they were replaced. The revisions, that is, can indicate what the revised text was intended *not* to mean, and thus can help to clarify what it means, in somewhat the same way that corrections in an author's preliminary drafts can shed light on the finished work.

A second reason for examining the earliest Book of Common Prayer is that although it was officially laid to rest after a three-year trial run, it did not remain buried. The original text has returned again and again to haunt the reception of the text that took its place, and its influence continues to be felt. There are those who would say that the Prayer Book of 1549 represents a half-hearted attempt to do what the classical versions do far better. Others see it as a tragic might-have-been, the liturgy that the Church of England could

The Book of Common Prayer. Charles Hefling, Oxford University Press (2021). © Oxford University Press.
DOI: 10.1093/oso/9780190689681.001.0001.

have had instead of the sorry substitute it got. Either way, the difference between the first and second Prayer Books of Edward VI calls attention to issues that bear on what this text is for and what made it the serious and sacred text it has been.

Authorship

To ask who wrote the Book of Common Prayer in the first place is to ask, in a way, the wrong question. For one thing, *compiled* would be a better word than *wrote*. Most of the Prayer Book text is transcribed *verbatim* from the Bible. Some of it is translated from far older liturgical texts. Some of it is on loan, borrowed and adapted from service books that were being used elsewhere. Some of its formal arrangement is novel, much of it very traditional. There is reason to think that the work of putting all this together was done in a hurry, but who did it and how it was done have never been altogether clear.

Thomas Cranmer, the prelate who wrote the two prefatory essays discussed in the previous chapter, is sometimes said to have been responsible for the rest of the Prayer Book as well. Possibly he was. Contemporary sources, among them King Edward's diary, report that an unspecified number of unspecified bishops and other learned divines were involved; presumably the archbishop of Canterbury was one of them. But it would be more than a hundred years before a list of names, Cranmer's and a dozen others, appeared in print.[1]

---

[1] Thomas Fuller, *The Church-History of Britain; From the Birth of Jesus Christ, Until the Year M. DC. XLVIII* (London, 1656), book 7 386. On this list and others that depend on it, see Francis Aidan Gasquet and Edmund Bishop, *Edward VI and the Book of Common Prayer*, 2nd ed. (London: John Hodges, 1891), 138–143. For learned speculation, see Robert J. Hetherington, *The Compilers of the Book of Common-Prayer of the Church of England. A Historical Inquiry* (Birmingham, UK: privately published, 1968).

Figure 5.1 The Compilers of the English Liturgy

Frontispiece in Anthony Sparrow, *A Rationale, or Practical Exposition of the Book of Common-Prayer*, 1722.

The chronicler who published the list was not always quite accurate on points of fact, and he does not say where he got the names, although none of them is improbable. By the beginning of the eighteenth century, in any case, his list had become canonical and even iconic. It takes pictorial form in an engraving of Cranmer with his twelve colleagues, portrayed in a way that suggests, perhaps on purpose, Jesus Christ at table with his twelve disciples (Figure 5.1).[2] While the scene is no doubt fanciful, there may in fact have been a committee, which may have met to compile an English service book, with the Holy Bible, ancient liturgies, and the writings of the church fathers spread out for consultation, as they are in the engraving. Or, if a committee met at all, which is not entirely certain, it may only have met to register pro forma assent to decisions already taken.[3]

Those decisions may well have been Cranmer's. Before he was nominated to the archbishopric by King Edward's father, Henry VIII, Cranmer was a scholar and probably knew as much as anyone in England about what would today be thought of as liturgics. He also became a strong proponent of the religious and political movement that is now called the Reformation; and while there can be some question as to just how much of the original Book of Common Prayer represents Cranmer's own beliefs, there is not, nor was there at the time, any question but that the new English liturgy was meant to further the reformation of the English church.

[2] The engraving is the frontispiece in a 1722 edition of *A Rationale, or Practical Exposition of the Book of Common-Prayer* by Anthony Sparrow, which was originally published with a slightly different title in 1655 and will be discussed here in a later chapter.
[3] There is some evidence that a "Windsor Commission," somewhat misleadingly so called, met in September, 1548 at Chertsey Abbey, not far from Windsor. On reconstructing this shadowy gathering, see William Page, "The First Book of Common Prayer and the Windsor Commission," *Church Quarterly Review* 98.195 (April 1924): 51–64, esp. 58–62; and Diarmaid MacCulloch, *Thomas Cranmer: A Life* (New Haven, CT: Yale University Press, 1996), 395–397.

Reformation

The Reformation in England was odd. On that, if not on much else, historians seem to agree. Its oddness makes a lexical excursus necessary.

In continental Europe, the movement of reform that is conventionally said to have begun in 1517, when Martin Luther lodged his famous protest, divided Christians, their institutions, and their religious practice in two. Today the divisions are usually labeled *catholic* and *protestant,* and the usual connotations of the labels are, respectively, continuity with the past and adherence to a new, refashioned Christianity. This taxonomy has its problems. Christians on the protestant side of the division have insisted that their religious reforms in no way abandoned the holy catholic church that the ancient creeds affirm. For a long time, accordingly, those who rejected the Reformation, and who maintained allegiance to the institutional church headed by the pope and headquartered in Rome, were referred to in protestant circles not as catholics but as Romanists or papists, or more politely as Roman Catholics. At the same time, there were fissures within reformed Christianity, notably between the followers of Luther and those who adopted the even less traditional Swiss and southern German variety of protestantism associated with the name of John Calvin.

With the understanding that anachronism is unavoidable, and that there is no neutral, unambiguous nomenclature to be had,[4] this book will use *protestant* and *catholic,* uncapitalized, in the modern, generalized sense of reformed and unreformed respectively. The word *reformed* itself is thus an umbrella term; it will not be limited here, as it sometimes is, to Swiss or Helvetian or Calvinist protestantism. The word *protestant* is not limited to Lutherans, as it was at

---

[4] See Thomas H. Clancy, "Papist—Protestant—Puritan: English Religious Taxonomy 1565–1665," *Recusant History* 13.4 (1976): 227–253; and Peter Marshall, "The Naming of Protestant England," *Past and Present* 214 (2012): 87–128, esp. 108.

first, and the word *catholic* is not limited to Roman Catholics, but will keep its older and wider connotations.

Turning now to the odd case of England, this much can be said about it: "In almost every respect, the English Reformation is Act II of a Continental drama played out earlier and on a different stage."[5] The question is whether Act II was a reprise of Act I—whether the form of Christianity of which the Book of Common Prayer is a foundational text can or cannot be subsumed within continental protestantism and understood in the same terms.

In some accounts it cannot. Act II, as they understand it, was only superficially similar to Act I. There was, to be sure, a juridical, administrative, political rupture; Henry VIII did cut institutional ties with the papacy and the Roman church. In public worship, Latin did give way to English and the services were simplified. But for all that, the independent Church of England did not go on to become a protestant church as the word applies to any of the European churches of the Reformation. It went its own way, on its own. This narrative, in its extreme form, has been called the myth of the English Reformation, meaning the myth that in England the Reformation never really happened.[6] There are less exaggerated, more defensible forms of this account, but on the whole historians at present are inclined the other way, toward assimilating religious change in sixteenth-century England to developments elsewhere. The English church not only separated itself from Rome; it aligned its doctrine, discipline, and worship with international protestantism, mainly the Swiss variety. This narrative too comes in an exaggerated form, which would dismiss as mere fossils, interesting but irrelevant flies in amber, the anomalies, compromises, and

---

[5] Peter Newman Brooks, *Thomas Cranmer's Doctrine of the Eucharist*, 2nd ed. (London: Macmillan, 1992), xxii.

[6] The phrase comes from Diarmaid MacCulloch, "The Myth of the English Reformation," *Journal of British Studies* 30.1 (1991): 1–19, which outlines the complexity of the relevant issues, and points to a source of the myth.

continuities with the catholic past that set the reformed Church of England apart.

They did set it apart, though, and they cannot simply be dismissed. "All Reformed Protestant churches had their idiosyncrasies, but the English one was more idiosyncratic than most."[7] Of its many idiosyncrasies, the most important one, arguably, was the Book of Common Prayer. None of the other churches of the Reformation set any great store by a prescript liturgy, let alone a liturgy that retained so much that had long been traditional. In itself, the idiosyncratic English Prayer Book may not have made the English church catholic. It did, from the first, call its protestantism into question.

The question arises at several points in the Prayer Book, but most insistently in the service which in 1549 was entitled The Supper of the Lord, and the Holy Communion, commonly called the Mass (owc 19–40). It is certainly not the only important text in the Book of Common Prayer. It takes up only a few pages. It might not be there at all, for anything Cranmer's two essays have to say. It was most often used, until the nineteenth century, not in its entirety but in the curtailed form of "table prayers" in which bread and wine play no part. It has, nevertheless, been subjected to more scrutiny than the rest of the Prayer Book's contents put together; and it is the text that was altered most significantly when the original book was replaced in 1552. Most of this chapter from here on will examine it.

Justification and the Mass

To say of a liturgy that it is commonly called the Mass is to assert its continuity with a form of worship which, for most Christian

---

[7] Alec Ryrie, "The Reformation in Anglicanism," *OHAS* 35–45 at 38. See also Eamon Duffy, "The Shock of Change: Continuity and Discontinuity in the Elizabethan Church of England," *Ecclesiastical Law Journal* 7.35 (2004): 429–446, esp. 429, 437, 444.

people, clergy and laity, had long been the substance of their religion. Around the axis of the Mass a whole world of belief and practice revolved. It is important to ask how far the new Prayer Book service does in fact maintain continuity with this venerable rite, because whether a service meant for a reformed church should be continuous with the Mass at all is perhaps the most contentious issue that the Book of Common Prayer has been embroiled in.

The source of the contention is a theological impasse, a contradiction. The Mass, as it was understood at the time of the Reformation, was irreconcilable with the Reformation's cardinal tenet, the doctrine by which Luther reportedly said the whole church either stands or falls: the doctrine of justification by faith.

To be justified, in the relevant sense, is to be accepted, pardoned, and deemed just or righteous by a just and righteous God. When God so favors anyone, it is exactly that—a favor, a gift. That is the vital point. Justification, in Reformation teaching, is in no sense an achievement; it does not belong to any economy of reciprocation, reward, or desert. No one has a right to God's favor, nor can anyone earn it. The only exception is Jesus Christ, God's own Son, whose righteousness alone is the righteousness on account of which anyone whom God justifies is justified. The reward that Christ has merited, especially by his suffering and death, God gratuitously bestows on others, sinners though they are. A logic of payment and exchange is incapable of comprehending this divine largesse; the truth that God pardons sinners because Christ has done what sinners inevitably fail to do for themselves is a truth that can only be taken on trust. To believe in this gift is to possess it, which is to say that those who are justified are justified freely, by grace, through faith.

Such was the official teaching of the reformed Church of England, as expounded at length in the authorized collection of homilies that the Prayer Book refers to, and especially in one of them, the Homily of Justification, which is generally attributed to Cranmer and which is formally endorsed in the Thirty-nine

Articles of Religion.[8] The practical consequences of this teaching were enormous; for if faith in Christ—not piety or acts of devotion or virtuous "works" or worthy effort—is the human corollary of divine benevolence, then a whole religious ecology is drained of its meaning and value. Pilgrimages, processions, statues, relics, shrines, ceremonies, the saints in heaven and the clergy on earth—none of these has or can ever have any efficacy. In no way do they mediate or condition divine favor. To suppose they do can only be superstition, if not idolatry. Saints cannot help the living, the living cannot help the dead by their prayers, nothing is made inherently sacred by priestly blessings, pious acts will never expiate sin, and God cannot be appeased by ritual sacrifices.

The last of these protestant disavowals is the one that is most directly relevant in the present context, inasmuch as it applies to the Mass. To describe the Mass as a ritual sacrifice is to describe it very inadequately, but the description does point to an aspect of this complex act of worship which is especially germane to the genesis of the Book of Common Prayer. In the liturgy of the western Mass, bread and wine are consecrated, offered, and consumed at an altar by the priest who celebrates the rite. He alone recites the long, composite prayer known as the *canon* of the Mass. In the course of this prayer the bread and wine cease to be bread and wine and begin, without any perceptible change, to be the body and blood of Christ. This event, which by the time of the Reformation was termed *transubstantiation*, occurs at the place in the canon where the priest speaks the words that were spoken, according to the New Testament accounts, by Jesus Christ at his Last Supper: "This is my

---

[8] The first of the two volumes of *Certain Sermons or Homilies* was issued 1547. The printed title of the third homily is "Of the Salvation of All Mankind by only Christ our Savior, from Sin and Death Everlasting." By common consent, however, this is the Homily of Justification referred to by that name as authoritative doctrine in the eleventh of the Thirty-nine Articles. The next two homilies, "Of the True and Lively Faith" and "Of Good Works," also Cranmer's work, extend the argument.

body . . . This is my blood . . . Do this in remembrance of me." From that moment on, Christ himself is really present.

To signal his presence, the consecrated wafer of bread known as the host is at that point "elevated": the priest, who faces the altar at which the sacrifice is being offered, lifts the host high enough for anyone behind him to see and venerate it as Christ's body. This ceremony is the climax of the rite as a visible performance, and for many laypeople it was the most intense moment of their religion.[9] What follows the elevation is the offering to God of the consecrated elements in which Christ is present, in remembrance of his sacrificial death on the cross, which the sacrifice of the Mass effectually represents. This offering the priest makes in the name of the congregation, praying that God will accept the sacrifice, to the benefit alike of living worshipers and the faithful departed. He then consumes what has been consecrated, adored, and offered.

It will be evident that this very partial and abbreviated account of the Mass is at odds with the very partial and abbreviated account of Reformation teaching presented earlier. That is the point. On protestant grounds, to believe that the Mass is a meritorious deed, that it presents God with a propitiatory offering which compensates for the sins of anyone on whose behalf the priest offers it, is to rely on human activity that usurps faith in the efficacy of Christ's death. In the Mass, merely natural effort is credited with the utterly supernatural value of a divine gift that can only be received. From that mistaken inversion spring all the disastrous errors of the pope's religion. Thus it was Luther's stated opinion that "having triumphed over the Mass, I think we have triumphed over the whole papacy."

The context of this pronouncement is worth mentioning. Luther made it in 1522, in his refutation of a treatise that had recently been written to defend the Mass, both as a righteous work and as

---

[9] See the comments of Carlos M. N. Eire on late medieval piety in *War against the Idols: The Reformation of Worship from Erasmus to Calvin* (Cambridge: Cambridge University Press, 1986), 8–27.

a placating sacrifice—written by Henry VIII, king of England.[10] At least Henry put his name to it. At the time, he had no sympathy with the agitation for reform that had begun to percolate into his kingdom; not that he ever had much. It was in reward for his vindication of received teaching that he was given the honorific title borne by his royal successors ever since: *Fidei Defensor*, Defender of the Faith.

The Lord's Supper

What the young King Henry defended, Luther and other reformers deplored. Nevertheless most of the churches of the Reformation continued to observe their own ritual meal of bread and wine, which, like the Mass, found its warrant in Christ's command to "do this in remembrance of me." On exactly what doing this was doing, however, they were deeply and painfully divided. "No theological theme, not even justification, was more keenly debated in the Reformation."[11]

Much of the debate about what was variously called the Sacrament of the Altar, the Eucharist, or, as in the Prayer Book, the Lord's Supper or Holy Communion, turned on the notoriously difficult notion of presence, and specifically on the presence of Christ. To reject transubstantiation, as all protestants did, was not necessarily to deny Christ's genuine presence in the Supper. Some reformed churches taught that anyone who receives the sacrament eats and drinks Christ's body and blood together with bread and wine, on the basis that Christ meant what he said. "This *is* my body" must be understood in the plain, literal sense of the words, yet

---

[10] *Martinus Lutherus contra Henricum Regem Angliæ*, in *Martin Luthers Werke*, Weimarer Ausgabe 10/2 (*Schriften* 1522) 175–222 at 220 line 13: "Triumphata vero Missa puto nos totum Papam triumphare." Note the date.

[11] B. A. Gerrish, "The Reformation and the Eucharist," in *Thinking with the Church* (Grand Rapids, MI: William B. Eerdmans, 2010), 229–258 at 229.

without implying that the bread is ever anything other than bread. This interpretation was not acceptable to all. One alternative was to agree that the bread remains bread, but not that what Christ said about it should be taken literally. By "this is" he could only have meant "this signifies." To "do this," following his commandment, is therefore to be mindful of what Christ himself did and does for those who have faith in him. Only in this conscious remembering can it be said that he is present.

These two positions on Christ's eucharistic presence came to be associated, respectively, with the names of Martin Luther and the early Swiss reformer Ulrich Zwingli. Arguably the association rests on dubious grounds, especially where Luther is concerned, but it was a widely accepted usage, especially among English writers. By whatever name, the first position affirms both that Christ is really present and also, against transubstantiation, that the sacramental bread and wine remain in their substance or essential being as well as their empirical qualities. It does not attempt to explain how that can possibly be true. The conventional name for this teaching is *consubstantiation*. The second, so-called Zwinglian position asserts that since Christ is really in heaven, seated, as the creeds put it, at the right hand of his Father, it can*not* possibly be true that his natural body and blood are really anywhere else. Hence there is no reason to ascribe any special status or valence to earthly bread and wine. They are signs of something they are not. A rather dismissive name for this teaching is "real absence."

These were not the only ways to understand the Supper, but what other estimable reformers believed and taught is more difficult to state concisely. Some sought to have it both ways: the eucharistic bread and wine are signs, but not bare signs; what they signify is Christ present, not absent; his presence is not imaginary or metaphorical only, although it is not localized or material either. The positive meaning of these largely negative assertions is not always clear, perhaps because what they refer to is itself a mystery that words cannot adequately express. In any case the Lord's Supper was a matter of sharp and constant debate throughout the sixteenth century within and between the churches of the Reformation, not least the Church of England. It was a debate with obvious implications for deciding what ought to be done and said in any eucharistic liturgy meant to correct and displace the traditional liturgy of the Mass, as the Communion office in the Book of Common Prayer was meant to do.

Reforming the Mass in England

The aim of the preceding section was to sketch a context in which to understand the first version of the Book of Common Prayer, with a view to its Communion office in particular. It can now be asked: What is that office *for?* The next several sections will suggest that the purpose of Holy Communion as prescribed in 1549 is definitely not adoration; that there may be a particular, limited sense in which it can be called sacrifice; but also that to participate in the Lord's Supper is not to *offer* so much as to *receive*. The service takes place primarily for the sake of communion.

Communion, in the sense of accepting and consuming the sacramental bread and wine, was a part of every Mass, but for most people, most of the time, a marginal part. There was always one communicant, the celebrating priest; almost always, he was the only one, even when a congregation was present, for by custom (though not by rule) laypeople received communion very rarely, perhaps once a year at Easter. There were reasons for doing things this way, but to the protestant reformers there were better reasons for doing them differently. Whatever Christ meant by "Do this," he surely intended everyone to eat and drink—to receive the sacrament, to receive it frequently, and to receive both wine and bread, not bread only, as was the ordinary practice when anyone besides the celebrant did take communion at Mass.

The Order of the Communion

Just this agenda—frequent, general communion, in both "kinds"—
was introduced into the Church of England by Act of Parliament
early in the reign of Edward VI. Liturgical prescriptions for
implementing the agenda followed, in the shape of a booklet
entitled *The Order of the Communion*. The texts printed there would
be printed again, a year later, in the first Book of Common Prayer,
but for the time being they were simply to be added to the Mass.

The Prayer of Humble Access
as in *The Order of the Communion*, 1548

We do not presume to come to this thy table (O merciful Lord)
trusting in our own righteousness, but in thy manifold and great
mercies: we be not worthy so much as to gather up the crumbs
under thy table: but thou art the same Lord, whose property is
always to have mercy: grant us therefore, gracious Lord, so to eat
the flesh of thy dear Son Jesus Christ, and to drink his blood, [in
these holy Mysteries,] that we may continually dwell in him, and
he in us, that our sinful bodies may be made clean by his body,
and our souls washed through his most precious blood. Amen.

*In the classical Book of Common Prayer, the bracketed words
are omitted, and the last two clauses are rearranged.*

The *Order* requires a set exhortation to be delivered in advance;
then, after Mass has been celebrated in Latin as usual, an English
rite for receiving the sacrament begins with another exhortation.
Following a general confession, said on behalf of everyone, the
priest pronounces absolution and adds "comfortable words," scriptural sentences that give assurance of mercy mediated by Christ. He
then kneels to say what would later be known as the *prayer of humble*

access, and rises to deliver the sacrament, in both kinds, using two formulas which allude to the end of that prayer: "The body of our Lord Jesus Christ, which was given for thee, preserve thy body unto everlasting life" and "The blood of our Lord Jesus Christ, which was shed for thee, preserve thy soul unto everlasting life."[12]

Laypeople who took part in this augmented rite may or may not have understood the Latin words said or sung by the priest as he celebrated the Mass. Presumably they did understand the English words he spoke afterward. What then were they given to understand?

The two exhortations which the Sacrament Act had ordered, and which *The Order of the Communion* prints in full, convey much the same message. The sacrament of Christ's body and blood is "comfortable," fortifying and encouraging. To receive it is to be assured and made certain of the benefits, above all the forgiveness of sins, that Christ obtained for sinners by shedding his blood and giving his body to death. But this strength and confidence are to be had only by those who receive worthily, with sorrow for their own sins, charity toward the world, and firm intent to amend their lives.

For all who come so prepared, Christ has left a pledge and remembrance of his love, namely his body and blood, on which the faithful may spiritually feed, and by feeding be united with him as children of God. Inversely, unworthy recipients eat and drink their own damnation, provoking God's anger and retribution. Repentance, then, is necessary. Penance, however, is not. If the prescribed general confession will not suffice for a quiet conscience, a personal, "auricular" confession may be made to a priest beforehand; but penance in that sense is optional, and individuals

---

[12] Joseph Ketley, ed., *The Two Liturgies* A.D. *1549, and* A.D. *1552: with Other Documents Set Forth by Authority in the Reign of King Edward the Sixth* (Parker Society; Cambridge University Press, 1844), 8; H. A. Wilson, ed., *The Order of the Communion, 1548*, Henry Bradshaw Society 34 (London, 1908), 44. Wilson's edition gives the text of the *Order* twice, first in facsimile and then within a reconstruction of the whole Mass as it might have been celebrated on Easter Day, 1548.

are left to decide for themselves whether they will use one form or the other.

What the English rite is evidently meant to teach above all is that the sacrament exists for the benefit of communicants—not as a sacrifice made to obtain mercy, but as a gift that testifies to mercy obtained. If they are to benefit from it, therefore, those who receive communion must receive it, not as the means to some further end, but because receiving it is beneficial in itself. Then and there, in the spiritual eating and drinking of Christ's body and blood, worthy recipients dwell in Christ and he dwells in them; they are washed and adopted; they enjoy the comfortable assurance of having been forgiven.

The boons these expressions refer to, whatever they are, depend ultimately on Christ's fruitful and glorious passion. Proximately, they would seem to depend as well on what receivers receive. The English rite in the *Order of the Communion* does not stand on its own; it only delivers what was produced at the moment of consecration in the Mass it is attached to. At the same time, although the *Order* forbids altering the Mass itself, adding it to the Mass does alter what the Mass means. While the consecrated bread would be elevated for veneration, as usual, it is not consecrated only in order to be an object of reverence and adoration; it is consecrated to be distributed and consumed. To that extent, the English supplement shifts the point and purpose of the service as a whole toward the act of receiving the sacrament. Communion is now a reason, and a necessary reason, for celebrating the liturgy. Eventually it would be the sole, sufficient reason.

The First English Communion Service

In the original Book of Common Prayer, the texts that first appeared in the *Order of the Communion* reappear toward the end of the service "commonly called the Mass." It might therefore be supposed that the entire service is a reiteration, in English, of the traditional Mass, now extended to include a general distribution of consecrated bread and wine. Up to a point, that would be a fair description of the 1549 office for the Lord's Supper.

Like the Mass, the office has two main parts. The first part, ante-Communion, which includes readings from the New Testament and the recitation of the Nicene Creed, can take place without the second; in that case it follows Mattins and the Litany, in much the same way as was described in chapter one. The second part, which provides for the administration of the sacrament, may be carried out only if there are others present who intend to receive communion with the priest. It is this second part that carries most of the theological freight, both in the wording of its prayers and rubrics, and in the structural logic of its components, which are listed in Table 5.1.[13]

The texts that the *Order of the Communion* had prescribed are now the fourth item in the table, except the exhortations, with which the second part of the service begins. Between these exhortations, which expound the benefits of receiving communion, and the devotions that lead to the act of receiving it, the Prayer Book service places the items numbered 2 and 3 in the table, the offertory and what may be called the sacramental prayer. Formally speaking, both of these have counterparts in the Latin rite of the Mass. Whether they have the same meaning is another question.

Offertory

The English words *offering, oblation,* and *sacrifice,* used substantively, belong to the same semantic field. It would be natural, then,

---

[13] Since labeling is always an exercise of interpretation, it should be pointed out that, as with previous tables, the 1549 Prayer Book itself does not name all the items listed. In particular, the table borrows *consecration* and *memorial/oblation* from later versions of the Book of Common Prayer.

Table 5.1 Holy Communion (second part)
1549 Book of Common Prayer

---

1 *exhortations* (OWC 22–25)

2 *offertory* (OWC 25–27)

3 *sacramental prayer* (OWC 27–32)

    preface and *Sanctus*

    canon

        first division: intercession

        second division: consecration

        third division: memorial / oblation

    Lord's Prayer

4 *communion* (OWC 32–34)

    invitation to confession (short exhortation)

    general confession, absolution, comfortable words

    prayer of humble access

    administration

5 *postcommunion* (OWC 34–36)

    Agnus Dei

    sentences

    prayer of thanksgiving

---

to suppose that an *offertory* involves oblation and that something is offered. In the 1549 Communion office, however, the word denotes an ensemble of scriptural sentences, which are to be said or sung while a number of other things are happening. First, members of the congregation who are so minded move to the choir or chancel, where the altar stands, and put their donations of money into a "poor men's box" (OWC 27). If they intend to receive communion, they "tarry still in the choir." The priest, presumably after counting those who have tarried, lays out on the altar sufficient bread and wine. Whether by doing so he *offers* them is debatable. Analogy with the Mass would suggest that he does, but nothing in the prayers or rubrics says so. Whatever he is doing, he does it as the offertory *sentences* are being recited, but those sentences are all about generosity and almsgiving and cannot, without special pleading, be referred directly to the bread and wine.

After preparing the elements, if not offering them, the priest begins the central, sacramental prayer, the third item in the table, which calls for close examination. It opens, as does the corresponding section of the Mass, with a dialogue. The congregation is invited to give thanks to their Lord God, since "it is meet and right so to do." After a thankful introduction, the *preface* in liturgical parlance, comes an ancient hymn, drawn from scripture, which begins with the acclamation, "Holy, holy, holy, Lord God of hosts" and so is known as the *Sanctus*. The priest then turns to the altar to say or sing "plainly and distinctly" a long prayer that occupies the same position as the canon does in the Mass and is so named.[14] This text falls fairly clearly into the three divisions listed under item 3 in Table 5.1. First comes an intercessory prayer, then a prayer of consecration, which leads to a memorial or prayer of oblation.

The Canon (1): Intercession

The first division of the canon is a self-contained unit, with a coherence of its own and no very evident connection to what follows. It opens with a bidding: "Let us pray for the whole state of Christ's church." The beginning of this prayer has already been discussed; in the classical Prayer Book it is relocated in the first part of the service, ante-Communion. To recall what was said about it in chapter one, intercession is made for the king, his council and other authorities, the clergy, the people, persons in adversity, and

---

[14] The name *canon* is used, however, only in the order for the Celebration of the Holy Communion for the Sick (OWC 80). It may have got there by inadvertence. Still, there it is.

the present congregation. In its 1549 form, the bidding does not add "militant here in earth," and the prayer is not concerned only with the living; it goes on to thank God for the saints in heaven and commends to his mercy the departed who "rest in the sleep of peace."

After these intercessions, the meaning of the canon hinges on three pairs of nearly synonymous verbs: *bless and sanctify, celebrate and make,* and *offer and present.* The first of these duplets refers to what the prayer asks God to do. The other two express what the priest, and those in whose name he prays, are doing by praying the prayer.

The Canon (2): Consecration

The canon's second division (owc 30–31) is central in more ways than one. It begins very abruptly after the intercessions for the whole state of the church, and moves toward a narrative recital, not unlike the one in the Latin canon, of what Christ did and said at supper on the night before he was crucified. This second division consists of one long, involved sentence in the form of a hypertrophic collect. There is an address, which characterizes God in a certain way, followed by a petition, which asks God to do something specific, and an aspiration, which states the resulting benefit. Here the petition is that God will bless and sanctify bread and wine, so that, as the aspiration clause puts it, they may "be unto us" Christ's body and blood (see Table 5.3, first column).

The top half of Figure 5.2 shows this sentence as it was printed in 1549.[15] When its complex of relative clauses is untangled, it affirms:

- that in order to redeem (rescue, buy back) sinners, God gave Jesus Christ, his Son, to be crucified;

[15] The earliest date on a printing of the 1549 Prayer Book (of which there were several) is March 7. The illustration shows folio cxvi *verso* in a printing dated May 4 (Griffiths 1549/8; STC 16270).

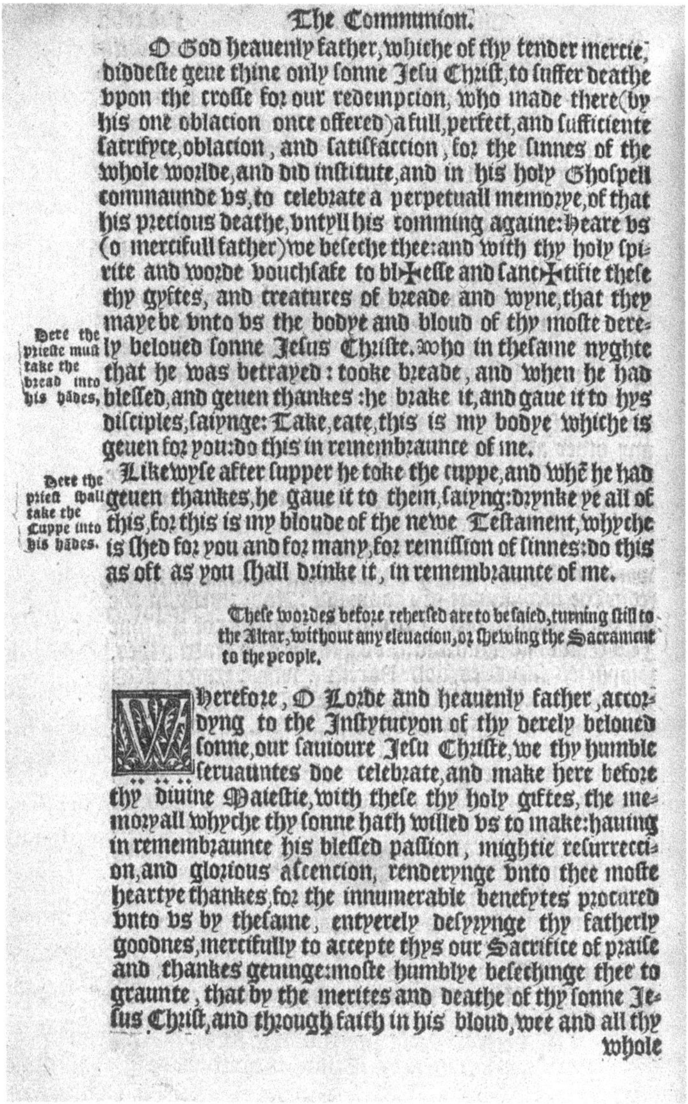

O God heauenly father, whiche of thy tender mercie, biddeste geue thine only sonne Jesu Chiist, to suffer deathe vpon the crosse for our redempcion, who made there (by his one oblacion once offered) a full, perfect, and sufficiente sacrifyce, oblacion, and satiffaccion, for the sinnes of the whole worlde, and did institute, and in his holy Ghospell commaunde vs, to celebrate a perpetuall memorye, of that his precious deathe, vntyll his tomming againe: Heare vs (o mercifull father) we besethe thee: and with thy holy spirite and worde vouchsafe to bl✠esse and sanc✠tifie these thy gyftes, and creatures of breade and wyne, that they maye be vnto vs the bodye and bloud of thy moste derely beloued sonne Jesus Chiiste. Who in thesame nyghte that he was betrayed : tooke breade, and when he had blessed, and geuen thankes : he brake it, and gaue it to hys disciples, saipnge: Take, eate, this is my bodye whiche is geuen for you: do this in remembraunce of me.

Here the priest must take the bread into his handes,

Likewyse after supper he toke the cuppe, and whẽ he had geuen thankes, he gaue it to them, saipng: drynke ye all of this, for this is my bloude of the newe Testament, whyche is shed for you and for many, for remission of sinnes: do this as oft as you shall drinke it, in remembraunce of me.

Here the priest shall take the Cuppe into his handes.

These wordes before rehersed are to be saied, turning still to the Altar, without any eleuacion, or shewing the Sacrament to the people.

Wherefore, O Lorde and heauenly father, accordyng to the Institucyon of thy derely beloued sonne, our sauioure Jesu Chiiste, we thy humble seruauntes doe celebrate, and make here before thy diuine Maiestie, with these thy holy gyftes, the memoryall whyche thy sonne hath willed vs to make: hauing in remembraunce his blessed passion, mightie resurreccion, and glorious ascencion, renderynge vnto thee moste heartye thankes, for the innumerable benefytes procured vnto vs by thesame, entyerely desyrynge thy fatherly goodnes, mercifully to accepte thys our Sacrifice of praise and thankes geuinge: moste humblye besechinge thee to graunte, that by the merites and deathe of thy sonne Jesus Chiist, and through faith in his bloud, wee and all thy whole

Figure 5.2 Prayer of Consecration in the First Prayer Book
Edition printed by Edward Whitchurch, May 4, 1549.
Courtesy of the Beinecke Rare Books Library, Yale University.

- that by suffering and dying on the cross, Christ offered himself as a sacrifice;
- that this self-oblation on his part was valuable enough to make satisfaction (compensation, restitution) for the sins of everyone else;
- that before he died, Christ established a memory (commemoration, memorial) of his sacrificial death, to be observed ever after; and in particular
- that he blessed and gave thanks for bread and wine, which he distributed, using words that refer to them as his body and blood.

Two typographical details on the page shown in the illustration should be noted. They prescribe "manual acts," ceremonial gestures that the priest is to perform with his hands as he recites the prayer. All these actions involve the bread and wine on the altar. The two crosses in line 10 at "bl✠ess and sanc✠tify" would have been recognized by any priest who knew the old Latin books; they are instructions to trace a cross, presumably over the "gifts and creatures" that are the objects of the two verbs, while those words are being said. Then, having signed the bread and the cup with the cross, the priest is to take each of them into his hands, at the places indicated by the marginal rubrics, printed in smaller type, that line up with "took bread" and "took the cup" in the prayer.[16]

These gestures associate words with things. It is *this* bread and *this* wine that God is asked to bless and sanctify. The meaning of the verbs is almost certainly the same as that of two other duplets, *bless and consecrate* and *hallowed and consecrate(d)*, used in the *Order of the Communion*. It would follow that blessing, sanctifying, hallowing, and consecrating are equivalent names for an act that singles out something—here, the bread and wine—as holy, or

---

[16] In these rubrics *hãdes* is a contraction of *handes*, hands. The omission of *n* is similarly indicated in *whẽ* (line 18).

imparts sacredness to it. Accordingly, this division of the canon can be called the *consecration*, and has generally been so called, although no form of that word is used in the 1549 text.

On the assumption that the prayer is granted, the bread and wine to which the priest's words and his manual acts refer are sanctified—but not venerable or adorable. The rubric immediately after the consecration, just before the ornamental *W* in the illustration, rules out what has already been mentioned as the ceremonial acme of the Latin Mass: the "elevation, or showing the sacrament to the people." As blessed and sanctified, the bread and wine are devoted to a sacred purpose, which is to "be unto us" Christ's body and blood. Yet clearly this does not mean "unto us as objects of our worship." What it does mean, the canon goes on to say in its third division.

The Canon (3): Memorial/Oblation

The prayer of consecration is a request. It is about what God does. The third division of the canon (owc 31–32) is about what we do, we being those unto whom the bread and wine are and are to be Christ's body and blood. With those "gifts and creatures," now sanctified, "we thy humble servants do celebrate and make," before God, the memorial that Christ willed. So much is clear enough. The duplet *celebrate and make* (line 29) can be understood as a speech-act or performative utterance, like "I baptize thee" or "with this ring I thee wed." To say the words, as the priest does and as worshipers do through his agency, is to realize or make real the fact they refer to. Celebrating and making are what happens then and there.

What it is to celebrate a memorial, or to do this "with" bread and wine, is less obvious. Certainly it is to have in thankful remembrance Christ's passion, resurrection, and ascension. The prayer says so (lines 31–32). Moreover, giving thanks for the benefits his passion has procured, especially forgiveness of sins, is a "sacrifice of praise" (line 36). This sacrifice, however, and the remembrance of Christ to which it corresponds, are connected only loosely, if at all, to the "holy gifts." The consecrated bread and wine happen to be on the altar while thanks and praise are being offered, but there does not seem to be any reason why they must be there.

Be that as it may, the canon goes on from *celebrate and make* to another duplet and another speech-act: "we *offer and present*." What takes place in this utterance is oblation, the handing over of an offering or sacrifice, which is said to be "reasonable, holy, and lively" (living, alive). Earlier the prayer spoke of a sacrifice of praise and thanksgiving; here the sacrifice which is offered and presented is "our self, our souls and bodies." The prayer then switches abruptly to a request for worthy reception of the sacrament and for mutual indwelling with Christ, before returning to the idea of oblation. After a final acknowledgment of unworthiness to offer any sacrifice, God is asked to accept, even so, "this our bounden duty and service."

It may be that this last, rather unspecific phrase refers to the earlier self-offering, or to the whole Communion office, or to the prayers and supplications that are brought up to God's holy tabernacle by the angels that the prayer asks him to employ. What has *not* been offered, however, to judge by the text of the canon, is Christ—not Christ himself, not his own sacrifice, not his body and blood in or with or under the material forms of bread and wine. Christ has been offered already, by Christ himself. The second division of the canon, with its intricate relative clauses, makes that quite clear. On Christ's self-oblation, and on that alone, the remission of sins depends. Neither the sacrifice of praise and thanksgiving nor the oblation of "our self, our souls and bodies" is the same as the "full, perfect, and sufficient sacrifice" that Christ once and only once offered for the benefit of believers.

The canon in the 1549 Communion office is a complex and subtle composition. It is also, probably, the most debated and debatable text in any Prayer Book. The fact that there is a canon at all, complete with a consecration formula and manual acts, is remarkable in itself. Other reformed eucharistic liturgies, if they include an institution narrative, do not build it into a prayer addressed to God; instead, it functions as a lesson from scripture, read out to instruct and edify the congregation. On the other hand, although the involved and high-sounding language[17] of the 1549 prayer can be heard as a paraphrase of the traditional Latin canon, and may have been designed to give that impression, it is not the same. With respect to bread and wine there is neither oblation nor adoration. The fact that both of these had been left out was noticed and decried when the House of Lords debated the Prayer Book before passing the first Act of Uniformity.[18]

Why there is no adoration or oblation of the sacramental bread and wine is explained, by implication, in the rite itself. It consistently expresses the relation between the Christian and Christ in terms of spiritual communion, not active confrontation, whether material or physical or sensible. If Christ is present, his presence does not make him the object of anything that anyone does. Priest and people cannot be said to offer, present, touch, or behold him. What they do is receive; what they give is thanks; and what they offer is themselves. To do so is their "bounden duty"—almost the first words of the canon, and almost the last.

"Commonly Called the Mass"

The English service "commonly called the Mass" evidently means something different from what the Mass, considered as a meritorious work and a propitiatory sacrifice, had meant. Whether

---

[17] The phrase is borrowed from Colin Buchanan.

[18] See Gasquet and Bishop, *Edward VI and the Book of Common Prayer*, 404–405. A more recent and more exact transcription is printed in Colin Buchanan, ed., *Background Documents to Liturgical Revision 1547–1549* (Bromcote, Notts: Grove Books, 1983), 15–33; see esp. 18.

the difference was evident when the Prayer Book script was first performed is a further question. For many and perhaps most people, the obvious difference would not have had to do with the meaning of words as understood; it would have been the fact that they were understandable. To hear the whole Mass said or sung in English, if the Mass is what it was, must have been startling.

The novelty should not be exaggerated. In 1549 liturgical devotions in English were readily available for private use, and at Mass the gospel and epistle were being read from the English Bible.[19] The *Order of the Communion* too, if it was used at all widely, would have made the transition less of a jolt. But it was a big transition, all the same. What the eucharistic liturgy gained in intelligibility it must consequently have lost in loftiness, remoteness, mysteriousness, and in that respect holiness. It had been an elaborate, exalted rite, set apart from everyday concerns; now it was being conducted in the same tongue as worldly affairs. Not that the language is colloquial. Even in 1549 the diction was a little old-fashioned; the syntax is formal. Still, it is English, not Latin.

On the other hand, the modest and gradual infusions of vernacular language that had so far occurred did not change what was done at the altar, and neither did the new English liturgy, except at one point, the elevation of the host. Perhaps the disappearance of this conspicuous moment, combined with a general communion in both kinds, was enough to shift the experiential center of gravity from adoration to reception. But perhaps not. Most of what people saw at the new service of Holy Communion could have been what they were used to seeing at Mass. The scenery and costumes did not change, or if they did, it was not because the Prayer Book demanded it. The rubrics do not give directions about the location of the altar, and they do allow the priest, the clerks, and any assisting clergy to

---

[19] The point is emphasized in Stanley Morison, *English Prayer Books: An Introduction to the Literature of Christian Worship* (Cambridge: Cambridge University Press, 1949), 58, 67, 71.

wear much the same special clothing as had always been worn at Mass.[20] Furthermore, gestures and postures—"kneeling, crossing, holding up of hands, knocking upon the breast"—are explicitly left to individual choice (owc 98). Assuming that this permission applies to the celebrating priest, all the customary ritual actions, apart from elevation, could still be used. In sum, whatever the audible words that the Prayer Book ordered may have been intended to mean, and however far that meaning may have diverged from the medieval rite, it would have been quite possible for the service "commonly called the Mass" to look as though it *was* the Mass.

What it was possible to do, some parish priests evidently did—they made the new English service as much like the familiar Latin one as they could. There is no way to know whether they did it from laziness or recalcitrance, or whether by doing it they made the Prayer Book more acceptable to their parishioners, or perhaps less. They certainly did not commend themselves to anyone who regarded the Mass as an abomination that ought to be eliminated, not imitated. From that standpoint, the whole purpose of a reformed Communion rite was being defeated by more or less willful misrepresentation.

Meanwhile, the new Prayer Book was being anatomized and appraised by scholarly reformists from abroad, who had been brought to England to teach in the universities and cooperate in the establishment of the new religion. The opinions of these "foreign divines" were various, especially on the Lord's Supper, and it is difficult to know how far their criticisms and recommendations influenced the decision to issue a new service of Holy Communion, in a new Book of Common Prayer, three years after the first one. The official reason, as stated in the new Act of Uniformity which imposed the new liturgy in 1552, was that "there hath arisen in the use and exercise of the foresaid common service"—the 1549

---

[20] See Table 6.2, first column, with Appendix 1.

liturgy—"diverse doubts for the fashion and manner of the ministration of the same, rather by the curiosity of the minister and mistakers, than of any other worthy cause."[21] There was nothing wrong with the former book, but "in some places . . . it is necessary to make the same prayer and fashion of service more earnest and fit to stir the Christian people to the true honoring of almighty God." The necessity has been met, the Act goes on to say, and the book is now "explained and made fully perfect."[22]

The perfected book came into use on All Saints Day, November 1, 1552. It did not last long; officially, a little more than a year, though in fact rather less. But it was this book that Queen Elizabeth reinstated, and that was refurbished in 1662. In other words, it was the prototype of the classical Prayer Book (see Table 4.1). As compared with the original version, which it "explained and made fully perfect," it is much the same in some places, much different in others. The difference is most significant in the Communion office.

Holy Communion Revised

Both parts of the Communion office were affected by the 1552 revisions. In the original Prayer Book, ante-Communion began with a Psalm and two ancient hymns (owc 20), known to musicians and liturgists as the *Kyrie* ("Lord, have mercy upon us") and the *Gloria in excelsis* ("Glory be to God on high") or Greater Doxology. These were all removed. In their place the revised rite has the

---

[21] The complexity of the question can be seen in Basil Hall, "Cranmer, the Eucharist and the Foreign Divines," in *Thomas Cranmer: Churchman and Scholar*, ed. Paul Ayris and David Selwyn (Woodbridge, UK: Boydell, 1993), 217–258. Hall judges that the "curiosity of the ministers" was more important than the radical views of (some of) the imported Continental reformists.

[22] The second Act of Uniformity, in Ketley, ed., *The Two Liturgies* 214–215. The practice of including within the Book of Common Prayer the legislation that authorizes it began in 1552 with the second Edwardine book, although different printings put the Act in different places and some of them omit it.

Ten Commandments at the beginning; the *Gloria in excelsis* is repositioned at the end of the whole service; the *introit* or opening Psalm has disappeared. As a result, the first part of the 1552 liturgy has the form discussed in chapter one. The rearrangement of the second part is more significant, especially as it affects the canon. Many of the words and some of the components are still there, but their meaning is no longer what it was in 1549.

In the "perfected" office of the Lord's Supper nothing remains of the 1549 canon except the second division, the one that includes the narrative of institution. Some of the first division is relocated in ante-Communion, as a separate prayer for the whole state of the church; some of the third division is relocated at the end, *after* communion, as an alternative to the concluding prayer of thanksgiving. Confession, absolution, comfortable words, Lord's Prayer, prayer of humble access—all these are placed differently also.

This structural reshuffle will be clearer in Table 5.2, which should be compared with the more detailed outline in Table 5.1. In the revised sequence (right-hand column), those who intend to communicate confess their sins and are given absolution. The priest then invites them to lift up their hearts and join in the *Sanctus* "with angels and archangels and with all the company of heaven." Having done so, they somewhat jarringly declare once again, in the relocated prayer of humble access, that they are not worthy so much as to gather up the crumbs under the Lord's table. While they are still kneeling, the priest stands to say all that is left of the canon, which is the long sentence, somewhat revised, that includes the institution narrative. And that is all. There are no speech-acts by which priest and people "celebrate and make" a memorial or "offer and present" themselves to God. The liturgy passes at once, with no *Amen*, to the administration of communion, followed by the Lord's Prayer.

Only after bread and wine have been distributed is there a prayer, cut down from what had been the third division of the 1549 canon, that asks for acceptance of the congregation's sacrifice of praise.

Table 5.2 Structural Comparison of Communion Rites

The original Book of Common Prayer 1549	The classical Book of Common Prayer 1552 / 1559 / 1662
	invitation, confession, absolution, comfortable words
3 *sacramental prayer*	
preface and *Sanctus*	preface and *Sanctus*
	prayer of humble access
canon	
1 intercession	
2 consecration	consecration (?)
3 memorial / oblation	
Lord's Prayer	
4 *communion*	
invitation, confession, absolution, comfortable words	
prayer of humble access	
administration of communion	administration of communion
	Lord's Prayer
5 *postcommunion*	
Agnus Dei, sentences	
prayer of thanksgiving	prayer of thanksgiving *or*
	prayer of oblation

Because this abridged prayer of oblation, usually still so called, has become an alternative to the prayer of thanksgiving, it need never be said at all. Even if it is said, its new position keeps it from being associated, as it could be in 1549, with bread and wine on the table—it is no longer called an altar—for by the time the prayer is said, bread and wine are not there, having been distributed and consumed. Otherwise stated, what is meant by "this our sacrifice"

in the reduced, repurposed prayer of oblation can only be the whole
of the preceding service. Nor can the bread and wine be thought of
as an offering on the ground that they are set out during the offertory. There is no offertory. Nor are bread and wine set out. There is
a *collection*; the churchwardens gather up the people's "devotions"
for the poor; but no rubric even mentions the bread and wine until
the point at which they are distributed. It would be consistent with
the text if they were never placed on the table at all.[23] Their role
is to be received and consumed. To receive them, evidently, is to
"do this." The emphasis which the *Order of the Communion* and the
first Prayer Book had put on communion as the main event is even
stronger in the "perfected" rite; conversely there is even less openness to the idea of offering Christ in or with or by means of bread
and wine.

Besides these structural alterations there are changes in the
wording of the 1552 service that bear on how the eucharistic
elements are to be regarded in themselves. Probably the most
significant of these verbal changes appears in the pared-down
canon. The side-by-side comparison in Table 5.3 will make it
evident.

Originally the tenor of the request was: "bless and sanctify these
gifts, that they may be unto us." As altered in 1552 it is: "grant that
we, receiving these gifts, may be partakers." The difference is subtle,
but the alteration would seem to imply that communicants par-
take *because* they receive but not necessarily because of *what* they
receive. To put it another way, participation in Christ's body and
blood is what occurs in the act of eating and drinking the sacramental bread and wine; but the fact that this participation occurs
does not mean the bread and wine are in fact Christ's body and
blood. Nor does it mean they are not. Logically, the two facts are

---

[23] Colin Buchanan makes the point in "What Did Cranmer Think he Was Doing?" in
An Evangelical among the Anglican Liturgists (London: SPCK, 2009), 71–113 at 98 note
86. Neither he nor anyone else supposes that the elements actually *were* not placed on
the table.

Table 5.3 The Petition in the Sacramental Prayer at Holy Communion

The original Book of Common Prayer 1549	The classical Book of Common Prayer 1552 / 1559 / 1662
Hear us, O merciful Father, we beseech thee, and with thy Holy Spirit and Word, vouchsafe to bl✠ess and sanc✠tify	Hear us, O merciful Father, we beseech thee, and grant that we, receiving
these thy gifts and creatures of bread and wine,	these thy creatures of bread and wine, according to thy Son our Savior Jesus Christ's holy institution, in remembrance of his death and passion,
that they may be unto us the body and blood of thy most dearly beloved Son Jesus Christ: Who in the same night that he was betrayed . . .	may be partakers of his most blessed body and blood: Who in the same night that he was betrayed . . .

independent. Rhetorically, no doubt, the altered prayer is phrased so as to associate them intimately. But whereas the original prayer asked God for a change in the material gifts ("that they may be"), the revised version eliminates the words *bless and sanctify*, and asks instead for a change in the communicants who receive what is given ("that we, receiving . . . may be").

Much the same shift of emphasis seems evident in the words of administration, which are entirely different in 1552 (see Table 6.1 in the next chapter). Just after people have heard the priest recite Christ's words, "Take, eat: This is my body . . . ," they hear him say to each of themselves, "Take and eat this . . ." The proximity and similarity of the two phrases would make it natural to hear the administration formula as meaning, "Take and eat this, the body of Christ." The wording does allow of being so construed, but does not demand it. "This" can be understood as "this bread (and nothing else)." It need not even mean "this consecrated bread," since what is left of the former sacramental prayer need not be interpreted as a prayer of consecration—although it can be, and commonly has been, so interpreted.

Granted, however, for the sake of argument, that the prayer indeed consecrates, whatever sacredness it may impart is impermanent. If any bread or wine happen to be left over after the service, the minister "shall have it to his own use." Since the bread was baker's bread to begin with, not the thick, unleavened wafers that were prescribed in 1549 (OWC 38–39), the minister could take it home and have it for dinner.[24] Nothing could be much further removed from the elevation of the host.

None of these changes is unambiguous or decisive in itself. All of them do point in the same direction: away from affirming a presence of Christ intrinsically conjoined with what communicants physically take, eat, and drink. It is very likely that the relocation of the prayer of humble access was similarly motivated. Placed as it was in the 1549 Prayer Book, between the consecration and communion (see Table 5.1 and Table 5.2, first column), and recited as it was, by the priest kneeling with his face toward the altar, the prayer could imply veneration of the consecrated sacrament. Its new, awkward position, after the *Sanctus*, makes any such implication almost impossible to draw, since at that point the bread and wine have yet to be consecrated, if they are consecrated at all.

The Declaration on Kneeling

There is one place in the 1552 Communion service that might conceivably be construed as open to adoration of the sacrament. The original Prayer Book gave no directions concerning the posture of communicants, but the revised book directs the priest to deliver the

---

[24] The whole rubric can be seen in Figure 5.3, five lines from the bottom.

bread and wine "to the people in their hands kneeling." This new direction went unremarked until the book had gone to press. When a belated alarm was raised, the king's privy council decided to launch a pre-emptive strike, lest anyone suppose that the rubrical order to kneel was an order to venerate the sacrament.

The council's deterrent took the form of an explanatory declaration, which was to be inserted into the new Prayer Book. In Figure 5.3 it appears as the long paragraph in the middle of the page. Notice that it is printed no differently from the rubrics above it and below, although it is commonly called the Black Rubric, as though other rubrics were not black.[25] The Declaration on Kneeling, to use its formal name, avers that to kneel, as the earlier rubric requires, is not to adore anything: not bread and wine, for that would be abhorrent idolatry, and not—this is the important phrase—"any real and essential presence there being of Christ's natural flesh and blood," for that is impossible. To account for the impossibility a metaphysical syllogism is adduced. No body, not even Christ's, can be in more than one place at one time. But Christ's natural body is in heaven. *Ergo* it cannot be in the hands of kneeling communicants, or for that matter anywhere else.

The Declaration on Kneeling rules out both transubstantiation, at least as it was commonly understood, and consubstantiation, as taught by (some) Lutherans. Whether it rules out Christ's presence altogether—whether, that is, it necessarily implies a Zwinglian or "real absence" doctrine—depends on what is meant by Christ's "natural" body and on whether there can be a veracious, actual presence that is not "real and essential." Those questions must be left to theologians. For present purposes, it is enough to say that

[25] Both the nickname and the color of the ink will discussed in chapter eleven. The council's ukase came too late for the explanation to appear at all in some copies. The 1552 Prayer Book shown in the illustration (Griffiths 1552/12; STC 16285a) prints it among the rubrics at the end of Holy Communion, where it belongs; but the fact that the foliation is incorrect suggests some last-minute shuffling; *Fo*[*lium*] 97 is correctly 102.

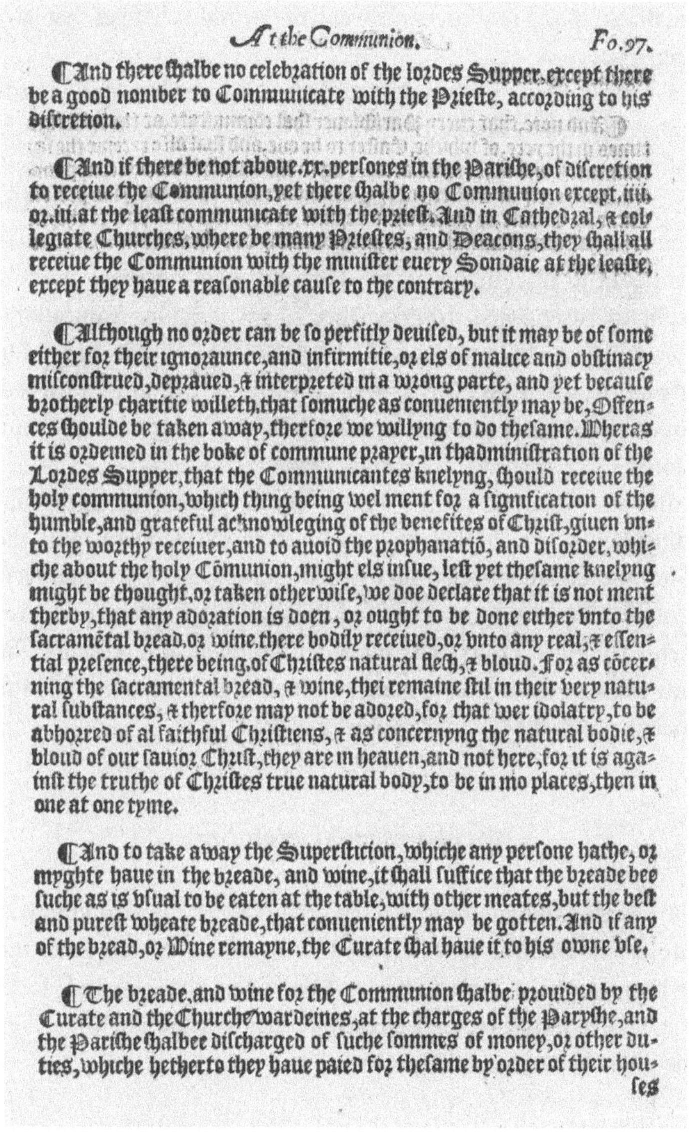

¶And there ſhalbe no celebꝛation of the loꝛdes Supper, except there be a good nomber to Communicate with the Pꝛieſte, accoꝛding to his diſcretion.

¶And if there be not aboue.xx.perſones in the Pariſhe, of diſcretion to receiue the Communion, yet there ſhalbe no Communion except, iiii, oꝛ.iii.at the leaſt communicate with the pꝛieſt. And in Cathedꝛal, ꞝ col=legiate Churches, where be many Pꝛieſtes, and Deacons, they ſhall all receiue the Communion with the miniſter euery Sondaie at the leaſte, except they haue a reaſonable cauſe to the contrary.

¶Although no oꝛder can be ſo perfitly deuiſed, but it may be of ſome either foꝛ their ignoꝛaunce, and infirmitie, oꝛ els of malice and obſtinacy miſconſtrued, depꝛaued, ꞝ interpꝛeted in a wꝛong parte, and yet becauſe bꝛotherly charitie willeth, that ſomuche as conueniently may be, Offen=ces ſhoulde be taken away, therfoꝛe we willyng to do theſame. Wheras it is oꝛdeined in the boke of commune pꝛayer, in thadminiſtration of the Loꝛdes Supper, that the Communicantes knelyng, ſhould receiue the holy communion, which thing being wel ment foꝛ a ſignification of the humble, and grateful acknowleging of the benefites of Chꝛiſt, giuen vn= to the woꝛthy receiuer, and to auoid the pꝛophanatiõ, and diſoꝛder, whi= che about the holy Cõmunion, might els inſue, leſt yet theſame knelyng might be thought, oꝛ taken otherwiſe, we doe declare that it is not ment therby, that any adoꝛation is doen, oꝛ ought to be done either vnto the ſacramẽtal bꝛead, oꝛ wine. there bodily receiued, oꝛ vnto any real, ꞝ eſſen= tial pꝛeſence, there being, of Chꝛiſtes natural fleſh, ꞝ bloud. Foꝛ as cõcer= ning the ſacramental bꝛead, ꞝ wine, thei remaine ſtil in their very natu= ral ſubſtances, ꞝ therfoꝛe may not be adoꝛed, foꝛ that wer idolatry, to be abhoꝛred of al faithful Chꝛiſtiens, ꞝ as concernyng the natural bodie, ꞝ bloud of our ſauioꝛ Chꝛiſt, they are in heauen, and not here, foꝛ it is aga= inſt the truthe of Chꝛiſtes true natural body, to be in mo places, then in one at one tyme.

¶And to take away the Superſticion, whiche any perſone hathe, oꝛ myghte haue in the bꝛeade, and wine, it ſhall ſuffice that the bꝛeade bee ſuche as is vſual to be eaten at the table, with other meates, but the beſt and pureſt wheate bꝛeade, that conueniently may be gotten. And if any of the bꝛead, oꝛ Wine remayne, the Curate ſhal haue it to his owne vſe.

¶The bꝛeade, and wine foꝛ the Communion ſhalbe pꝛouided by the Curate and the Churchewardeines, at the charges of the Paryſhe, and the Pariſhe ſhalbee diſcharged of ſuche ſommes of money, oꝛ other du= ties, whiche hetherto they haue paied foꝛ theſame by oꝛder of their hou=
ſes

Figure 5.3 Communion Rubrics in Edward VI's Second Prayer Book

Edition printed by Richard Grafton, 1552.

Courtesy of the Beinecke Rare Books Library, Yale University.

the Black Rubric reinforces the trend of the other changes that have been discussed.

Chiefly because of those changes, the 1552 version of the Lord's Supper has been called a communion without a Mass.[26] Certainly, compared with the 1549 rite, it puts more distance between itself and the tradition of the western church before the Reformation. The elements of bread and wine are further desacralized or demystified, the better to discourage superstition and idolatry. They are more explicitly disengaged from sacrifice as propitiation, from adoration, and from the presence of Christ, as these were conceived in relation to the Mass. The material "creatures" are to be received, not offered; to be eaten and drunk thankfully, not gazed upon and adored.

In later versions of the Prayer Book, small but significant adjustments, which will be examined in due course, pull the Communion office back from where it stands in the "perfected" version of 1552. As it stands, however, the text is a remarkable achievement. To quote a frequently quoted assessment, it represents "the only effective attempt ever made to give liturgical expression to the doctrine of 'justification by faith alone.'"[27]

Other Rites and Ceremonies

The more unambiguously reformed character of the second Prayer Book's Communion service is evident elsewhere as well. Since the revisions in other services brought them into the "classical" form that has been surveyed here already, in chapters one and three, they need only be noticed briefly.

---

[26] By A. H. Couratin in "The Service of Holy Communion, 1552–1662," *Church Quarterly Review* 163 (1962): 431–442 at 433.

[27] Gregory Dix, *The Shape of the Liturgy* (London: Dacre Press, 1945), 672. The assessment was not, for Dix, an accolade.

Mattins and Evensong

These two services, so named in 1549, are renamed Morning and Evening Prayer, although the old names lingered in popular usage. To each of them the revision of 1552 adds the penitential opening described in chapter one. In 1549 there was no alternative to any of the three canticles taken from the gospels, *Benedictus* at Morning Prayer, *Magnificat* and *Nunc dimittis* at Evening Prayer. The revised offices allow specific Psalms to be recited instead.

Baptism

Presumably for the sake of preventing superstition, a number of ceremonies are no longer prescribed in the Baptism service. In 1549 there was an exorcism; godmothers and godfathers laid their hands

---

The Exorcism in Public Baptism
Book of Common Prayer, 1549

Then let the priest looking upon the children, say

I command thee, unclean spirit, in the name of the Father, of the Son, and of the Holy Ghost, that thou come out, and depart from these infants, whom our Lord Jesus Christ hath vouchsafed to call to his holy Baptism, to be made members of his body, and of his holy congregation. Therefore thou cursed spirit, re-member thy sentence, remember thy judgment, remember the day to be at hand, wherein thou shalt burn in fire everlasting, prepared for thee and thy angels. And presume not hereafter to exercise any tyranny toward these infants, whom Christ hath bought with his precious blood, and by this his holy Baptism calleth to be of his flock.

on the baptized infant, who was clothed with "the white vesture, commonly called the crisom" as a token of innocence, and was also anointed with oil (owc 51). In the 1552 Prayer Book these symbolic features are omitted. The sign of the cross remains, although it is relocated to a different point in the rite. This ceremony has, however, been removed from both Confirmation and Matrimony, which otherwise remain largely the same (owc 62, 67, 69).

Burial

The Order for the Burial of the Dead changed significantly.[28] One of the prayers that was discarded had commended into the hands of God the soul of the sister or brother whose body is buried. As a prayer *for* the departed it was at odds with the reformers' insistence that the dead do not inhabit an intermediate state, purgatory, between heaven and hell, where the chastisement they must suffer can be alleviated by prayers and Masses offered in this world by the living.

Equally dubious, from a protestant standpoint, was a sentence said by the priest as he cast earth on the corpse: "I commend thy soul to God the Father almighty, and thy body to the ground, earth to earth, ashes to ashes, dust to dust, in sure and certain hope of resurrection to eternal life" (owc 82). Not only was this a commendation of the departed; it was spoken *to* the departed, as in some sense still a member of the earthly community who could in some sense be spoken to. Beginning in 1552 there is a committal, not a commendation; it is said while earth is cast "by some standing by," not by the priest; and it regards only the corpse, not the soul of the deceased, who is referred to in the third person, not the second: "Forasmuch as it hath pleased Almighty God of his great

---

[28] On the Burial office and its revisions in a wider context, see Peter Marshall, *Beliefs and the Dead in Reformation England* (Oxford: Oxford University Press, 2002), 108–113, 124–187.

mercy to take unto himself the soul of our dear brother here departed, we therefore commit his body to the ground; earth to earth," and so on.

The original Prayer Book provided for a celebration of Holy Communion in conjunction with the Burial Office. The revised version does not. Probably the provision was eliminated because such a service might be thought of as a Requiem Mass, or something like it, offered for the repose of the deceased.

The Visitation of the Sick

There is still provision in the 1552 Prayer Book for Communion to be celebrated with a sick person, at home, but the Visitation office no longer makes allowance for the sacrament to be "reserved" for that purpose. Reservation, in the liturgical sense, is setting aside consecrated bread and wine after a regular eucharistic celebration, either for distribution elsewhere at another time or—in pre-Reformation practice—for devotional purposes akin to veneration of the elevated host at Mass. There was no place for such devotions, of course, in the first Book of Common Prayer, any more than there was for the elevation; but the priest was permitted, following an open Communion service in church, to take some of the bread and wine with him when he visited the sick, and to administer them after the general confession, absolution, and comfortable words were said (OWC 79). The revised Prayer Book strikes this permission from the rubric. Only after a full celebration at which the invalid is present (with others) may she or he receive the sacrament elsewhere than in church. Any kind of reservation, it can be inferred, would suggest the superstitious idea that bread and wine have some inherent potency in virtue of consecration, apart from a congregational service.

Conclusion

The 1552 Book of Common Prayer cannot have seen much use. Once it was clear that Edward VI was dying and that he would not be succeeded by a protestant cousin but by his half-sister Mary, it was also clear that the days of the English liturgy were numbered.[29] For the most part, the royal supremacy orchestrated by Henry VIII had worked to the advantage of religious reform, as long as his protestant son was alive to exercise it. But what the reforming party managed to do during King Edward's brief reign, Queen Mary undid. She was a devout, not to say fanatical adherent of her Spanish mother's religion, which during her even briefer reign began to call itself *catholic* in an exclusive sense. For that religion she was determined to reclaim England; had she lived longer than she did her success might have been greater. As it was, all of her brother's religious legislation was rescinded; the Book of Common Prayer was explicitly abolished; the Mass was reinstated, together with papal authority; and a great many protestant heretics, as the queen believed them to be, were burned alive on account of their protestantism. One of them was Thomas Cranmer.

Others who had welcomed the Reformation left, while they still could, for protestant centers abroad—Strassburg, Geneva, Zurich. Some of these émigrés took their Prayer Books with them. Their exile came to an end when Mary Tudor, "the saddest woman in English history," died in 1558. She had borne no children. The next heir, by her father Henry VIII's will, was the daughter of the woman for love of whom he had divorced Mary's mother. The new queen was a protestant and her name was Elizabeth.

---

[29] See Table 4.1: the second Act of Uniformity came into effect on November 1, 1552; Edward died in July, 1553; Mary's first Statute of Repeal took effect on December 20.

Six

Settling In

Queen Elizabeth's accession leads back to the opening pages of the Book of Common Prayer, the Act of Uniformity passed by her first Parliament. It passed by a whisker, and how it came to be passed at all has been debated. The outcome is not in doubt; Queen Mary's repeal of legislation concerning religion was repealed and King Edward's second, more protestant Prayer Book was brought back into use, with certain small changes. The question is whether this was the outcome desired and intended by Elizabeth and her advisers.

According to one reconstruction of events, the 1552 Prayer Book was reinstated under pressure from zealous protestants, especially those who had returned to England after fleeing from Mary's fiery counter-Reformation. Parliament would never have accepted a liturgy less thoroughly reformed, although the queen herself favored a settlement of religion based on the liturgy of 1549. The more usual account, on the other hand, has been that restoration of the second, "perfected" Book of Common Prayer was intended all along, and that parliamentary opposition to Elizabeth's program came not from protestant extremists in the Commons, but from conservative members of the House of Lords, especially the bishops appointed by her late sister. On this interpretation, a few alterations of the 1552 Prayer Book were introduced to mollify adherents of the old faith, or even win their support. Not that they did.[1]

---

[1] On the shifting tides of scholarship, see Andrew Pettegree, "The Marian Exiles and the Elizabethan Settlement," ch. 6 in his *Marian Protestantism: Six Studies* (Aldershot, UK: Scholars Press, 1996), 129–150; and more recently Cyndia Susan Clegg, "The 1559 Books of Common Prayer and the Elizabethan Reformation," *Journal of Ecclesiastical History* 67.1 (2016): 94–121, esp. 97–105. Clegg's own argument, based in part on

The Book of Common Prayer. Charles Hefling, Oxford University Press (2021). © Oxford University Press.
DOI: 10.1093/oso/9780190689681.001.0001.

The Elizabethan Alterations

Either way, it was not the first Book of Common Prayer that the 1559 Act of Uniformity restored but the second, with three stated changes, "and none other, or otherwise." At Morning and Evening Prayer, the first lessons appointed by date in the kalendar give way to proper lessons on Sundays and holydays; at Holy Communion, longer sentences are prescribed at the delivery of the sacrament; and the Litany is modified.

The Act refers to these changes without specifying them. The only uncertainty as to exactly what they were meant to be arises in the Litany. The earliest surviving copies of the 1559 Prayer Book all agree in omitting from one of the deprecations a plea for deliverance from "the tyranny of the bishop of Rome and all his detestable enormities." Toward the end, however, there is some disparity. Editions from both of the authorized printers add several prayers to the original Litany, but not the same ones and not in the same order.

About the wording of the communion sentences, spoken by the priest to each communicant at the delivery of the sacrament, there is no disagreement. King Edward's first Prayer Book prescribes one form of words, his second Prayer Book another form, entirely different, and Queen Elizabeth's Prayer Book prescribes both. The original sentences and the later ones are simply stapled together with the single word *and* (Table 6.1). The result is a pair of long and slightly awkward speeches that can be understood in either of two ways, or both. The second half of each sentence, retained from the version of 1552, is more explicitly associated with faithful, thankful reception of the sacrament. In that sense it is more subjective. The first half, retrieved from the 1549 Prayer Book, is more hospitable to belief in Christ's presence in or with or through the bread and wine. In that sense, it is more objective. In fact, what the 1559

---

artifactual evidence, is meant to "put to rest all assertions that Elizabeth . . . sought to have the Elizabethan Reformation rest on Edward's 1549 Book of Common Prayer" (119).

Table 6.1 Words of Administration at Holy Communion

1549 First Prayer Book of Edward VI	1552 Second Prayer Book of Edward VI	1559 Prayer Book of Elizabeth I
The body of our Lord Jesus Christ, which was given for thee, preserve thy body and soul unto everlasting life.		The body of our Lord Jesus Christ, which was given for thee, preserve thy body and soul into everlasting life:
	Take and eat this in remembrance that Christ died for thee, and feed on him in thy heart by faith, with thanksgiving.	and take and eat this in remembrance that Christ died for thee, and feed on him in thine heart by faith, with thanksgiving.
The blood of our Lord Jesus Christ, which was shed for thee, preserve thy body and soul unto everlasting life.		The blood of our Lord Jesus Christ, which was shed for thee, preserve thy body and soul into everlasting life:
	Drink this in remembrance that Christ's blood was shed for thee, and be thankful.	and drink this in remembrance that Christ's blood was shed for thee, and be thankful.

Prayer Book directs the priest to say to communicants begins with the same words that had been said to them at Mass, while the *Order of the Communion* was in use.[2]

The importance of reintroducing those words should not be exaggerated.[3] They were evidently uncontroversial at the time, and they leave the rest of the Communion service just as it was in 1552. Still, the composite formulas do make it easier to reconcile

[2] The wording is not exactly the same. The 1549 Prayer Book had changed both "preserve thy body" and "preserve thy soul" to "preserve thy body and soul"; the Elizabethan version keeps the change.

[3] See Pettegree, *Marian Protestantism*, 135–136.

the whole service with an understanding of communion as not only remembering but receiving Christ. In that regard, the "masterpiece of theological engineering"[4] that produced the Elizabethan sentences is consistent with another revision, which the 1559 Act of Uniformity does not mention. The Black Rubric is gone.[5] It could be that this last-minute explanation of what kneeling does and does not mean was left out because it had no parliamentary authority; but omitting its explicit denial of Christ's "real and essential presence" would have been consonant with what little can be inferred about the new queen's personal beliefs. It is a plausible though unverifiable conjecture that she not only engineered the communion sentences but set aside the Declaration on Kneeling.

Possibly too, Elizabeth had something to do, indirectly, with another rubrical alteration, which would prove to be endlessly vexatious. Her taste for sartorial dignity in public worship is thought to be the reason for a clause in her Act of Uniformity which provides that "such ornaments of the church and of the ministers thereof shall be retained, and be in use, as was [sic] in this Church of England, by the authority of Parliament in the second year of the reign of King Edward the Sixth, until other order shall be therein taken by authority of the Queen's Majesty" (OWC 192). The operative words are *second year*, for the proviso appears to overrule a rubric in the Prayer Book of 1552, Edward's *fifth* year, that regulates what a clergyman may and may not wear "at the time of the Communion and all other times in his ministration." Somebody, no one knows who, altered this rubric to agree with the new legislation that overruled it, and added, for good measure, a reference to the legislation itself. The result, as it appears in the Elizabethan Prayer Book, is the third column of Table 6.2.

---

[4] Diarmaid MacCulloch, *The Later Reformation in England*, 2nd ed. (London: Palgrave Macmillan, 2001), 27.

[5] More exactly, the folio editions issued in 1559 omit it, as do all later editions. Quarto editions exist (Griffiths 1559/5 and 1559/6) that still print the Declaration, presumably by mistake.

Table 6.2 Rubrics ordering the Ornaments of the Minister

1549 rubric before The Supper of the Lord and the Holy Communion	1552 rubric before Morning Prayer	1559 Ornaments Rubric before Morning Prayer	1662 Ornaments Rubric before Morning Prayer
Upon the day and at the time appointed for the ministration of the holy Communion, the priest . . . shall put upon him the vesture appointed for that ministration, that is to say: a white alb plain, with a vestment or cope.	And here is to be noted, that the minister at the time of the Communion and all other times in his ministration, shall use neither alb, vestment, nor cope; but . . . being a priest or deacon, he shall have and wear a surplice only.	And here is to be noted, that the minister at the time of the Communion, and at all other times in his ministration, shall use such ornaments in the church as were in use by authority of Parliament in the second year of the reign of King Edward the Sixth according to the act of Parliament set in the beginning of this book.	And here is to be noted, that such Ornaments of the church and of the Ministers thereof at all times of their Ministration, shall be retained and be in use as were in this Church of England by the Authority of Parliament, in the second year of the reign of King Edward the Sixth.

The instructions in Edward's second Book of Common Prayer (second column) were simple: a surplice is to be worn at all services—no alb, no vestment, no cope.[6] The wording strongly implies that the intention was to reverse a rubric in the original Prayer Book (first column), which *requires* an alb and either a vestment or a cope at Holy Communion. The 1559 Act of Uniformity does not mention any "ornament" in particular, and neither does the rubric that reiterates it. They both simply order everything to be

[6] The ceremonial costume these terms (probably) refer to is explained in Appendix 1.

done the same way things were done in the second year of Edward's reign—however that was. If what these indirect directives mean is the way things were done while the first Book of Common Prayer was in use, they mean that alb, vestment, and cope are no longer forbidden. In other words, as of 1559 the minister at Holy Communion could again be vested as he could before the stringently protestant restrictions in the 1552 Prayer Book came into force.

Rubrics are one thing, though, and performance is another. If any Elizabethan minister did put on "a white alb plain, with a vestment," there is no evidence of the fact. There is plenty of evidence, however, that what ministers are permitted or forbidden to wear when they conduct the Prayer Book services was a contentious issue throughout Elizabeth's reign, as it would continue to be, on and off, into the twentieth century. Table 6.2 will come up again.

Apart from the changes discussed so far, which were few and fairly small though not unimportant, Queen Elizabeth's Book of Common Prayer is the same as the version revised in 1552. The kalendar was altered in 1561, chiefly by adding a number of minor holydays,[7] and with that the authorized text of the Book of Common Prayer arrived at the form it would have for the rest of the sixteenth century.

Which is not to say that what will be found between the covers of an Elizabethan Prayer Book is always the text, the whole text, and nothing but the text. The official contents were often added to and sometimes abridged. Parts of the book were combined with other texts. Divine Service was issued separately, modified for use on special occasions. Some of these reconfigurations were authorized; most were tolerated. All of them throw light on how the Book of Common Prayer was received, used, and understood.

---

[7] These new commemorations made no liturgical difference, since no proper collect, lessons, epistle, or gospel were assigned. Among other persons, Valentine was added on February 14, George on April 23, Nicholas on December 6, and Lucy on December 13. Also added were the Invention of the Cross (its discovery) on May 3 and the Conception of Mary on December 8.

Supplements: Psalms in Verse
and Godly Prayers

The earliest editions of the Book of Common Prayer were folios, eleven inches tall, more or less, legibly printed in large type, as shown in Figures 5.2 and 5.3, for the minister and perhaps the clerk to use in public prayers. This was the normative format—not necessarily the most common one—throughout Elizabeth's reign. The 1559 Act of Uniformity did not extend to the Psalter or to the Ordinal, which was formally authorized later and incorporated much later. The Psalter, however, was sometimes printed continuously with the Prayer Book services; sometimes it was bound up with them, at the back of the volume, though separately printed with a title page of its own; sometimes it was issued by itself, as the Ordinal generally was. For personal use there were handier Prayer Books, often quartos, eight inches tall or a bit taller, as well as smaller octavos and a few editions smaller still. Like most books, these could all be purchased unbound, or bound according to the buyer's taste or affluence. In either case they were very frequently combined with one or both of two other texts: a collection of Psalms rewritten in verse, and a set of personal, as contrasted with common or liturgical, prayers.

Sternhold and Hopkins

The so-called singing Psalms will come up again when music is discussed in chapter twelve. The name was used colloquially for the contents of *The Whole Book of Psalmes: Collected into English Metre, by Thomas Sternhold, John Hopkins, and Others.* For almost two centuries the title page of this collection went on to announce that its rhyming, metrically regular paraphrases were "allowed to be sung in all churches, of all the people together, before and after Morning and Evening Prayer; and also before and after sermons." Permission to use them at public prayers was granted, at least by implication, in a set of injunctions that Queen Elizabeth issued in 1559. She liked music in church, and her injunctions not only encouraged the singing of Prayer Book services, but also allowed that "an hymn or such-like song" might be sung before or afterward.

There was a demand in England for such-like songs, which were a regular part of protestant services abroad. The collection that came to be known as Sternhold and Hopkins cornered the market. In it were included not only the 150 Psalms but the Prayer Book canticles, the Lord's Prayer, the Ten Commandments, and even the Athanasian Creed, all paraphrased in rhymed stanzas. Some editions added musical notation for "apt tunes to sing withal," sturdy, straightforward melodies that were easy to learn and sing. So common was it for an edition of Sternhold and Hopkins to be bound at the back of a Book of Common Prayer that even learned writers spoke of the singing Psalms as though they belonged officially to its contents.[8]

Godly Prayers

Under the title of "Certain Godly Prayers," sixteenth- and seventeenth-century Prayer Books frequently include a floating collection of prayers that are not directly related to the liturgical offices, and are plainly intended for personal use. Like metrical Psalms, these prayers made their first appearance in Prayer Books issued during Edward VI's reign, although a few of them can be traced to the English primer published under the auspices of Henry VIII. Primers were vernacular versions of the traditional Book of Hours; they contained devotional texts and short

[8] For example, Edmund Reeve, *The Christian Divinitie contained in the Divine Service of the Church of England* (STC 20829; 1631), 116: "In the title of the Psalmes in meeter in the Booke of Common prayer it is thus said. . . ."

liturgical services that could be used anywhere, by individuals or families. A few prayers from Henry's official version were evidently borrowed by the printers, who added them, with others, to the Prayer Book. They may have been following official instructions, or they may have wanted to make the authorized liturgy more like a primer, more widely usable and perhaps more marketable. In any case the precedent they set was followed for the better part of two hundred years.

Godly Prayers

A Prayer for Patience in Trouble

How hast thou, O Lord, humbled and plucked me down! I dare now unnethes [scarcely] make my prayers unto thee, for thou art angry with me, but not without my deserving. Certainly I have sinned, Lord, I confess it, I will not deny it. But, O my God, pardon my trespasses, release my debts, render now thy grace again unto me, stop my wounds, for I am all-to [utterly] plagued and beaten: Yet, Lord, this notwithstanding, I abide patiently, and give mine attendance on thee, continually waiting for relief at thy hand, and that not without skill; for I have received a token of thy favor and grace towards me, I mean thy word of promise concerning Christ, who for me was offered on the cross for a ransom, a sacrifice and price for my sins: wherefore, according to that thy promise, defend me, Lord, by thy right hand, and give a gracious ear to my requests, for all man's stays are but vain. Beat down therefore mine enemies thine own self with thy power, which art mine only aider and protector, O Lord God Almighty. Amen.

The Godly Prayers are usually phrased in the first-person singular, rather than the plural of common prayer, and they are usually longer and more effusive. One group of about twenty begins with a confession and a prayer to be said in the morning, and finishes with a bedtime prayer and a prayer for the hour of death.[9] Other prayers were added later, but there was never a settled number or arrangement. Despite having no official status, use and wont gave them a prescriptive right to be included in Prayer Books meant for personal use, and they sometimes made their way into folio editions, from which they had to be expelled more than once.[10]

Adaptations: Occasional Forms of Prayer

The Book of Common Prayer has no services concerned specifically with contingent events and circumstances that affect everyone. It only provides a few special prayers that may be added to Divine Service "if the time require." In the Elizabethan Prayer Book, the times that would require these optional prayers are times of public calamity—drought, famine, flood, plague, war—and these woes are interpreted, as the Visitation office interprets sickness, in terms of divine displeasure, warning, and punishment. The prayers are penitential requests not only for succor but for forgiveness.

In 1563, however, when plague broke out in London, a program of penitence, fasting, and public supplication was ordered by royal authority, and the booklet which ordered it prescribes, among other things, a whole form of service which is to be "used in common prayer twice a week" to demonstrate remorse and plead

---

[9] On sources of the Godly Prayers, see William Keatinge Clay, ed., *Liturgies and Occasional Forms of Prayer Set forth in the Reign of Queen Elizabeth* (Parker Society; Cambridge University Press, 1847), xix–xxi; and for texts, 246–271.

[10] In 1637, Archbishop William Laud ordered Godly Prayers to be taken out of the Book of Common Prayer for Scotland; see Paul Morgan, "Some Bibliographical Aspects of the Scottish Prayer Book of 1637," *The Bibliotheck* 5 (1967): 1–23 at 17–19. In 1661, when England's Prayer Book was being rehabilitated, two such prayers were deleted in the House of Commons, as chapter eight will mention, and Godly Prayers were deleted again by the revisers of the final text.

for mercy. For this service appropriate readings from scripture are appointed and a long scripted sermon is printed, together with a composite or cento "psalm." All these texts are set within the structure of Divine Service as it stood in the recently restored Book of Common Prayer. The liturgy thus modified and interpolated would be the first in a long series of special, one-off forms of prayer, each of which adapts the whole of the regular service in response to particular circumstances.[11]

The circumstances were not always dire. In addition to "fast books," as they were called, special forms of prayer were published for times of celebration and thanksgiving, notably the anniversary of Queen Elizabeth's "entry into her reign," which was one of the minor holydays added to the Prayer Book kalendar (on the wrong date) when it was revised in 1561.[12] The Queen's Day or Accession Day was observed as a feast, with popular revelry following public prayers, which took the form of Divine Service as it would be conducted on a Sunday. Booklets published for use on this and other special occasions often printed all the offices in full, with the appointed Psalms and Bible readings inserted into the Prayer Book text, so that everything could be read "without turning to and fro." The Queen's Day service issued in 1576 provides three alternatives for the first lesson, each of them a condensed narrative of a virtuous Old Testament monarch who purged his kingdom of idolatrous worship. The symbolic or typological parallel with the protestant Queen Elizabeth, England's defender against popery

---

[11] The series is being studied and catalogued in an ongoing research project, "British state prayers, fasts and thanksgivings 1540s–1940s." The first volume of Natalie Mears, Alasdair Raffe, Stephen Taylor, Philip Williamson, and Lucy Bates, eds., *National Prayers: Special Worship since the Reformation* (Woodbridge, UK: Boydell Press, 2013) covers the years as far as 1688; the second volume (2017) continues through 1870. See also Natalie Mears, "Special Nationwide Worship and the Book of Common Prayer in England, Wales and Ireland, 1533–1642," in *Worship and the Parish Church in Early Modern Britain*, ed. Natalie Mears and Alec Ryrie (Farnham, Surrey and Burlington, VT: Ashgate, 2013), 31–72.

[12] It appeared in the kalendar, which at the time used only Roman dating, on the line for 14 Kal. Decembris, the eighteenth day of November, instead of the seventeenth.

and superstition, is plain and plainly intentional. Interestingly, the rubrics call for a Psalm "in meter," presumably from Sternhold and Hopkins, before and after the sermon.[13]

The Prayer Book in the Bible

As other texts could be added to the Book of Common Prayer, so too the Book of Common Prayer, or parts of it, could be added to another book, the Bible. The practice of combining these sacred texts in one volume began while the original Prayer Book was still in use. Printed at the front of one edition of the Bible are the 1549 offices of Mattins and Evensong, the Litany, and a compilation of all the Sunday and holyday collects.[14] The same excerpts, as revised, can be found in Bibles published in the early 1560s. A Bible with these additions would provide all the texts needed for reciting both of the daily offices, or for following those services as conducted in church.

In the earliest examples of Bibles augmented in this way, the translation is the one used in the Prayer Book itself, the "Great" Bible that Miles Coverdale revised and translated in 1539. When this version gave way in 1568 to the so-called Bishops' Bible as the Church of England's authorized scripture, it might have been logical to change the biblical excerpts in the Prayer Book, the epistles and gospels especially, to match the new translation, which was meant to be used in reading the chapters at Morning and Evening

---

[13] *A fourme of Prayer with thankes geyuing, to be vsed every yeere, the .17. of Nouember, beying the day of the Queenes Maiesties entrie into her raigne* (STC 16479; London: Richard Jugge, [1576]).

[14] *The Byble in Englishe* (STC 2089; London: Nicholas Hill [1552]). The wording of the *Te Deum*, the *Benedicite*, and the Litany shows that the Prayer Book excerpts come from the version of 1549, despite the (conjectural) date of the Bible. Ian Green surveys the various ways in which parts of the Book of Common Prayer were added to Bibles, in "'Puritan Prayer Books' and 'Geneva Bibles': An Episode in Elizabethan Publishing," *Transactions of the Cambridge Bibliographical Society* 11.3 (1998): 313–349.

Prayer. But nothing was changed. The Prayer Book continued to follow the Coverdale translation.

So too did the Psalter. Properly speaking, the Psalms were no part of the Book of Common Prayer; if necessary, they could be read, like the lessons, from a Bible. Since 1549, however, clerks and choirs had made use of separately printed Psalters, with headings and marginal labels to indicate the daily portions, and in this convenient form the Psalms were frequently bound up with the Book of Common Prayer. With the introduction of the Bishops' Bible, the Church of England had, in effect, two versions of the Psalms. The translation in the Bishops' Bible could in principle be recited instead of Coverdale's at Morning and Evening Prayer, and in some editions the book of Psalms is in fact divided into portions, evidently for that purpose. Some other editions, remarkably, print the Psalms from the Great Bible in place of the Bishops' Bible's own version. At least one edition includes both versions, in parallel columns. The outer half of each page has the "translation after the Hebrews"; on the inner half the "translation used in the common prayer" is printed in different type.[15] Coverdale had not translated his Old Testament directly from the original language, and in point of accuracy the Bishops' translation "after the Hebrews" is perhaps superior. But in public worship the Great Bible Psalms held their own.

With yet another Bishops' Bible, as its title page announces, is "joined the whole service used in the Church of England."[16] At the front are all of the Prayer Book offices, plus the Coverdale Psalter; only the liturgical epistles and gospels are left out. Instead, after each of the Sunday and holyday collects there are two citations, which take advantage of the fact that the Bishops' Bible numbers verses as well as chapters. Added to each citation are the first few

---

[15] *The holie Bible* (Bishops' Bible, STC 2197; London: Richard Jugge, 1572).

[16] *The Holy Byble, conteynyng the Old Testament, and the New. Set foorth by aucthoritie; Whereunto is ioyned the whole service vsed in the Churche of Englande* (Bishops' Bible, STC 2115; London: Richard Jugge, 1576).

words of the passage it refers to. Together, these indicators made it easy to find the appointed epistle and gospel in the adjoining Bible. Possibly the expectation was that ministers would read those passages from the new translation at public prayers. In that case, a Prayer Book would not be necessary at all, and neither would a separate Psalter. The enlarged Bible could serve as a one-volume liturgical compendium.

Two years later, the new Queen's Printer brought out a similar omnibus, a folio Bible evidently meant for use in church, with a condensed Prayer Book at the beginning and two versions of the Psalms, printed in double columns.[17] This handsome volume is noteworthy for two reasons. The Bible is a Geneva Bible, named for the capital of advanced protestantism where English refugees had begun the translation during Queen Mary's reign. In England the Geneva version was widely read and studied, especially by the "hotter sort of protestants" conventionally known as puritans. Officially, this version could not be used to read the lessons at Divine Service, but the inclusion of the Prayer Book text in a chancel-size edition suggests that it was intended to be so used.

The Prayer Book text it includes is the second noteworthy feature. It is not quite "the whole service used in the Church of England." Three offices are missing, all of them obnoxious to puritans: Private Baptism, Confirmation, and the Churching rite. There are also changes in the services that remain. Most obviously, *minister* is printed at several points instead of the offensive term *priest*. Although no one seems to have complained when it was published, this bowdlerized abridgment later became mildly notorious. In the next century a stridently anti-puritan writer reported its publication as a great abuse, "designed to no other purpose, but by degrees to bring the Church of *England* into some conformity

---

[17] *The Bible, Translated according to the Ebrew and Greeke . . . With most profitable Annotations vpon all the hard places . . . Whereunto is added the Psalter of the common translation agreeing with the booke of Common prayer* (Geneva Bible, STC 2123; London: Christopher Barker, [1578]).

to the desired orders of *Geneva*."[18] This insinuation of miching mallecho was passed on by nineteenth- and twentieth-century writers, and the tale grew in the telling. At some point the name "puritan Prayer Book" attached itself to this edition as well as to others that were similarly customized, even though they all leave untouched much that puritans detested. A more recent investigation suggests, however, that there was probably no conspiracy to purify the Book of Common Prayer "by degrees." A more likely explanation of the whole episode is the printer's commercial interest in selling Bibles.[19]

By the middle of Elizabeth's reign, abridged Prayer Books were quite common and for the most part quite unexceptional. Instead of being included at the front in Bibles, these "Bible versions," sometimes misleadingly so called, were printed and marketed independently, each with its own title-page. Usually the Act of Uniformity and Cranmer's two essays are left out, along with the full texts of the Communion readings; otherwise most "Bible versions" of the Prayer Book are complete and accurate. Some include the Coverdale Psalter. Typically they are quartos, which could be bound together with a Bible of the same size in whichever translation the purchaser preferred, although guide words for the epistles and gospels in some editions show they were expected to be matched with a Bishops' Bible or with the Geneva version. By the end of the sixteenth century, as many of these shortened Prayer Books were being published as were complete editions; in the first half of the seventeenth century there were twice as many. Unabridged lectern-size printings continued to be the norm, but

---

[18] Peter Heylin, *Aërius Redivivus: or, The History of the Presbyterians* (Oxford: John Crossey, 1670), book 7 283. Heylin appears to admit that he got his information at second hand. He also says the culprit was Richard Jugge, the Queen's Printer. It was not. Christopher Barker became Queen's Printer in 1577, and is named as such on the title-page.

[19] This is Ian Green's conclusion; see " 'Puritan Prayer Books' and 'Geneva Bibles' " 316.

increasingly it was these smaller, handier Prayer Books that made the text familiar.

The Elizabethan Prayer Book in Use

It did not take long for the Book of Common Prayer to become a best-seller,[20] and the physical dispositions of its text that have been discussed indicate some aspects of its use. For how the offices it prescribes were actually conducted in the early years there is indirect evidence; complaints about abuses, for example, are often exceptions that prove the rule. But descriptions are few. As with Shakespeare's plays, the printed scripts exist; they were certainly performed; but by and large what happened in performance can only be conjectured.[21]

The Harrison Description

One Elizabethan text that does present itself as a straightforward report of common prayer in the Church of England was published in Holinshed's *Chronicles*, the encyclopedic compendium that Shakespeare is thought to have drawn upon for historical information. Folded into the *Chronicles* is "The Description of England," written by Holinshed's collaborator William Harrison in 1577, which among many other things describes the English church and its worship.[22]

[20] Ian Green, *Print and Protestantism in Early Modern England* (Oxford: Oxford University Press, 2000), 239–265, esp. 247–250.

[21] See Patrick Collinson, "Shepherds, Sheepdogs, and Hirelings: The Pastoral Ministry in Post-Reformation England," in *The Ministry: Clerical and Lay*, ed. W. J. Sheils and Diana Wood (Ecclesiastical History Society Papers; Basil Blackwell, 1989), 185–220, esp. 190–192, 207–211.

[22] On Harrison's "Description," see Christopher Marsh, *Popular Religion in Sixteenth-Century England* (New York: St. Martin's Press, 1998), 27–95, esp. 35–37; John Booty,

Harrison was himself a parish minister, so it is reasonable to suppose he knew what he was writing about. His account puts first things first. "There is nothing read in our churches," it begins, "but the canonical scriptures." The Psalter is read every month, the Old Testament once a year, the New Testament gospels in the morning, the epistles in the afternoon—all as the Prayer Book prescribes. There may be "some exposition or exhortation . . . unto amendment of life," a sermon, that is, if the minister of the parish knows enough about the Bible to qualify him for the bishop's license to preach. If not, he could read one of the doctrinal or pastoral homilies issued by public authority.[23]

"After Morning Prayer," Harrison goes on, "also we have the Litany and Suffrages, an invocation in mine opinion not devised without the great assistance of the spirit of God," and then the Communion service, although this might be what some call a "dry communion" with no distribution of the sacrament.[24] The liturgy is conducted somewhat differently in different churches. The Psalms, for instance, might be sung "by note," chanted in some fashion. In greater churches and cathedrals there might be a choir to sing the responses. But Harrison is at pains to point out that everything, whether sung or spoken, can be heard and understood. The minister "saith his service commonly in the body of the church with his face toward the people," addressing them from a sort of cubicle, the reading pew, which Harrison describes as "a little tabernacle of wainscot." Not only do unlettered parishioners "learn divers of the Psalms and usual prayers by heart, but also such as can read do pray together with him [the minister], so that the whole

---

"History of the 1559 Book of Common Prayer," in *The Book of Common Prayer 1559: The Elizabethan Prayer Book* (Washington, DC: Folger Shakespeare Library, 1976), 327–382 at 375–378; Glyn J. R. Parry, *A Protestant Vision: William Harrison and the Reformation of Elizabethan England* (Cambridge: Cambridge University Press, 1987).

[23] The second, much longer book of *Certain Sermons or Homilies*, which the first book had promised in 1547, was published in its final form in 1571.

[24] William Harrison, *The Description of England: The Classic Contemporary Account of Tudor Social Life*, ed. Georges Edelen (Ithaca, NY: Cornell University Press, 1968), 34.

congregation at one instant pour out their petitions unto the living God for the whole estate of his church in the most earnest and fervent manner."[25]

Conformists and Nonconformists

If Harrison's description typifies the English church in general, it would seem that after fifteen or twenty years the Act of Uniformity was taking effect and the Elizabethan church was settling into the "Elizabethan settlement." But there were nine or ten thousand parishes in England, and there is reason to think that their ministers followed the Book of Common Prayer in quite disparate ways—if they followed it at all.

In that regard it is instructive to set Harrison's account alongside a list of "Varieties in the service and administration used" that was written a few years previously and may have been compiled from information reported by the church's bishops.[26] "Some," the list begins, "say the service in the chancel," at the far end of the building; "others in the body of the church," as Harrison reports. Some remain in a special seat, Harrison's "tabernacle" probably, but others go to the pulpit. Some observe the order of the Prayer Book to the letter; others "intermeddle Psalms in meter," most likely from Sternhold and Hopkins. In some churches the Lord's Supper was administered from a table in the nave, the body of the church. In some the table stood in the chancel. Sometimes it was aligned east and west, along the main axis of the building; sometimes it stood "altar-like," north and south. When the sacrament was administered, communicants might receive it sitting or standing or, as the Prayer Book directs, kneeling. Baptism sometimes took place at the font, but sometimes

---

[25] Harrison, *Description of England*, 36.

[26] Patrick Collinson considers it to have been such a report; see *The Elizabethan Puritan Movement* (Oxford: Oxford University Press, 1967), 367. The list is transcribed in John Strype, *The Life and Acts of Matthew Parker*, book 2 ch. 19.

a portable bowl was used instead. Some ministers always made the prescribed sign of the cross, others never. In short, public worship was conducted diversely and not always in keeping with the Prayer Book's instructions.

Harrison's "Description" is silent, perhaps deliberately, on one of the most contentious items on the list of "varieties in the service": the surplice, a long white smock that members of the clergy were expected to wear in church. No one thought that this or any other article of clothing was supremely important. Scripture says nothing about clerical attire, one way or the other. For just that reason, conformists could argue that in the interest of order and decency, which scripture does enjoin, the church is competent to require the surplice to be worn, and to enforce the requirement. Nonconformists, on the other hand, could argue that what is harmless in itself may nevertheless be harmful in its significance. Ministers of a reformed church should not be seen wearing any of the same apparel that was once worn to conduct the superstitious ceremonies of unreformed religion. Even if the surplice never connoted propitiatory sacrifice, as the Mass vestments supposedly did, it is none the less meaningful, and what it means is popery. By similar reasoning, wafer bread, kneeling, and altar-like communion tables could all be judged guilty by association and condemned as the noxious residue of false worship.

And so too could the Book of Common Prayer. Despite its vernacular language and its reliance on scripture at every turn, the Prayer Book services themselves, text and rubric, were too much like the old, discarded Latin rites to be acceptable to some of the more advanced English protestants. As they conceived the matter, their church, as reformed, must be defined by contrast with what it was not, identified by its exclusion of the *other* that was Rome. They might be willing to say that the Book of Common Prayer was a step in the right direction, but not that it had gone far enough.

To the godly, as these zealous Christians at times called themselves, or to puritans, as others called them, it was clear that the

Elizabethan establishment should resemble much more closely than it did the "best reformed churches," by which they meant the hubs of non-Lutheran protestantism in Zurich, Strassburg, Frankfort, and especially Geneva. Worship was not the only point at issue; there were theological and therefore political disparities as well; but inasmuch as worship is the most concrete manifestation of a church's identity and character, the Prayer Book was bound to be one focus of a complex dispute.

Attempted Reforms

In 1559, no one could know whether the new queen's religious policies would be permanent. They might have been, as many hoped they would be, stopgap measures, soon to be followed by the thoroughgoing reformation that godly protestants longed for. In 1562, at the church's first Convocation[27] after Parliament passed the Act of Uniformity, there were already proposals to make the Book of Common Prayer more puritan-friendly: no more saints' days, no crossing in Baptism, no obligatory kneeling.[28] But these were sorties in a larger campaign. What Parliament had enacted, Parliament could alter, and to Parliament militant puritans turned for relief from the constraints of the Prayer Book. Not long after a bill concerned with rites and ceremonies went nowhere—the queen saw to that—and partly, it seems, as a result, a famous tract entitled *An Admonition to the Parliament* was published. The language of the bill is appropriately sober; the *Admonition* is still worth reading

[27] The name *Convocation* is shorthand. Properly speaking there were two convocations of the clergy in the Church of England, one for the small northern Province of York, the other for the vastly larger Province of Canterbury. The two commonly met together as an ecclesiastical legislature, concurrently with the national Parliament, in which the bishops, who constituted the upper house of Convocation, also sat.
[28] There were other proposals as well; see the summary in William Haugaard, *Eizabeth and the English Reformation: The Struggle for a Stable Settlement of Religion* (Cambridge: Cambridge University Press, 1968), 125–126.

for its rumbustious rhetoric. Each in its way takes aim at the Book of Common Prayer.

The preliminary "whereas" section of the rites-and-ceremonies bill openly admits what everyone knew anyway: godly ministers routinely flouted the statutory liturgy and sympathetic bishops did nothing to stop them. By way of defending this lawlessness, the bill avers that the Book of Common Prayer was all very fine when Queen Elizabeth reinstated it, but things have changed. There were not many preachers then; now there are. To make time for their sermons and for other godly exercises that will instruct and edify their congregations, these earnest ministers admittedly leave unsaid some things that strict obedience to the Prayer Book would require them to say. Yet in so doing they have "conformed themselves more nearly to the imitation of the ancient apostolical church and the best reformed churches in Europe . . . to the great increase of true knowledge, furtherance of God's glory, and extinguishing of superstition."[29] Had the bill been enacted, licensed preachers would have been allowed to omit anything they chose to omit. They might even set the Prayer Book aside entirely.

The *Admonition to the Parliament* is a feisty set of variations on a parallel theme: the supposedly reformed church in England still falls short of the real thing. Too many popish abuses have yet to be extirpated, many of them displayed for all to see in the Book of Common Prayer. Kneeling to receive communion amounts to idolatrous worship of a "breaden god"; signing with the cross imports a new sacrament, which only Christ has a right to do; the surplice is a popish rag, redolent of superstition. It is true that the canticles are scriptural; but *Magnificat* and *Nunc dimittis* are not prayers that anyone who is not the Virgin Mary or Simeon is entitled to say. It is true that the liturgical gospels are scriptural; but to stand up while they are being read is to imply that the rest of the Bible is

---

[29] The Bill concerning Rites and Ceremonies (1572), in W. H. Frere and C. E. Douglas, eds., *Puritan Manifestoes* (London: SPCK, 1907), 149–151 at 150.

not equally inspired. All this and much else is summed up in the *Admonition's* famous indictment of the Book of Common Prayer as "an unperfect book, culled and picked out of that popish dunghill, the Mass-book, full of all abominations."

Moreover, even if the existing liturgy had none of these particular defects, it would still be a *liturgy*, a gallimaufry of mere "reading services" that can be conducted by persons who may be able to read but who cannot and do not preach. That is no way to feed the sheep of Christ's flock; they need and long for sermons. Besides, repeating printed words from a book stifles the godly practice of "conceived prayer" uttered freely and *ex tempore*. In better times, the *Admonition* insists, it was not so. "Then ministers were not tied to any form of prayers invented by man, but as the spirit moved them, so they poured forth hearty supplications to the Lord. Now they are bound of necessity to a prescript order of service, and book of common prayer."[30] Not that this necessity did much to hinder godly pastors from curtailing and rearranging the prescript order they were bound to. On the contrary, "there may have been almost as many versions of a Prayer Book service as there were puritan incumbents."[31]

What the more zealous Elizabethan protestants might have put in place of the Book of Common Prayer can be gathered from an alternative text that they did present to Parliament, together with a petition asking that it might be authorized and put in use. *A booke of the Forme of common prayers . . . agreable to Gods worde, and the vse of the reformed Churches* is a short book with a long and rather complicated history that begins in Calvin's Geneva and passes through Frankfort to Middleburg in the Low Countries, where an English translation was printed on the sly.[32] In the Middleburg

---

[30] *An Admonition to the Parliament*, in Frere and Douglas, eds., *Puritan Manifestoes*, 8–19 at 11.

[31] Collinson, *Puritan Movement*, 366. An incumbent is the minister who is (permanently) in charge of a parish church.

[32] *A booke of the Forme of common prayers, administration of the Sacraments, &c. agreable to Gods worde, and the vse of the reformed Churches* (STC 16568; Middelburgh

liturgy the people's part (when they are not singing Psalms) is to listen to the minister declaim two very long prayers, one before and one after the sermon. These specific prayers are not obligatory, however; conceived prayer is expressly permitted. At the Lord's Supper a lengthy exhortation warns communicants against believing that Christ is in any way present in earthly and corruptible things, and instructs them that the true eating of Christ happens when they lift up their minds by faith so as to enter heaven, where alone he can be received. There are echoes of Prayer Book phrases throughout this exhortation, but it may also be the only liturgical text that has ever used the word *buggerer*.[33]

Conclusion: The Prayer Book and the Queen

Discussions of the Elizabethan church run the risk of letting the puritans take over. It is understandable that the complaints of the godly get a lot of attention: they did a lot of complaining. But it would begging the question to assume that theirs was the one genuinely reformed position just because they said it was. There were "Prayer Book protestants" too, as Judith Maltby calls them; laypeople who took no offence at the official liturgy, who accepted it, absorbed it, adapted their piety to it, and in time became attached to it. Usually there is no sure way to distinguish them from their timid or apathetic neighbors. "Practitioners of commonplace prayer-book religion, unlike the more strident religious minorities, do not pluck at the historian's sleeve."[34] But it does not follow that

---

[sic]: Richard Schilders, 1586); text in Thompson, *Liturgies*, 322–341; modern-spelling edition in Peter Hall, ed., *Reliquiæ Liturgicæ: Documents Connected with the Liturgy of the Church of England*, vol. 1: *The Middleburgh Prayer-Book* (Bath: Binns and Goodwin, 1847).

[33] *A booke of the Forme of common prayers*, sig D2; Thompson, *Liturgies* 336. Hall, *Reliquiæ* I: 53 declines (in Latin) to print the word.

[34] Patrick Collinson, *The Religion of Protestants: The Church in English Society 1559–1625* (Oxford: Oxford University Press, 1982), 192.

their conformity was merely passive. They complained too. They complained when the Book of Common Prayer was *not* used, or was used improperly; when their minister left out parts of Divine Service, or would not let his congregation say their responses in the Litany and the Ten Commandments, or did not use the first half of the prescribed administration sentences at communion, or refused to celebrate the sacrament at Easter, or preached that people who looked in their books were papists.[35]

The fact that people had Prayer Books to look in, as Harrison's "Description" suggests many of them had, is itself significant. Parish churches were required to own copies. Parishioners were not; they were only required to go to church for common prayers. Yet the book that prescribed those prayers was selling briskly when the *Admonition to the Parliament* vilified it as pickings from the popish dunghill. It is true, of course, that the Act of Uniformity gave the statutory liturgy a big advantage to begin with. Conformity was the default setting, the de jure norm. Still, Prayer Book protestantism might not have caught on de facto, had it not been for "the life—unexpectedly prolonged—and the beliefs—unexpectedly ambiguous—of Elizabeth of England."[36]

The ambiguity has never been resolved to everyone's satisfaction. Elizabeth did not want it to be resolved at all. Sooner or later every investigation comes back to the constantly quoted remark she is reported to have made about her unwillingness to make windows into men's hearts and secret thoughts. The secrets of her own heart she kept to herself. At least part of her antipathy to the tactics of her more implacably Calvinist clergy was aversion to their window-making. They longed for "a nation ruled by God through the hearts of the people, while Elizabeth was interested in ruling the nation for

---

[35] Judith Maltby, *Prayer Book and People in Elizabethan and Early Stuart England* (Cambridge: Cambridge University Press, 1998), 14, 43, 45, 49.

[36] Charles Williams, *The Descent of the Dove: A Short History of the Holy Spirit in the Church* (London: Longmans, Green & Co., 1939), 179.

God."[37] To that end she insisted on conformity. If it was sincere conformity, so much the better; but with whether it was sincere or not she declined to concern herself.

By conformity was meant, chiefly though not only, conformity with the lawful liturgy, about which Elizabeth was as reticent as she was about what she believed. There is evidence for the way she wanted the Prayer Book services to be conducted. She was partial to vestments and choral music. For a time, the "little silver cross" in her private chapel was a minor *cause célèbre*, and her impatience with polemical preaching is well known.[38] The story is told that she was horrified when the dean of St. Paul's Cathedral in London gave her as a New Year's present a Book of Common Prayer with added engravings of saints and martyrs. But it turns out to be only a story. It was always an intrinsically improbable story; devotional images were not the sort of gift that the godly dean would give, and the queen would more likely have been pleased than horrified if he had given it. But it appears he did not. The episode was fabricated.[39]

As for what Elizabeth herself thought about the Prayer Book, there is probably just one reliable source, a letter she wrote when marriage to a royal Roman Catholic was under discussion. If, she told her ambassador in France, the prince in question did become her husband, he would of course attend Divine Service with her. And why not? In it there is not one thing that the Church of Rome does not use also; or if there is, it comes from the Bible. The English service does not compel anyone to "alter his opinion in the great matters now in controversy in the Church." For it consists in reading and hearing scripture, and praying with the Psalter and "the ancient

[37] Norman L. Jones, *The Birth of the Elizabethan Age: England in the 1560s* (Oxford: Blackwell, 1993), 34.

[38] On her cross (of which more than one appeared, and which was sometimes called a crucifix) and its significance, see Margaret Aston, *England's Iconoclasts*, vol. 1: *Laws Against Images* (Oxford: Oxford University Press, 1988), 312–315.

[39] For the story, see Ralph Churton, *The Life of Alexander Nowell* (Oxford: Oxford University Press, 1809), 71–73. For its fabrication, see Diarmaid MacCulloch, "Forging Reformation History: A Cautionary Tale," in *All Things Made New: The Reformation and Its Legacy* (Oxford: Oxford University Press, 2016), 321–358 at 353–358.

prayers, anthems and collects of the church, even the same which the universal church hath used, and doth yet use."[40] That is no bad description of Morning and Evening Prayer. Elizabeth has been called "the only determined 'Anglican' in England."[41] Perhaps she was. If the English church never became one of the "best reformed churches," its supreme governor, last of the Tudor sovereigns, deserves much of the blame, or the credit.

[40] Elizabeth to Francis Walsingham, May 1571, in Dudley Digges, *The Compleat Ambassador: or Two Treatises of the Intended Marriage of Queen Elizabeth* (London: Bedell and Collins, 1655), 98–99.
[41] Christopher Haigh, *Elizabeth I*, 2nd ed. (London: Longman, 1998), 38.

Seven
Disruption

When Queen Elizabeth's unexpectedly prolonged life did come to an end, godly protestants thought they would be given another chance. The settlement of religion which they expected would be temporary had turned out to be "ever the same"—the queen's motto. Her successor, though, was James Stuart, king of Scotland, where protestantism had won its way to a Genevan polity and Genevan worship. The Scottish Kirk was presbyterian, not episcopalian, and if any formal liturgy was used, it was likely to be a close cousin of the Middleburg Liturgy. King James had grown up environed by this thoroughly reformed religion. He was something of a theologian himself. He had publicly disparaged the Book of Common Prayer. All in all, it looked as though his reign in England might restart the unfinished reformation that Elizabeth had deliberately stalled.

Such was the hope of the puritan leaders who greeted James with a list of desiderata as he made his way to London. The name "Millenary Petition" has stuck to their address, although there were never a thousand signatures, and none at all when it was delivered.[1] Three of its four clauses have to do with institutional problems that undoubtedly needed to be dealt with, but the petition opens with liturgical grievances. For twenty years English clergy had been required to consent and subscribe to the proposition that "the Book of Common Prayer, and of ordering bishops, priests, and deacons, containeth nothing in it contrary to the word of God"; and they were obliged to commit themselves to the use of that book, only,

---

[1] Roland G. Usher, *The Reconstruction of the English Church* (2 vols.; London: D. Appleton, 1910), I: 291, 290 note 1.

The Book of Common Prayer. Charles Hefling, Oxford University Press (2021). © Oxford University Press. DOI: 10.1093/oso/9780190689681.001.0001.

in public worship.[2] The petitioners, "groaning as under a common burden of human rites and ceremonies," would have had their way if there existed no prescriptive liturgy to subscribe to, but if there must be one and they must subscribe to it, then at least the parts of the Prayer Book that godly ministers had long complained of should be removed, amended, or qualified.

King James, His Bible, and the Book of Common Prayer

The new king was not unwilling to discuss revising the Church of England's liturgy. He quite enjoyed theological disputation. Presently, therefore, a conference was convened at the royal residence at Hampton Court. It was not a debate, meant to help the undecided make up their minds, but it was not entirely rigged either, although James was always in control of the proceedings, acting as "an unconventional umpire who from time to time took hold of both bat and ball."[3] Some of his own contributions were witty, not to say scabrous; a few of them let his boredom show ("Is there anything *else?*"); one of them was his famous dictum, "No bishop, no king." Of the puritans who took part, none was a firebrand and one has been described as an extreme moderate,[4] but even so nearly all of their most important requests went unmet.

James, it turned out, had no objection to the four "nocent ceremonies," the surplice, kneeling, the marriage ring, and what he called the airy cross in Baptism. He saw nothing wrong with the term *priest* or with the sacerdotal language of the absolution

---

[2] "Articles touching preachers and other orders for the church" (1584), Cardwell, *Annals*, I 466–471 at 468–469. It was not a new requirement.

[3] Patrick Collinson, "The Jacobean Religious Settlement: The Hampton Court Conference," in *Before the English Civil War: Essays on Early Stuart Politics and Government*, ed. Howard Tomlinson (New York: St. Martin's Press, 1984), 27–51 at 36.

[4] Collinson, "Jacobean Religious Settlement," 38.

formula in the Visitation office.[5] He did agree in part, however, with objections to Private Baptism.

The rubrics in that service allowed a newborn to be baptized at home, rather than in church, though not "without great cause and necessity." Parents might perform the service if their child was unlikely to live, and by extension anyone, ordained or not, might baptize in an emergency. Women, midwives in particular, had been known to do so. By permitting such exceptions in exceptional circumstances, the Prayer Book implied that the necessity of baptism *per se* is greater than the necessity of an ordained clergyman to administer it. Puritans saw things otherwise. Since eternal salvation depends entirely on divine election, baptism was not, in their view, absolutely necessary. It was, however, a divinely commanded ordinance of the church, and so must necessarily be performed by the church's authorized ministers—not by laymen, and certainly not by women.

The royal umpire split the difference: baptism is indeed necessary for salvation, but a minister is necessary for baptism. Accordingly, although the service of Private Baptism kept its place in the Prayer Book, it was redefined—or rather, "explained." The title became, in effect, a rubric that restricts the administration of the rite to "the Minister of the Parish, or any other lawful Minister, that can be procured."[6] The existing rubrics were altered on the same lines. The service as such, however, remained as it was, in keeping with James's strategy of "contriving how things might best be done, without appearance of alteration." If it was possible to explain the Prayer Book's prescriptions, without changing any of the words they prescribed, no parliamentary approval would be necessary. The authority of the church's supreme governor, James himself, would suffice.

[5] Colin Buchanan, ed., *The Hampton Court Conference and the 1604 Book of Common Prayer.* Grove Liturgical Studies 68 (Norwich, UK: Hymns Ancient and Modern, 2009), 26.
[6] Buchanan, *Hampton Court Conference*, 49.

On what counts as explanation, the supreme governor's ideas were fairly broad. The Confirmation service, like Private Baptism, was given an amplified title, so as to emphasize that candidates must be able to render an account of their faith, as set out in the Catechism. More notably, the Catechism itself was enlarged. Twelve new questions "explain" the (unchanged) sacramental rites of Baptism and Holy Communion.[7] One of the new answers would become a *locus classicus* as the Anglican definition of a sacrament: "an outward and visible sign, of an inward and spiritual grace."[8]

These adjustments and a few others may have made affirming the godliness of the Book of Common Prayer somewhat easier for scrupulous ministers, but not much. The puritans at Hampton Court were more successful in regard to a request which, at the time, made no difference in public worship, but which would eventually have a profound effect not only on the Book of Common Prayer but on all English-speaking protestantism and all English speaking. They asked for a new English Bible. King James agreed.

The Bishops' Bible had never caught on. The Geneva Bible had, but James thought it the least satisfactory English translation of all. He is said to have been particularly annoyed by the copious and sometimes contentious notes in its margins. That might be why the new translation, which alone would be permitted in Divine Service, was not allowed to be annotated. When it was published in 1611, this Bible, now inseparable from the name of the king who in some sense authorized it, displayed at the outset the purpose for which it had been authorized. The first edition opens with twenty-two pages of the Book of Common Prayer: the tables, kalendar, almanack, rules for finding Easter—everything necessary for determining which chapters should be read at Morning and Evening Prayer.

The Prayer Book itself, with its Hampton Court explanations, is sometimes counted as a new version, although that is just what it

---

[7] See Ian Green, *The Christian's ABC: Catechisms and Catechizing in England c. 1530–1740* (Oxford: Oxford University Press, 1996), esp. 509–515.

[8] Buchanan, *Hampton Court Conference*, 51; OWC 429.

was not, as far as the king was concerned. Like Queen Elizabeth's additions to the kalendar, the alterations he agreed to left spoken words untouched, and were deemed to be covered by the existing Act of Uniformity, which continued to be printed at the front of the book. But James did add his own Proclamation for the Authorizing and Uniformity of the Book of Common Prayer, which warns his subjects "not to attempt or expect any further alteration in the common and public form of God's service."[9] Nor was there further alteration. The Elizabethan Prayer Book, very lightly amended, held its ground for another forty years. When English puritans were at last relieved of their "common burden of human rites and ceremonies," it was not because the Book of Common Prayer had been altered. It was because it had been abolished.

Its abolishment belongs to the "late unhappy confusions" that a new Preface would allude to when the Prayer Book was restored in 1662. Of those confusions, it had been not only a casualty but also, in some sense, a cause. The ordinance that made using it a penal offense was promulgated in the midst of civil warfare that had begun in 1637 when the imposition of a Book of Common Prayer was attempted in Scotland. The next quarter-century was as turbulent a time as any in the history of the British Isles. Historians have yet to agree on how best to understand what the Prayer Book would later call the Great Rebellion—as a puritan revolution, a bourgeois uprising, a war of religion, or something else. What is true is that afterward, when the banished Prayer Book came back into use, it was a different book—not because of what it said, for that had not changed much, but because of what it meant. A well-worn adage has it that things which are truly valuable are truly valued only when they have been taken away. That could be said of the Book of Common Prayer. Fifteen years of enforced absence brought its value to light. It became, in a way it had not been, a sacred text.

[9] Buchanan, *Hampton Court*, 45–46.

The Unsettling Laudians

In any account of what happened to and because of the Prayer Book in the mid-seventeenth century, the name Laud inevitably stands out. William Laud was archbishop of Canterbury. Whether he was also the next thing to a saint, as surely an Anglican martyr as King Charles I, or instead "the greatest calamity ever visited upon the English Church,"[10] can be debated. Either way, his name is attached to a trend or movement within that church, which Laud himself undoubtedly promoted although he neither started it nor took it as far as others did.

Laudian, like *puritan*, is a convenient, conventional, and contentious label for a type of protestant Christianity, a style of worship, a stance *vis-à-vis* the Reformation, and an attitude toward catholicism as represented by the Roman church. In all these respects, Laudianism was a kind of counter-puritanism. The principle from which it developed was one that King James had laid down at the Hampton Court conference when he said it was his "constant and resolute opinion, that no church ought further to separate itself from the church of Rome . . . than she had departed from her self when she was in her flourishing and best estate, and from Christ her Lord and Head."[11] To say that James himself was a Laudian might be an exaggeration, but not a big one.[12] Those who shared and developed his "constant and resolute opinion," avant-garde conformists as they are sometimes called, extended the same principle from liturgical details to public worship generally. The upshot was a constellation of practices, policies, and teachings that came to be labeled Laudianism.

---

[10] Patrick Collinson, *The Religion of Protestants: The Church in English Society, 1559–1625* (Oxford: Oxford University Press, 1982), 90.

[11] Cardwell, *Conferences*, 200 lines 19–24.

[12] Alan Cromartie virtually says it in "King James and the Hampton Court Conference," in *James VI and I: Ideas, Authority, and Government*, ed. Ralph Houlbrooke (Burlington, VT: Ashgate, 2006), 61–80; see 78–80.

"In all ages of the church," Laud declared, "the touchstone of religion was not to hear the word preached but to communicate."[13] Laudians made that touchstone their own. By shifting the center of religious gravity from sermon to sacrament and from preaching to prayer, they were following what they believed to be authentic, ancient Christian precedent. The most conspicuous plank in this platform was the "altar policy" for which Laud was vilified, fairly or otherwise.[14] Since Elizabethan times, it had been common practice to keep the communion table in the main part of the church, or else to move it there for the Lord's Supper and put it back in the chancel afterward. To have an honest wooden table standing in the midst of the congregation meant something; it announced that what took place around the table was emphatically not the Mass. The Laudian policy conveyed a different meaning. In churches where it was complied with, the table was lodged permanently at the east end of the building, raised on steps, aligned north and south, surrounded with a railing, and covered with a drapery or carpet. Table though it might still be, it had the look of an altar.[15]

Related to this policy, as an expression of the priority of prayers over preaching, was the Laudian insistence on conformity with the rubrics of the Prayer Book, which were not to be set aside to make way for sermons but followed punctiliously and without exception. All the prescribed services must be performed on Sundays and holydays; times of fasting and abstinence and the eves or vigils of feasts must be observed; lessons and Psalms must never deviate from the kalendar.[16] Ceremonies that the rubrics did not

[13] *The Works of... William Laud* 4 (Oxford: John Henry Parker, 1854), 284.

[14] See Kenneth Fincham and Nicholas Tyacke, *Altars Restored: The Changing Face of English Religious Worship, 1547–c. 1700* (Oxford: Oxford University Press, 2007), 159–160, 176, and ch. 6, "The Beauty of Holiness," 227–273, esp. 249–265.

[15] On the altar policy, see Julian Davies, *The Caroline Captivity of the Church: Charles I and the Remoulding of Anglicanism 1625–1641* (Oxford: Oxford University Press, 1992), together with Kenneth Fincham, "The Restoration of Altars in the 1630s," *The Historical Journal* 44.4 (2001): 919–940.

[16] Kenneth Fincham, "Clerical Conformity from Whitgift to Laud," in *Conformity and Orthodoxy in the English Church, c. 1560–1660*, ed. Peter Lake and Michael Questier (Rochester, NY: Boydell, 2000), 125–158; see esp. 146–149.

explicitly order assumed a greater importance—not in themselves, as Laudians were careful to stress, but in relation to the high privilege and sacred duty of public prayer, especially at Holy Communion. Kneeling, bowing, and standing were all, in their degree, sacramental gestures, outward signs that both expressed and nourished inward devotion. Laudians never changed a word in the Prayer Book, but they did change the meaning of the liturgy it prescribes, by imbuing its performance with what they took to be dignity, decency, and comeliness.[17]

Others, not surprisingly, took it to be superstition and popery. Certainly Laud's own language was at times more catholic than a protestant prelate might be expected to use. In the same speech that includes the "touchstone" passage quoted earlier, he compared the pulpit with the altar as sites of divine presence, and pronounced the altar to be the greater of the two. What can be ascribed to the pulpit, he said, is at most *hoc est verbum meum*, "this is my word," whereas in respect of the altar it can and must be *hoc est corpus meum*, "this is my body." To Laud's opponents, this unabashed allusion to the consecration formula in the Latin missal could only mean that the archbishop believed in transubstantiation. He did not, to judge by what he wrote; but he did believe that once those words are duly spoken, "be the minister never so unworthy, yet 'tis infallibly *hoc est corpus meum* to every worthy receiver."[18]

The words that Laud held to be infallible had been made to call attention to themselves in a remarkable "Laudian" edition of the Book of Common Prayer issued in 1627. The printed words of the

---

[17] See especially Peter Lake, "The Laudian Style: Order, Uniformity and the Pursuit of the Beauty of Holiness in the 1630s," in *The Early Stuart Church, 1603–1642*, ed. Kenneth Fincham (Stanford, CA: Stanford University Press, 1993), 161–185 and 275–282. Also Peter White, "The *Via Media* in the Early Stuart Church," in the same volume, 211–230.

[18] Laud, *Works*, 4 284, quoting himself in an earlier oration. It is just conceivable that "little hocus-pocus," one of several opprobrious nicknames used for Laud, was a parody of *hoc est corpus*.

central prayer in the Communion office are the same, as words, as they had been in every Prayer Book since 1552. As printed, they are not. There is a visual jolt, which can be seen in Figure 7.1, at the point that corresponds to *hoc est corpus meum*. The words of

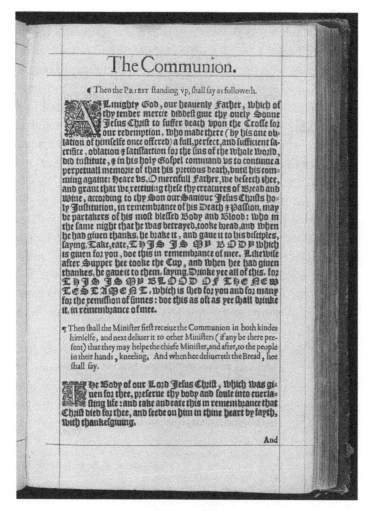

Figure 7.1 "Laudian" Typography in a 1627 Prayer Book
Courtesy of the Beinecke Rare Books Library, Yale University.

institution are set in capital letters: THIS IS MY BODY and THIS IS MY BLOOD OF THE NEW TESTAMENT. Capitals were routinely used in Roman Catholic missals to signal the importance of these words in the canon of the Mass, but never had any such typographical emphasis appeared in a Book of Common Prayer.

Who was responsible for its appearance in 1627 is not recorded, but such evidence as there is points to a likely suspect. The next year, John Cosin, a Laudian if anyone was, found himself accused of tampering with the Prayer Book, and wrote to Laud, then dean of the chapel royal, to explain. The King's Printers had indeed asked for advice about amending certain mistakes, mainly in the kalendar; but "other alterations," Cosin says, "I made not, unless it were here and there for the beautifying of the book with sundry characters and fairer letters than before, or for the printing of the *Pater noster* at large."[19]

Now, the 1627 folio Prayer Book prints the Lord's Prayer in full at three places where earlier editions had simply indicated that it was to be recited.[20] Cosin's letter makes it fairly certain that in those places "the printing of the *Pater Noster* at large" was his doing; and since the use of capital letters for the words of institution in the same edition is also an innovation, it seems equally likely that those are the "fairer letters" which his letter says he also ordered.

It would not be surprising if he did order them. Cosin had a penchant for imitating Roman Catholic books. In the same year that saw the publication of the Prayer Book with the extraordinary typography, he published an adaptation of the seven liturgical

[19] Cosin to Laud, June 1628, in George Ornsby, ed., *The Correspondence of John Cosin, D.D. Lord Bishop of Durham*, Part I (Publications of the Surtees Society 52; Durham: Andrews & Co., 1869) 138–141 at 139.

[20] The three places are the end of Morning Prayer, the beginning of Evening Prayer, and the beginning of Holy Communion. For the 1559 text see OWC 110, 111, and 124. It is unchanged in the folio Prayer Book of 1625 (STC 16304) at A5 *verso*, A6 *verso*, and M3 *verso*. There was no folio edition in 1626. In the 1627 edition (STC 16368) the corresponding pages, now with the Lord's Prayer printed "at large," are A6, A7, and M6 *verso*.

services known as the canonical hours. Into this *Collection of Private Devotions* . . . *Called the Houres of Prayer,* Cosin put as much of the Prayer Book as he could, and he included no distinctively Roman Catholic prayers; but the whole ethos of his *Private Devotions* exemplifies the Laudian conviction that the English church, although it had been reformed, had not been reinvented.[21] In their own way, the conspicuous capital letters in the 1627 Prayer Book do the same.

There appears to be no evidence for modern statements that this "Laudian" edition was suppressed or withdrawn, but the next full-sized printing did revert to the usual typography, and Cosin's capitals, if they were his, were never repeated.[22] Nor were they forgotten. In 1641 a committee appointed by the House of Lords delivered its considered opinion that the "words in the form of consecration" were "not to be printed hereafter in great letters."[23] This ruling was one of several "considerations upon the Book of Common Prayer" included in the report of an inquiry concerned with innovations in the doctrine and discipline of the church. Reaction against the "altar policy" and other Laudian disturbances had set in; Laud himself was under house arrest. After a trial in which justice played no part, he was publicly beheaded in 1645 for subverting the word of God, insinuating popish superstition and idolatry, and laboring to draw the English church into Roman obedience. Such, anyhow, were the charges.

[21] See P. G. Stanwood, "Introduction" in John Cosin, *A Collection of Private Devotions,* ed. P. G. Stanwood (Oxford: Oxford University Press 1967), xiii–liii, esp. xxii–xxvii; and Bryan D. Spinks, "What Was Wrong with Mr Cosin's Couzening Devotions? Deconstructing an Episode in Seventeenth-Century Anglican 'Liturgical Hagiography,'" *Worship* 71.4 (2000): 308–329.

[22] The idea that the 1627 edition was somehow called in, as the "Wicked Bible" was a few years later, seems to have started as conjecture on the part of a mid-nineteenth-century Bodley's Librarian, which was mentioned in passing by Frederick George Lee in *The Directorium Anglicanum,* 3rd ed. (London: Thomas Bosworth, 1866), 75–76 note 3, and later repeated with embellishments; see J. F. Gerrard, *Notable Editions of the Prayer Book* (Wigan: J. Starr & Sons, 1949), 16–17; and *But One Use,* 90–91.

[23] On the Lords committee, see Cardwell, *Conferences,* 275.

The Prayer Book for Scotland

Among the means that Laud was accused of using to undermine reformed religion was a new and allegedly Romanized Book of Common Prayer that had been issued in 1637 for use in the Church of Scotland. It was soon called Laud's Liturgy, and still is. That it owes something to its namesake is clear enough, though just what it owes is not. The book was long in the making, and if Laud was one of its makers so too were the Scottish bishops, as well as King James, who initiated the project, and King Charles, who revived it.[24]

Charles appears to have had an agenda of his own. Although his death would later be commemorated as martyrdom for the Church of England, in life he was as partial to the Church of Rome as he could safely be. His strenuously Roman Catholic queen Henrietta Maria is reported to have said, years later, that he brought a copy of the new Scottish Prayer Book to her room one evening and urged her to read it, saying he was sure it would show her that between the beliefs of her church and his there was very little difference. As the queen's story goes, it was the archbishop of Canterbury, himself "a good catholic at heart," who had inspired Charles to restore the liturgy, and had advised him to begin with Scotland, where there would be less to fear from troublemakers. If that advice was in fact Laud's, he was gravely mistaken. What the queen called *ce livre fatal*, that fatal book, caused a great deal of trouble, and not only in Scotland.[25]

---

[24] The standard account, which includes the text of the Prayer Book for Scotland, is Gordon Donaldson, *The Making of the Scottish Prayer Book of 1637* (Edinburgh University Press, 1954), challenged on certain points by Joong-Lak Kim, "The Scottish-English-Romish Book: The Character of the Scottish Prayer Book of 1637," in *The Experience of Revolution in Stuart Britain and Ireland*, ed. Michael J. Braddick and David L. Smith (Cambridge: Cambridge University Press, 2011), 14–32. See also Leonie James, *'This Great Firebrand': William Laud and Scotland, 1617–1645* (Rochester, NY: Boydell, 2017), 80–111, esp. 92–98.

[25] For Henrietta Maria's story, see "Récit de la reine d'Angleterre" in *Mémoires de Madame de Motteville*, ed. M. F. Riaux (Paris: Charpentier, 1855), I ch. 9, esp. 190–191: "Ce livre fatal étant arrivé ne manqua pas de faire aussitôt beaucoup de bruit."

Laud himself maintained that it was the other way around. What little he did to bring about the Scottish Prayer Book was done at the behest of the king, if his own account is to be believed. As to the contents of the book, he would have preferred no change at all: if there was to be any prescript liturgy in Scotland, it had better be the same as the one used in England. Not he but the Scottish bishops had been responsible for revising the text, although he did vet the revisions and said publicly that they were improvements. Whether to absolve or condemn the archbishop need not be decided here. Probably, on the whole, "the safest judgment that the jury of history should return on Laud's part in introducing 'that fatal book' is the appropriately Scottish one of 'non-proven'."[26] But even if "Laud's Liturgy" is a misnomer, the book it names is in many respects a Laudian liturgy, which is worth examining on that account and for two further reasons: because of the effects which its reception in Scotland soon had on the Book of Common Prayer in England, and because of its long-term influence on Anglican liturgy everywhere.

"Laud's Liturgy"

When it came from the press in 1637, after prolonged negotiation and at least one false start, the Scottish Prayer Book looked much like an English edition. For that, at least, Laud was partly responsible: he saw to it that the printer used blackletter type, which for a book printed in Scotland was unusual.[27] The printing itself is admirable, superior in some ways to English Prayer Books, and perhaps

---

[26] Charles Carlton, *Archbishop William Laud* (London: Routledge & Kegan Paul, 1987), 161.

[27] On blackletter type, see chapter eleven; also James, *Firebrand*, 96. The printing has been studied extensively; see Paul Morgan, "Some Bibliographical Aspects of the Scottish Prayer Book of 1637," *The Bibliotheck* 5 (1967): 1–23. For Laud's instructions, see his letter to John Maxwell, Bishop of Ross, September 19, 1635, in Laud, *Works*, 6.2 434.

a little more opulent where decorative initials and the use of red ink are concerned.

As for the text, the most extensive and noticeable difference appears in the biblical extracts. With a few exceptions they come from the version of the Bible recently launched by the Scottish King James, which in Scotland had come to be the preferred translation. The Lord's Prayer remains as it had been—"forgive us our trespasses," not "our debts"—but the sixth Commandment, for example, is "Thou shalt not kill" instead of "Thou shalt do no murder." The epistles and gospels follow the King James translation to the point of replicating its typography: words added by the translators are set in roman type. The Psalter even prints the gnomic word *Selah*.

In the rubrics and tables, some of the many alterations seem likely to have been made with an eye to the concerns and sensibilities of Scottish protestants. The *Benedicite* is omitted and there are no lessons from the Apocrypha in the ordinary schedule of course reading, although a few chapters are assigned to holydays. The word *presbyter* is used; never *priest*. In a few places *Pasch* and *Yule*, Scots words for Easter and Christmas, appear. At the time, however, none of these changes seems to have drawn attention to itself in Scotland.

What did draw attention, and has drawn it ever since, is the Communion office. In other services, differences from England's Book of Common Prayer are interesting but mostly insignificant; in this one, they change the meaning substantially. To put it briefly, the Scottish version of Holy Communion undoes much of what was done to it in 1552. In particular, it restores three texts that had been purposely cut out of the central prayer, the canon.

One of these texts is the clause that asks God to "bless and sanctify" the bread and wine. Another is the statement of what this request intends, namely that the bread and wine "may be unto us the body and blood" of Christ. As chapter five has discussed, this clause was changed in 1552 so as to make it instead a request "that we may be partakers" of Christ's body and blood, which is not quite the same thing (see Table 5.3). The Scottish consecration prayer, which is so named, keeps the newer formula ("that *we* may be") but splices it together with the older one ("that *they* may be"). The third restored text is the memorial or prayer of oblation, which again is so named. Before it was demoted and truncated in 1552, this prayer had been the last division of the canon, following the institution narrative (see Tables 5.1 and 5.2). The Scottish Prayer Book puts it back.

Related to these three restorations are two other changes. In the consecration prayer, manual acts are ordered, as they had been in 1549, at the words "took bread" and "took the cup." And when the presbyter delivers the sacrament he is to say the first half of the long Elizabethan formula—the original words—but not the entirely different words substituted in 1552, which in 1559 became the second half of the formula (see Table 6.1). In response to this benediction, as a rubric calls it, "the party receiving shall say, *Amen.*"

Although it was Laud's stated opinion that these revivals made the Communion office in Scotland's Prayer Book better than England's, he took no credit for them. The chief agent was James Wedderburn, the most Laudian of the Scottish bishops. If Laud, the king, or both had not vetoed some of his proposals, Wedderburn would have pushed the Communion service still further in a conservative direction. As it was, the renovated text went far enough to raise the specter of popery.

Behind the sometimes hysterical language used to attack the Scottish Prayer Book in general, and in particular its Communion office, there is usually a logical argument along the following lines. Ever since the Reformation, the great wall of division between protestants and papists has been the Mass. No one who affirms the Mass can be a true protestant and no true protestant affirms the Mass; there is no middle ground. But to all intents and purposes the Scottish Prayer Book brings back the Mass. *Ergo*, it must be rejected if the Scottish church is to remain truly protestant. To acquiesce in the imposition of this "Popish-English-Scottish-Mass-Service

Book"[28] would be to open the door to superstition, idolatry, and all the detestable enormities of the bishop of Rome.

Among those who argued for the minor premise of this syllogism—that the new Communion office is the Mass *redivivus*—was Robert Baillie, one of the Scottish commissioners who added their accusations to the many others that were brought against Archbishop Laud. Baillie could draw on respectable Roman Catholic authors to prove that the same constituents which they considered essential to their Mass appear, in the same order, in the Scottish service.[29] While the rhetoric he uses to make his case can be excessive, he cannot be accused of seeing what is not there to be seen. If King Charles hoped his queen would find in the Scottish Prayer Book a religion not unlike her own, that is just what Baillie found, and detested. Nor was he alone in finding it.

The Inaugural Debacle

Before learned critics such as Baillie had time to make their case in print, popular reaction to the Prayer Book for Scotland delivered much the same verdict in more dramatic and more consequential form. "That fatal book" instigated a riot; the riot touched off a war. Although the riot soon took on a mythical aura, it was real enough. It happened in Edinburgh, at the great church of St. Giles, which had recently been made the cathedral of a new diocese. There, on a Sunday in July, the archbishop of St. Andrews and several of his episcopal colleagues assembled for the inaugural reading of Divine Service according to the new Scottish liturgy. With the new bishop

---

[28] The phrase comes from John Row (1568–1646), *The History of the Kirk of Scotland from the Year 1558 to August 1637*, ed. D. Laing (Edinburgh: Wodrow Society, 1842), 398.

[29] Robert Baillie, *Ladensium ΑΥΤΟΚΑΤΑΚΡΙΣΙΣ, the Canterburians Self-Conviction*, 3rd ed. (Wing B462; London: Nathaniel Butter, 1641), 90–113, esp. 104, 107; and *A Parallel or Brief Comparison of the Liturgy with the Masse-Book, the Breviarie, the Ceremoniall, and Other Romish Rituals* (Wing B465; London: Thomas Paine, 1641), 38–60, 89–90.

of Edinburgh in the pulpit and the new cathedral's dean at the reading desk, Morning Prayer began.

What happened next is fulsomely commemorated at St. Giles' on a plaque marking the place where "a brave Scotch woman ... struck the first blow in the great struggle for freedom of conscience which after a conflict of half a century ended in the establishment of civil and religious liberty." Someone, that is, threw a stool. Who threw it the earliest accounts do not say. It may have been Janet or Jenny Geddes, whose name is on the plaque,[30] and her target may have been the "arch-prelate," as a contemporary print has it (Figure 7.2), though it was more likely the dean. What she is supposed to have shouted—something like "How dare you say Mass in my

Figure 7.2 The Prayer Book Riot in Edinburgh, July 1637
Illustration in John Vicars, *A Sight of the Trans-actions of these latter yeares*, 1646.
Courtesy of the Beinecke Rare Books Library, Yale University.

---

[30] Barbara Hamilton has nearly as good a claim; see David Stevenson, *The Scottish Revolution 1637-1644: The Triumph of the Covenanters* (Newton Abbot: David & Charles, 1973), 56–87, esp. 62–63.

ear!"—may have been a reaction to the liturgy, or it may have been a prearranged signal to begin a skirmish which is known to have been planned in advance, and for which the first reading of the new Prayer Book was a convenient pretext. In any case, greater turmoil was soon to follow.

The disruptions that began in 1637—the Bishops' Wars and the Wars of the Three Kingdoms, the regicide and the Interregnum, the Commonwealth and Oliver Cromwell's Protectorate—need not be rehearsed in detail here. Eight years after the commotion at St. Giles' had put a stop to Prayer Book liturgy in Scotland, a parliamentary ordinance put a stop to it in England; and a week after the Book of Common Prayer was done away with, so was Archbishop Laud.

The Church of England without the Prayer Book

Neither a royal pardon for Laud nor a royal proclamation commanding continued use of the Book of Common Prayer made any difference. The king and Parliament were at war, the first of the English Civil Wars. Charles had never had much use for Parliaments, which tiresomely kept him from doing what he thought a monarch should be free to do. For eleven years—not co-incidentally, the heyday of Laudianism—he ruled without a legislature. When at length he needed money to pay for a military expedition against the rebellious Scots, he reluctantly convened first one Parliament, then another, which soon demonstrated that it had its own agenda. Among the grievances that demanded redress, the king's ecclesiastical policies were by no means the least. As supreme governor of the Church of England he ought to have promoted true religion. Far from doing so, he—or his henchman Laud, or both—had deformed the church as it was in the time of Elizabeth and James, ignoring the threat of popery and promoting popish practices. Somehow, the Prayer Book in Scotland and the altar policy in England were all of a piece.

From this "Caroline captivity" the Long Parliament that began to sit in 1640 was determined to rescue the church. At first there was some agreement that what was needed was a weeding of the ecclesiastical garden and a return to the Elizabethan settlement. But before long it was being urged that the garden would have to be dug up and replanted, the settlement dismantled, the Reformation reformed. The whole structure of the English church must be restructured, Prayer Book, bishops, and all. The intricacies of how this more radical view came to prevail are less important here than the fact that it prevailed. Its weakness was that when everything had been uprooted there was little consensus on what kind of garden to plant.

The Directory

One symptom of this weakness was the *Directory for the Publique Worship of God*, which the parliamentary ordinance that took away the Prayer Book put in its place. The compilers of this small book were "agreed on the *delenda* but not on the *agenda*," on what should be demolished but not what should be done to replace it.[31] Presbyterians, English or Scottish, might have been content to use a set liturgy drawn up on Genevan lines; independents—the name used at the time for protestants who held that every local congregation is a law unto itself—wanted no liturgy at all. The *Directory* tried to have it both ways.[32] It does not prescribe any form of words,

[31] Horton Davies, *The Worship of the English Puritans* (1948; rpt. Morgan, PA: Soli Deo Gloria Publications, 1997), 130.

[32] On the *Directory*, Davies, *Worship of the English Puritans*, 127–142, 263–265. The text is printed in Thompson, *Liturgies*, 354–371. See also Peter King, "'The Reasons for the Abolition of the Book of Common Prayer in 1645," *Journal of Ecclesiastical History* 21.4 (1970): 327–339; E. C. Ratcliff, "Puritan Alternatives to the Prayer Book: The *Directory* and Richard Baxter's *Reformed Liturgy*," in *The English Prayer Book 1549–1662* (London: SPCK, 1963), 56–81, esp. 63.

but does make detailed recommendations. Five of its thirty-six pages list what the minister may suitably pray for or about before he preaches. His prayer and his sermon, together with his reading of two chapters from the Bible, if not more, make up nearly all of the usual Sunday service. The *Directory* assumes that metrical Psalms will be sung; there are even instructions for how to sing them. Otherwise, the minister gives a solo performance as "the mouth of the people unto God."

The *Directory* was supposed to be what the Book of Common Prayer had been: the one lawful standard for public worship throughout the English church. Quite apart from its intrinsic merits or flaws, however, it was a nonstarter. Many parishes did not buy it, despite orders to do so, and the Prayer Book continued to be used, despite orders to the contrary.[33] The forbidden liturgy was used to conduct services in private houses; in public, a few ministers were commended for the excellence of their "conceived" prayers, when in fact they were reciting from memory passages they were not allowed to read. Substitute services were composed, different enough from the Prayer Book to keep within the law, though the difference was often much less noticeable than the similarity.[34] Although many hundreds of conformist clergymen were ejected from their parishes, which were taken over by ministers acceptable to the parliamentary regime, the majority, perhaps a great majority,

---

[33] There may be more evidence for Prayer Book use than for use of the *Directory*. See Judith Maltby, "The Prayer Book and the Parish Church: From the Elizabethan Settlement to the Restoration," *OGBCP*, 79–92, esp. 89–90. On resistance to the *Directory* in Barbados, see Larry Cragg, *Englishmen Transplanted: The English Colonization of Barbados 1637–1660* (Oxford: Oxford University Press, 2003), 73–74.

[34] Judith Maltby, "'The Good Old Way': Prayer Book Protestantism in the 1640s and 1650s," in *The Church and the Book*, ed. Robert N. Swanson (Rochester, NY: Boydell and Brewer, 2004), 233–256; "Suffering and Surviving: The Civil Wars, the Commonwealth and the Formation of 'Anglicanism', 1642–60," in *Religion in Revolutionary England*, ed. Christopher Durston and Judith Maltby (Manchester: Manchester University Press, 2006), 158–180. For examples of memorization, see John Spurr, *The Restoration of the Church of England, 1646–1689* (New Haven, CT: Yale University Press, 1991), 14.

stayed put.[35] Not all of them risked heavy penalties by reading the Book of Common Prayer, but many did. If they did it quietly, with no Laudian extravagance, there was a fair chance they would be left alone.

The Ordinal was put to use as well. Parliament might abolish episcopacy and deprive bishops of civil jurisdiction, as it did, but no legislature could take away their episcopal character and powers. They were bishops still, and they exercised their ministry, inconspicuously, by ordaining deacons and priests. It has been estimated that from 1646 to 1660, unseated bishops conferred holy orders on some 2,500 individuals, of whom surprisingly many had previously received nonepiscopal ordination.[36]

Prayer Book Commentaries

Ban or no ban, the Book of Common Prayer had its users. It had its defenders as well. Arguments for banning it, such as those rehearsed in the *Directory*'s preface, did not go unanswered. It was not to be expected that ponderous reasoning like Henry Hammond's in *A View of the New Directory and a Vindication of the Book of Common Prayer* would change the minds of the militant nonconformists who had at long last got rid of a book they despised. But this and other polemical works, Jeremy Taylor's *Apology for Authorized and Set Forms of Liturgy against the Pretense of the Spirit*, for example, did sustain resistance to puritan policies by refuting the criticism of the Prayer Book on which, at least ostensibly, they were based.

---

[35] The numbers have been disputed from that day to this. John Spurr's estimate is "perhaps 70 per cent or even 75"; see Spurr, *Restoration* 7. See also Ian Green, "The Persecution of 'Scandalous' and 'Malignant' Parish Clergy during the English Civil War," *English Historical Review* 94 (1979): 507–531.

[36] Kenneth Fincham and Stephen Taylor, "Vital Statistics: Episcopal Ordination and Ordinands in England, 1646–1660," *English Historical Review* 126 (2011): 319–344; Spurr, *Restoration*, 9, 141–143.

By no means everything written about the outlawed liturgy was written to confute its enemies. It was for friends of the Prayer Book that *A Rationale upon the Book of Common-Prayer* was published in 1655. The first edition was anonymous, perhaps because Oliver Cromwell, ruling as Lord Protector, had issued a ukase that made it a penal offence to use the Prayer Book even in private. For reading it in public, the author of the *Rationale*, Anthony Sparrow, had already been driven from his rectory. But instead of writing a defense of the liturgy he would not abandon, Sparrow did something new. He wrote a commentary.

There was a long tradition of commentaries on books of the Bible, but not on the Book of Common Prayer. Sparrow does not call attention to the parallel, but it speaks for itself. His *Rationale* belongs to the genre of exposition and exegesis rather than disputation. Sparrow works through each office, explaining what is meant by words like *advent* and *font*, the arrangement of the kalendar, the order of Morning Prayer's components, the reasons for standing to say the Creed and for kneeling to say the General Confession. Each of these has an intelligible explanation. To grasp this rationale in all the parts of the liturgy is to see how admirably the whole of it is suited to its purpose. While using the Prayer Book for that holy purpose is of course a primary duty, its text is at the same time, like holy scripture, a text to "read, mark, learn, and inwardly digest."

Sparrow wrote, as he says, not to convert those who think ill of the Book of Common Prayer, but to show those who love it "and suffer for the love of it . . . why they should suffer on, and love it still more and more." Their suffering was a kind of martyrdom, and the Prayer Book itself was coming to be perceived, and revered, as a kind of martyr. Sparrow lived to see the end of suffering at the return of the English liturgy to the churches from which it had been banished. He also saw the publication of seven or eight editions of his *Rationale*. Evidently his calm, page-by-page explication of what he called "the ancient form" did for many readers what he hoped it would do.[37]

The ancient form was still officially outlawed when another tradition of commentary, less eclectic and more historically minded than Sparrow's, began with the publication of *An Alliance of Divine Offices Exhibiting All the Liturgies of the Church of England since the Reformation.* Hamon L'Estrange, a layman and like Sparrow a royalist, went to the trouble and expense of acquiring a copy of every version of the Book of Common Prayer, from the 1549 original to the recent, ill-starred Scottish Prayer Book. The text he expounds in his *Alliance* is the one that had been current in England, the Elizabethan version with its Hampton Court amendments. Around this text, he assembles extracts from the other Prayer Books. Separately, after each office, he adds his own commentary, which shows that like Sparrow he attached great importance to the Prayer Book's consonance with early Christian liturgy, before it was sullied by Roman accretions.

In that regard, *An Alliance of Divine Offices* is an exercise in apologetics. Chiefly, though, it is a portable compendium of all the authorized Prayer Book texts, distinguished on the page by means of different typefaces and arranged to facilitate comparison of the successive versions and call attention to changes and continuities. It was L'Estrange's main concern, as it was Sparrow's, to expound the meaning of the liturgy as it stood in his own day; but for L'Estrange understanding what the Prayer Book meant was partly a matter of understanding its ancestry and the revisions that had made it the text it was. For that insight, especially, he is honored as an originator of Anglican liturgics.[38]

---

[37] On the *Rationale*, see Kenneth Stevenson, "The Prayer Book as Sacred Text," *OGBCP*, 133–139.

[38] Paul V. Marshall, *The Voice of a Stranger: On the Lay Origin of Anglican Liturgics* (New York: Church Hymnal Corporation, 1993), esp. 247–253.

L'Estrange began his scholarly labors shortly before the Book of Common Prayer was outlawed, but he was prevented from publishing the fruits of them until 1659, shortly before the law became a dead letter. By then it was widely and, as things turned out, correctly expected that the English monarchy would soon be restored, and that its restoration would bring with it a restoration of the English liturgy. Those who relished their freedom from the prescriptions of the Prayer Book feared, also correctly, that they would again be required to use it. But first there would be yet another round of efforts to have their objections to using it met.

Eight

Establishment

However likely it seemed to be that the Book of Common Prayer would return to England's churches when Charles II returned to England, it was not inevitable. For his own part, the exiled king had made it clear that he would never abandon "the good old order in which he had been bred"; but he had also promised "a liberty to tender consciences, and that no man shall be disquieted or called in question for differences of opinion in matter of religion which do not disturb the peace of the kingdom." Presbyterians, many of whom actively supported political restoration, had reason to hope that if there was to be liturgical restoration as well, it would somehow take account of their conscientious objections to the Prayer Book. When the king did return in May 1660, they urged in a long, formal petition that "learned, godly, and moderate divines of both persuasions," presbyterian and episcopalian, might be appointed to compile a new book of public worship, or at least to revise the old one so that it would include "varying forms in scripture phrase, to be used at the minister's choice."

To this proposal the bishops, who were beginning to exercise their former authority, replied that they were not opposed to a review and revision of the Prayer Book, carried out by "such discreet persons as his Majesty shall see fit to employ."[1] Nor was his Majesty opposed. In a declaration that repeated both his solicitude for tender consciences and his high esteem for the Book of Common Prayer, Charles promised that the two parties would be equally

---

[1] George Gould, *Documents Relating to the Settlement of the Church of England* (London: W. Kent, 1862), 3, 5, 17, 35.

The Book of Common Prayer. Charles Hefling, Oxford University Press (2021). © Oxford University Press. DOI: 10.1093/oso/9780190689681.001.0001.

represented on a commission charged with recommending any liturgical alterations they might agree on.

Meanwhile, although the Prayer Book's official status had yet to be settled, it was making a rapid comeback.[2] Before the year was out, His Majesty's Printers, as they were once again known, brought out two folio editions for churches to use and two more in smaller formats. At Cambridge a deluxe edition was printed in one volume with the "last, best" translation of the Bible, which, as the dedication to King Charles pointed out, had been authorized by his royal grandfather.[3] There was a pirated edition too, or would have been, if the sheets had not been seized before they could be bound. The enterprising printers defended themselves on the ground that they were acting to meet an emergency and did not know who the King's Printer was.[4] As they had been quick to appreciate, there was a need and a market for new editions of the old Prayer Book. Before it was replaced in 1662, half the parishes in England, by one estimate, bought a copy.[5]

This resurgence did not go unopposed. Dozens of pamphlets attacked liturgy in general and the Book of Common Prayer in particular.[6] Some of them were simply reprints, and none of them had much to say that had not been said before. The principled objections of nonconformists had not changed since Elizabeth's

---

[2] For the reports of the celebrated diarists Samuel Pepys and John Evelyn, see N. H. Keeble, "Introduction: Attempting Uniformity," *Settling the Peace of the Church: 1662 Revisited*, ed. N. H. Keeble (Oxford: Oxford University Press 2014), 1–28 at 12. The parliamentary abrogation of the Prayer Book in 1645 was not formally annulled until the Treason Act of July 30, 1661.

[3] Wing B3618. This is not an abridged "Bible version," although it was printed at the front of a Bible. The epistles and gospels are there in full, still in the Coverdale translation.

[4] Henry Robert Plomer, "Eglesfield (Francis)," *A Dictionary of the Booksellers and Printers who were at Work in England, Scotland, and Ireland from 1641 to 1667* (London: Bibliographical Society, 1907), 69–70; State Papers, Domestic series, Charles II 1661–1662 (1861) 47: 208.

[5] Ronald Hutton, *The Restoration: A Political and Religious History of England and Wales 1658-1667* (Oxford: Oxford University Press, 1995), 172.

[6] For a masterly survey of this literature, see Christopher Haigh, "Liturgy and Liberty: The Controversy over the Book of Common Prayer, 1660-1663," *Journal of Anglican Studies* 11.1 (2013): 32–64.

Act of Uniformity imposed the liturgy that was now being revived. The pragmatic question was whether those who welcomed the revival and those who deplored it could share the same ecclesiastical space. The king appears to have thought they could, and tried to make it so. He appointed presbyterian chaplains; he offered to fill vacant bishoprics with presbyterians who were not utterly opposed to episcopacy; five months after promising a commission on liturgical revision, he appointed the commissioners and set a deadline for their deliberations.

The Conference at the Savoy

From the standpoint of anyone who hoped that the Prayer Book could be made less abrasive to tender consciences, the Savoy Conference—named for the bishop of London's residence, where the commissioners met—was about as successful as the Hampton Court discussions had been, which is to say not very successful at all. The bishops on the episcopalian side now had the upper hand, and they took the position that since the Prayer Book was perfectly adequate just as it was, the burden of proof fell on those who thought otherwise. Objections from the presbyterian side would have to be submitted all at once, as though to a panel of judges. This protocol put the presbyterians at a disadvantage from the first, but they accepted it and accordingly drew up a roster of "exceptions," general and particular.[7] As they acknowledged, the particular exceptions, about eighty in all, were not equally important. Trivial points and verbal quibbles were included, probably at the urging of Richard Baxter, one of the commissioners, who had his eye on the

---

[7] The most conveniently arranged presentation of the exceptions and the corresponding episcopal answers is Colin Buchanan, ed., *The Savoy Conference Revisited: The Proceedings Taken from the Grand Debate of 1661 and the Works of Richard Baxter* (Cambridge: Grove Books, 2002). Buchanan counts eighty-three particular exceptions; the conventional number is seventy-eight.

judgment of posterity and made sure every jot and tittle was put on record.

Baxter also composed and delivered a complete collection of services, evidently meant to supply "varying forms in scripture phrase to be used at the minister's discretion."[8] This prolix and repetitious text never stood much chance of being folded into the Prayer Book as a set of alternatives for puritans. The bishops ignored it, and in their written reply to the exceptions, they mostly stonewalled. To Baxter it seemed that "we spoke to the deaf." Nothing daunted, he answered the episcopal reply in a rebuttal of epic proportions.

The bishops were not completely deaf. There were a few points of agreement, the most important one being the adoption of the King James Bible for the liturgical epistles and gospels, and for some of the other biblical extracts, though not for the Psalter. In the Communion service, it was agreed that the consecration should be made more explicit by prescribing manual acts. The other concessions from the bishops' side were matters of detail, most of them not very significant. On the whole, for all the difference it made to the presbyterians, the Savoy Conference might not have happened at all.

While it was happening, a new and aggressively royalist Parliament assembled and set about framing a new Act of Uniformity. In the Commons, opposition to any liturgical innovation whatever was so strong that efforts were made to find a copy of Edward VI's second Prayer Book, which the Act of 1559 had reinstated, so that it could be reinstated again, just as it was in 1552, before Laud or anyone else could possibly have tinkered with the wording.[9] Returning to this pristine text would also have meant

---

[8] Text of Baxter's "Savoy Liturgy" in Thompson, *Liturgies*, 385–405; text and analysis in Glen J. Segger, *Richard Baxter's Reformed Liturgy: A Puritan Alternative to the Book of Common Prayer* (Burlington, VT: Ashgate, 2014).

[9] Paul Seaward provides an account of the parliamentary politicking in *The Cavalier Parliament and the Reconstruction of the Old Regime, 1661–1667* (Cambridge: Cambridge University Press, 1989), 162–195, emphasizing the importance attached to the 1552 Book of Common Prayer. See also C. J. Cuming, "The Prayer Book in Convocation, November 1661," *Journal of Ecclesiastical History* 8.2 (1957): 182–192.

canceling King James's explanations, dropping the first half of the administration formula at Holy Communion (Table 6.1), bringing back the Litany's plea for deliverance from papal enormities, reverting to the strictures of the original Ornaments Rubric (Table 6.2), and perhaps restoring the Declaration on Kneeling. All this may not have been what anyone had in mind. In the event, however, no 1552 Prayer Book could be found. Instead a copy printed in 1604—pre-Laud but post-James—was attached to the uniformity bill, though not until it had been purged of unauthorized accretions. Printed in this edition were two of the traditional Godly Prayers, which were deleted at the clerk's table by cutting out a whole leaf and obliterating the words on the previous page.[10]

If at that point the uniformity bill had been enacted, it would simply have restored officially the Prayer Book that was unofficially being printed, purchased, and used already—the Elizabethan version as amended at Hampton Court. The church, however, had not yet had its say, and it was only after Convocation had revised the whole book that the fourth Act of Uniformity restored it.

The Final Version: Additions and Enlargements

The many changes introduced by Convocation's review committee were mostly small, but in a few cases consequential. Among them were several though not all of the Savoy Conference agreements. There might have been more substantial renovation if two of the bishops—John Cosin, whose *Private Devotions* the previous

---

[10] No *authorized* prayers were removed, although there has been some confusion on the point. The edition will have been Griffiths 1604/2, in which Godly Prayers filled out the end of a gathering, as they often did. The last leaf (V4) was excised; V3 *verso* was stricken out. On the admittedly confusing parliamentary report, see [James Parker], *An Introduction to the Successive Revisions of the Book of Common Prayer* (London: James Parker and Co., 1877), lxxxv; C. A. Swainson, *The Parliamentary History of the Act of Uniformity* (London: George Bell, 1875), 11–12.

chapter mentioned, and Matthew Wren, uncle of Christopher the architect—had persuaded the rest of the committee to accept their recommendations.

Wren and Cosin were both Laudians of the deepest dye, and they had both aroused the hostility of parliamentary puritans at the beginning of the recent conflict. Cosin fled to France; Wren was imprisoned for eighteen years. Each had seen the discontinuation of the Book of Common Prayer as an opportunity to improve it, and had made note of specific improvements. Many of their ideas, as compiled by Cosin, appear in an extensively marked and annotated Prayer Book that the committee used in its deliberations.[11] Especially in the Communion office, the additions and corrections show the influence of the original English liturgy, channeled through the Scottish Prayer Book. But most of these amendments, which would have shifted England's Prayer Book in a less definitely protestant direction, were no more acceptable to the committee than were most of the presbyterians' proposals at the Savoy Conference, which would have shifted it the other way. Convocation, aware of what the Commons had been up to, was wary of shifting the Prayer Book at all. The changes it did recommend, which Parliament enacted with a little demur, were these:

(1) The two satellite books, the Psalter and the Ordinal, were formally incorporated, named in the full title, and listed in the table of contents. In the Psalms, revisions were editorial only; in the Ordination services they were very small but had large consequences.

(2) A number of individual liturgies were added: an office for baptizing persons no longer in their infancy, a set of services

---

[11] C. J. Cuming expounds these proposals in *The Durham Book: Being the First Draft of the Revision of the Book of Common Prayer in 1661* (Oxford: Oxford University Press, 1961); see esp. xvi–xxii.

and prayers for use on ships at sea, and the three annual commemorations known as the State Services.

(3) Many of the offices that the Prayer Book had always included were amended in various ways. Some of the most important amendments were silent; they made no difference in what is to be said or sung, but they did affect the rubrics that prescribe what is to be done.

The Psalter and the Ordinal

Despite the precedent of the Prayer Book for Scotland, the canticles and Psalms in the 1662 revision follow the Great Bible translation, as they had always done. One reason may be that in England, though not in Scotland, there was a tradition of singing them. Even when they were spoken rather than sung, the prose Psalms were familiar, and like the still more familiar canticles, they seem to have functioned less as instructive chapters of scripture than as vocal rituals or incantations. Their meaning was appropriated in reciting them as much as in understanding what was recited. That may be why the Psalms in the Bishops' Bible had never replaced Coverdale's Psalter, and why in 1662 the King James version did not replace it either.

A few outright mistakes, however, which the printers had carried over from one edition to the next, were put right. For many years, on the seventh evening of every month, the Psalter had warned that "the righteous shall be punished" (Psalm 37:29), although it had been pointed out again and again that *righteous* ought to be *unrighteous*. In 1662 this disconcerting error was at last corrected. Aside from that, and one or two other small repairs, the Psalter did not change.[12]

---

[12] It is sometimes said that the 1662 revisers altered the archaism at the beginning of the first Psalm from "hath not walked . . . nor *stand* . . . and hath not *sit*" to *stood* and *sat*. In fact both of these updates had appeared in earlier editions; if the revisers noticed the fact, they accepted it.

The Ordinal did. Two amendments, both slight, underscore the difference between the Church of England, as an episcopal church, and other churches of the Reformation. One change makes it explicit that bishops are not the same as priests; the other, that bishops are essential to the constitution of the church's ministry.

In the original Ordinal's service for the consecration of a bishop, the formula pronounced at the laying-on of hands was very nearly the same as the one used to ordain a priest, and neither formula specified the office of ministry that was being conferred. This made it possible to argue, if not very convincingly, that the Prayer Book draws no essential distinction between bishops and priests, and that by implication it comports with the parity of all ministers, which was the usual protestant understanding of ordination. To emphasize that this was not the Church of England's understanding, the revised Ordinal added to each of the two formulas the name of the ministerial order it imparts. The change was not substantive; it only made more explicit a distinction between the episcopate and the priesthood that had been fairly plain all along.

The other change in the Ordinal was more important. One corollary of the protestant theology of ordained ministry is that it belongs to all ordained ministers, as such, to ordain others. Until 1662, there could be some question whether a minister ordained by other ministers was thereby qualified for ministry in the Church of England. The preface of the original Ordinal was ambiguous in that regard. It required anyone who was not already a minister to be ordained by a bishop as a condition of assuming any ministerial office. This requirement would obviously apply to individuals who had never been ordained at all, but it might or might not apply to someone already ordained according to protestant practice, perhaps in a nonepiscopal church abroad. Otherwise stated, the question was whether episcopal ordination, which was certainly necessary in some cases, was necessary in all. The unambiguous answer in the preface of the revised Ordinal is *yes*. No one, as far as the Church of England is concerned, may act or be regarded as a genuine bishop, priest, or deacon without having been ordained at the hands of a bishop.

The point is somewhat technical, but its implications were (and are) momentous. After Parliament's abrogation of episcopacy in 1646, only nonepiscopal ordination was lawful, and ministers of various persuasions whom no bishop had ordained took charge of parish churches. By the standard of the 1662 Ordinal, their ordinations did not qualify them as clergy of the restored episcopal church. They must therefore relinquish their offices and ministries, which they had no authority to exercise, or else they must be ordained (again). This practical conclusion is only implicit in the Ordinal itself, but the Act of Uniformity by which the Ordinal was imposed draws it explicitly, and enforcement of its provisions in that regard had wide and painful consequences.

All the other changes in the Ordination services are minor. The ungainly paraphrase of the hymn *Veni Creator* was smoothed out a little, and a new, much shorter version was added as an alternative. In the original Ordinal, oddly, there were two rubrics in Latin. The revision eliminates them.[13]

Services Added

Enlarging the Prayer Book to include the Psalter and the Ordinal amounted to formal recognition of long-accepted practice. The 1662 revision also includes a number of services, most of them partly if not entirely new, that had never been contained in the Book of Common Prayer. In different ways, all these additions

---

[13] For the *Veni Creator*, see Brightman, *English Rite*, II: 977–979, 989–993; for the Latin rubrics, see 979.

reflect concerns of the re-established church at the time of its re-establishment.

One of the new liturgies pertains to sailors and another to unbaptized adults. Both were more numerous after the Commonwealth than before. The "Sea Service," tucked in between the Psalter and the Ordinal, was partly a response to the growth of England's navy and the expansion of commercial seafaring. It was also meant to replace *A Supply of Prayer for the Ships of this Kingdom, that want Ministers to Pray with Them*, which Parliament had issued in 1645 to supplement its new *Directory*.[14] Unlike the *Directory* itself, this pamphlet supplied scripted prayers, apparently because it was thought that if sailors had no script to follow they might neglect to pray at all, or might resort to the Book of Common Prayer, which would be almost as bad. For the restored Prayer Book a somewhat different supply of prayers, less verbose and more liturgical, was compiled. Daily Morning and Evening Prayer are ordered, with added prayers, as well as special thanksgivings after a victory or at the end of a storm, and a committal sentence adapted for burial at sea. A few verses from the King James Bible, included in the composite Psalms, prove that their composition was recent.

A third baptismal service was added in the 1662 Prayer Book owing to what its new Preface calls "the growth of Anabaptism through the licentiousness of the late times" (owc 211). Oliver Cromwell's tolerant regime had given free rein to radically reformed groups which insisted that Christian baptism must be a deliberate, personal act. Promises such as the ones that the Prayer Book allows godparents to make on behalf of infants ought to be made instead by the candidates themselves, who ought not to be baptized until they are capable of making them. Adults and older children whose baptism had been postponed on these grounds needed to be baptized before they could belong to the restored church; and

---

[14] See Bryan D. Spinks, *The Rise and Fall of the Incomparable Liturgy: The Book of Common Prayer 1559–1906* (London: SPCK, 2017), 77 and 161–169, which reproduces the original booklet.

since the existing baptismal office was unsuitable, meant as it was for infants, a modified rite was composed, in which "such as are of riper years" speak on their own behalf. As the Preface goes on to say, this new service could also be used when "natives in our plantations," presumably meaning the North American colonies, were converted to Christianity.

The "riper years" variant of the baptismal service was composed while Convocation was marking time as the Savoy Conference wound down. The three State Services were put into final form then as well. Like the special orders of prayer discussed in chapter five, these liturgies are all modifications of Divine Service, including Evening Prayer in one case. Each of them prescribes Psalms, lessons, epistle, and gospel, each selected for its relevance to the occasion. Composite Psalms replace the *Venite*; loquacious topical prayers replace the collect of the day and others are added to the Litany.

None of these three services was altogether new. One of them had been used for more than half a century. In 1606 Parliament ordered an annual commemoration of King James's deliverance in the previous year from "the most Traitorous and Bloody intended Massacre by Gunpowder." Since then the date of the failed Papists' Conspiracy, November 5, had been a red-letter day in the Prayer Book kalendar, but the form of prayers for the service of thanksgiving on that day was published from time to time in booklets of the usual kind. One of these provided the text that was added to the Book of Common Prayer.[15]

James escaped political murder. Charles I did not. Throughout the ensuing interregnum, the date of his execution, January 30, was kept by royalists as a solemn and mournful fast. One of his son's courtiers-in-exile compiled a long liturgy of lamentation, from which a remarkable prayer made its way into a form of service published in 1661 "by his Majesty's direction." It includes a request for

[15] On the Gundpowder service and its context, see Alexandra Walsham, *Providence in Early Modern England* (Oxford: Oxford University Press, 1999), 245–266.

grace to remember and provide for our latter end, by a careful studious imitation of this thy blessed Saint and Martyr, and all other thy Saints and Martyrs that have gone before us, that we may be made worthy to receive benefit by their prayers, which they in communion with thy Church Catholic offer up unto thee for that part of it here Militant, and yet in fight with and danger from the flesh.

The phrasing of this prayer manages, just barely, to steer clear of asking directly for intercession on the part of the saints in heaven, among whom the late king is numbered. Even so it went too far. In the reformed Church of England saints had always been exemplars, but never benefactors, by their prayers or otherwise. It took two revisions to make the wording acceptable for inclusion in the Prayer Book liturgy for January 30.[16]

Divine Service on that day nevertheless refers to the king as a martyr, and invites comparison between two blameless victims, King Charles and Jesus Christ, both of them maliciously executed by despicable enemies. The appointed prayers draw this parallel explicitly, and the appointed Psalms and Bible readings underscore it. The second lesson at Morning Prayer, however, was left as it stood in the ordinary sequence of course reading (see Figure 2.1). Since 1549 the chapter for January 30 had been Matthew 27, the narrative of Jesus' trial, execution, and burial on Good Friday. The king heard it read on the morning of his own execution.[17] For royalists, the anniversary of that day was a secondary Good Friday, and the special Prayer Book offices played a significant part in what became the cult of King Charles the Martyr.[18]

---

[16] For the office in its final form, see OWC 655–661; the much-revised collect begins at 660. The somewhat complicated bibliography of the January 30 service is discussed in Thomas Lathbury, *A History of the Book of Common Prayer and Other Books of Authority* (Oxford: James Parker, 1875), 334–336.

[17] Not at Holy Communion, as is sometimes stated. The king did receive the sacrament, but that service was preceded, as usual, by Mattins with the Psalms and lessons of the day.

[18] See esp. Andrew Lacey, "The Office for King Charles the Martyr in the Book of Common Prayer, 1662–1685," *Journal of Ecclesiastical History* 53.3 (2002): 510–526, expanded in *The Cult of King Charles the Martyr* (Woodbridge, UK: Boydell Press, 2003).

Collect at Holy Communion
January 30: The Day of the Martyrdom of King
Charles the First

Blessed Lord, in whose sight the death of thy saints is precious;
We magnify thy Name for that abundant grace bestowed upon
our late Martyred Sovereign; by which he was enabled so cheerfully to follow the steps of his blessed Master and Savior, in a
constant meek suffering of all barbarous indignities, and at last
resisting unto blood; and even then, according to the same pattern, praying for his murderers. Let his memory, O Lord, be ever
blessed among us, that we may follow the example of his patience, and charity: And grant, that this our Land may be freed
from the vengeance of his blood, and thy mercy glorified in the
forgiveness of our sins; and all for Jesus Christ his sake. *Amen.*

Because Charles II dated his de jure reign from the day of his
father's martyrdom, he did not observe an accession day. Instead,
the traditional service was reworked a little in 1662 to make it a celebration of his restoration on May 29, which happened to be his
birthday. The day had begun to be kept as a feast; including the office
in the Prayer Book made keeping it not only official but mandatory.

The services for these "solemn days" can be dismissed as political
propaganda. That, among other things, is what they are. Obligatory
exercises of public worship were a useful way of controlling the interpretation of the Civil Wars and of inculcating the sacredness of
kingship, the unqualified wickedness of rebellion, and the virtue
of passive obedience. But it does not follow that the State Services
were deliberately disingenuous. The Prayer Book had always been
a political text, and a theology of divine providence that conceives
God as deeply interested and directly involved in worldly politics,
English politics especially, was built into English protestantism.
What had happened to King James, his son, and his grandson
happened to anointed sovereigns, deputies of the same God who,

as scripture reports, set princes over his chosen people and took an active part in their history. Viewed in that light, the execution of Charles I was a national sin that called for national repentance, and the end of the Great Rebellion, like the frustration of the Powder Plot, was an intervention as miraculous as those recorded in the Bible. Whether that is the best light in which to view such events is of course a different question.

A General Thanksgiving

Almighty God, Father of all mercies, we thine unworthy servants do give thee most humble and hearty thanks for all thy goodness and loving kindness to us, and to all men; [*particularly to those who desire now to offer up their praises and thanksgivings for thy late mercies vouchsafed unto them.**] ** This is to be said when any that have been prayed for, desire to return praise.*
We bless thee for our creation, preservation, and all the blessings of this life, but above all for thine inestimable love in the redemption of the world by our Lord Jesus Christ; for the means of grace, and for the hope of glory. And we beseech thee give us that due sense of all thy mercies, that our hearts may be unfeignedly thankful, and that we show forth thy praise, not only with our lips, but in our lives, by giving up ourselves to thy service, and by walking before thee in holiness and righteousness all our days, through Jesus Christ our Lord, to whom with thee and the holy Ghost be all honor and glory, world without end. *Amen.*

Amendments, Audible and Inaudible

Besides adding a number of new services and incorporating the Psalter and the Ordinal, the revisers altered the liturgical epistles and gospels, as well as the sentences at Morning and Evening Prayer and other texts excerpted from the Bible, to match the "last translation," the King James version. They also made numerous changes, six hundred by one count, in the texts of the services.[19] Many of these are small verbal improvements, but a few are more substantive. Several optional prayers are added, among them the much admired General Thanksgiving. In the Elizabethan Prayer Book there was no proper collect, epistle, or gospel for the Sixth Sunday after Epiphany, which occurs in years when Easter is very late; nor was there a collect for Easter Even. All these are provided. A new clause at the end of the prayer for the whole state of the church at Holy Communion refers to "all thy servants departed this life in thy faith and fear" in such a way as to make it possibly though not unambiguously a prayer *for* them.

Elsewhere in the Communion office, changes in words sung or said are few and minor. Much more interesting are changes in the unspoken text—new and altered rubrics. The wording of the central sacramental prayer is virtually the same as it had been since 1552, but it is referred to explicitly as the prayer of consecration. One part of this prayer, the institution narrative, is specified as necessary (though not sufficient) for consecration to occur.[20] To show that the priest who recites this narrative is not merely reminding the congregation of what Christ did and said in the past, there is a new rubric in the margin which orders five manual acts that associate

---

[19] The count, which no one appears to have confirmed, was reported some years later by Thomas Tenison, who became archbishop of Canterbury. For extensive lists of the major changes, see W. K. Lowther Clarke, *Liturgy and Worship* (New York: Macmillan, 1932), 194–197; Cardwell, *Conferences*, 380–386.

[20] See owc 403 and Richard F. Buxton, *Eucharist and Institution Narrative*, Alcuin Club Collections 58 (Great Wakering: Mayhew-McCrimmon, 1976), 148–152.

the narration with the present bread and wine. Before the consecration prayer begins, those elements are to be placed on the holy
table during what is now termed the offertory, as they were before
the revision of 1552. Once they have been consecrated, whatever
may be left of them after the administration of communion must
be reverently put back on the table, where it is to be veiled, as befits
holy things, and reverently consumed immediately after the final
benediction. Only if *un*consecrated bread or wine remains may the
curate "have it to his own use" (owc 406).

Actions speak. In its wording, the prayer of consecration did not
change.[21] In its meaning, it did. The new rubrics order ceremonial
acts that situate the uttered prayers in a new and different context,
such that the words which are spoken and heard can be understood
in a sense that pulls back from the intentions of the 1552 revision.
"The pattern of the older Eucharist is restored—by rubric."[22]

At the same time, as if to counterbalance these ceremonial
rubrics, the 1662 revision also brings back the so-called Black
Rubric, the Declaration on Kneeling. Last seen in the short-lived
Prayer Book of 1552 (Figure 5.3), the Declaration had not been
forgotten. It came up at the Savoy Conference, where the bishops
disallowed it as unnecessary, but in the end the presbyterians,
who had proposed restoring it, got their way.[23] There is one small
change. The original Declaration denied that sacramental bread
and wine can be adored in virtue of any "real, and essential" presence of Christ's natural body and blood. As restored in 1662, the
text denies "corporeal" presence instead. The difference may or may

---

[21] To be precise, four words were added: "we *most humbly* beseech thee"; "for *the* remission of sins"; and *Amen*. At one point *who* replaces *which*. See Brightman, *English
Rite*, II: 693.

[22] A. H. Couratin, "The Service of Holy Communion, 1552–1662," *Church
Quarterly Review* 163 (1962): 431–442 at 442. See also Bridgett Nichols, *Liturgical
Hermeneutics: Interpreting Liturgical Rites in Performance* (Frankfurt-am-Main: Peter
Lang, 1996), 82.

[23] Buchanan, *Savoy Conference*, 52–53.

not be merely verbal. Even if it is not, however, the Declaration still asserts that Christ's body and blood are in heaven, not here, and that the bread and wine remain unchanged (owc 407). These assertions do not logically imply that there is no true though noncorporeal sense in which Christ is present, but they evidently do exclude transubstantiation, as they did in 1552.

The revisions that Convocation agreed to were recorded in a large 1639 Prayer Book, from which a complete fair copy was written.[24] This thick manuscript, duly signed late in December 1661, was accepted by Parliament and physically "annexed and joined" to the engrossment of the Act of Uniformity. On May 19 the Act received the royal assent. On August 6 it was announced that the new Book of Common Prayer had been printed and was available for purchase. On Sunday, August 24, the Feast of St. Bartholomew, the Act went into effect.

The Settlement of 1662

On St. Bartholomew's Day the Book of Common Prayer was established—finally established, in two senses. The Act of Uniformity fixed its text, permanently as it turned out. There has been no further revision of anything said or sung. At the same time, the Act defined and sanctioned the status of this text as the exclusive form of public worship in the Church of England, and required of the church's clergy public assent and consent to all and everything it contained.[25] Thus St. Bartholomew's Day saw the return of an old problem: whether a church defined in part by a prescribed,

---

[24] The date usually given is 1636, but see Griffiths, *Bibliography*, 100 and the entries there for 1636/1 and 1639/2.

[25] See Gould, *Documents Relating*, 389; George R. Abernathy, "The English Presbyterians and the Stuart Restoration, 1648–1663," *Transactions of the American Philosophical Society* n.s. 55.2 (1965): 1–101 at 43.

invariant, obligatory liturgy could be *the* church of England, coextensive with the political nation; whether it was possible for "all the whole realm" to have "but one use"; whether liturgical uniformity was compatible with ecclesiastical comprehensiveness.

The concrete reality of the problem was painfully evident in the exit of perhaps as many as 1,800 clergymen, who resigned or were ejected from their parishes and other posts, either because they were unwilling to subscribe to the oath that the Act required, or because they were unwilling to be episcopally (re)ordained, as it also required, or both. For these nonconformists, *dissenters* as they may now be called, August 24 was "Black Bartholomew." To some conformists, many of whom had themselves been expelled during the Commonwealth, it seemed only fair that those who refused to abide by the reinstated Prayer Book should be forced out in their turn. But not everyone was so minded. There were episcopalians, *Anglicans* as they may now be called, who entertained hopes that the stringent settlement of religion imposed by the Act of Uniformity and reinforced by subsequent legislation was not the last word, and that the question of where the established church stood in relation to dissenting protestants had not been closed. For the time being, however, lawful worship, Anglican worship, and worship according to the Book of Common Prayer were all one and the same.

Although Charles II tried in various ways to introduce a measure of the "liberty to tender consciences" he had guaranteed, his efforts met with opposition in so far as they would have benefitted papists as well as dissenting protestants.[26] Popery was still a byword for perfidious, alien, absolutist political aggression. If the king himself became a Roman Catholic, as he was said to have done, he did it *sub rosa*. His brother James, on the other hand, who succeeded him in 1685, had made no secret of his

---

[26] The king's own motives have been variously interpreted. See R. A. Beddard, "The Restoration Church," in *The Restored Monarchy 1660–1688*, ed. J. R. Jones (Totowa, NJ: Rowman and Littlefield, 1979), 155–175 at 161, 167–170.

own secession to Rome. The anomaly of becoming the supreme governor of a church he had repudiated did not stop him from altering its liturgy. James put himself into the State Services and added a new one, the King's Day, to celebrate the anniversary of his accession. When his second, Roman Catholic wife became pregnant, a special form of prayer was issued, followed by another when she gave birth; both of these were printed in at least one edition of the Book of Common Prayer.[27]

The baby, born in 1688, was a boy. The fact that he took precedence over his two Anglican half-sisters in the royal line of succession, and would certainly be brought up as a Roman Catholic, made a political crisis inevitable. Before the year was out, James's nephew William, sovereign prince of Orange, came to the rescue, or invaded, and James found it prudent to leave. A few months later William and his wife Mary, James's Anglican daughter, jointly accepted the throne that was deemed to be vacant. This Glorious Revolution, as it was called by those who approved of it, had two important consequences for the Book of Common Prayer. One of these, which the next chapter will discuss, took effect outside any ecclesiastical establishment. The other was an attempt to make the establishment in England more inclusive by adjusting its liturgy.

Comprehension

The 1662 Act of Uniformity draws a map of English religion with a clear boundary separating those who do not accept the doctrine, discipline, and worship of the national church from those who do. The actual landscape was more variegated. Besides

---

[27] Griffiths 1688/1; Wing B3682. The service celebrating the birth of the Old Pretender (as he grew up to be) actually begins immediately after the one for his mother, the pregnant Queen Mary of Modena, on the same page.

recusant Roman Catholics, there were protestant groups—
baptists, quakers, independents—who had no interest in liturgical worship or a national church as such. But there were also
nonconforming presbyterians who held, despite their nonconformity, that in principle the Christian church ought to be a
single institution, organized and established on a national basis,
and that some sort of liturgy scripted in advance was not entirely
out of the question.

From the standpoint of the ecclesiastical establishment, which
drew the boundary and policed it, "liberty to tender consciences"
might therefore take either of two forms, toleration or comprehension, or some combination of both. A policy of toleration would relinquish the principle of liturgical uniformity, by
acknowledging the legitimacy of at least some forms of worship
other than those set out in the Book of Common Prayer. A policy
of comprehension, on the other hand, would maintain uniformity
but redefine what it consists in, by altering the standard to which
legitimate public worship must conform. Comprehension would
change the rule; toleration would permit exceptions. In 1661 King
Charles's hope had been that the Savoy commissioners could
agree on liturgical changes that would allow the re-established
episcopal church to comprehend moderate presbyterians. Such
was not the temper of the time. In 1689 King William, himself
a Dutch Calvinist presbyterian, set up a new commission with a
mandate to try again.

This time, no nonconformists took part, but a number of the
commissioners were sympathetic, and several of those who were
not absented themselves.[28] Amendments accepted by members of
the commission who chose to participate were written into a Prayer
Book specially prepared with extra blank pages, which still exists.

---

[28] The standard study is Timothy J. Fawcett, *The Liturgy of Comprehension 1689: An
Abortive Attempt to Revise the Book of Common Prayer*, Alcuin Club Collections 54
(Southend-on-Sea: Mayhew-McCrimmon, 1973).

Table 8.1 The Collect for the Nineteenth Sunday after Trinity

1662	1689 (proposed)
O God, forasmuch as without thee we are not able to please thee; Mercifully grant, that thy Holy Spirit may in all things direct and rule our hearts; through Jesus Christ our Lord. Amen.	O God, forasmuch as without thee we are not able to please thee; Mercifully grant that thy holy Spirit may in all things direct, and rule our hearts, and *renew us in the spirit of our mind:* that *putting away all bitterness and wrath, anger and malice,* and every other evil affection, and *being kind one to another, tenderhearted, forgiving one another, even as thou, O God, for Christ's sake hast forgiven us;* we may comfortably look with an assured hope for the *day of redemption* from all evils, unto eternal life, through Jesus Christ our Lord. *Amen*

As might be expected, longstanding puritan objections were at last taken seriously. It was agreed, for example, among other things, that lessons from the Apocrypha should be omitted, and that objectionable ceremonies—wearing the surplice, making the sign of the cross in Baptism, kneeling to receive communion—should all be optional.

The commissioners also addressed the old complaint that the Prayer Book collects are too brief and too general. The more expansive and specific replacements they proposed all take for granted that a proper collect ought to allude, as a few of them already did, to the liturgical epistle that is read immediately afterward at Holy Communion. Table 8.1 illustrates the commission's approach. The Prayer Book collect, on the left, is a translation, almost certainly Cranmer's, that was lightly touched up in 1662.[29] In the more copious version of 1689, all the italicized words are quoted or borrowed from the corresponding epistle, Ephesians 4:17–32 (owc 359). As revised, the collect is not

---

[29] Brightman, *English Rite*, II 527; Fawcett, *Liturgy of Comprehension*, 96, 231–232 and 206–208.

notable for winsome phrasing. It does supply an aspiration or result clause, but packs into it, between *that* and *we may comfortably look*, as many words as there are in the whole original collect. Even an attentive worshiper might be pardoned for losing the connection.

Enlarging the collect has also modified what it means. As in the Prayer Book, it opens with an acknowledgment that prevenient grace is necessary: without God, pleasing God is not possible. Then, in the added phrases, the revised version makes a rhetorical and thematic turn and begins to sound less like a prayer than an exhortation to moral virtue meant for the congregation to hear. This shift of emphasis, evident in several of the 1689 collects, is perhaps a reflection of reordered priorities in the ethos of the Church of England. Without denying that divine initiative is always necessary, Anglicans were less and less inclined to keep up the rancorous theological quarrels about divine initiative that had preoccupied the early seventeenth century, and more and more inclined to concern themselves instead with holy living, practical religion, applied righteousness, and moral duty.[30] Such a comparatively undogmatic and broad-minded attitude was apt to bring with it an openness to reunion with dissenters, which many of the royal commissioners shared.[31]

Although the commission had been instructed to present its recommendations at the next meeting of Convocation, nothing was ever presented. To judge by the record of what the commissioners had done, they still had work to do; but for various reasons not even an interim report came before Convocation before it adjourned, and after its adjournment the commission did

---

[30] The conventional but not very helpful name for this trend is *latitudinarian*. See John Spurr, "'Latitudinarianism' and the Restoration Church," *The Historical Journal* 31.1 (1988): 61–82; Spurr, *Restoration Church of England* 279–330; and Bryan D. Spinks, *Liturgy in the Age of Reason: Worship and Sacraments in England and Scotland, 1662–c. 1800* (Farnham, UK: Ashgate Publishing, 2008), 49–50.

[31] Note, in this regard, John Marshall, "The Ecclesiology of the Latitude-men 1660–1689: Stillingfleet, Tillotson and 'Hobbism'," *Journal of Ecclesiastical History* 36.3 (1985): 407–427.

not reconvene. "So ended, and for ever, the hope that the Church of England might be induced to make some concession to the scruples of the nonconformists."[32] To some historians it has seemed that Anglicans, presented with a propitious opportunity to repair the defects of the Restoration settlement, fumbled and lost it.[33] At the time, however, even strong proponents of comprehension saw in the miscarriage of the revision project "a very happy direction of the Providence of God."[34] No one would have been satisfied. The interleaved Prayer Book used to record the abortive proposals was put away, with instructions to keep it secret. Not until the nineteenth century were the commission's efforts made public. A précis, however, fairly detailed though not entirely accurate, found its way into print in 1702, and its description of what has come to be known as the "Liturgy of Comprehension" was discussed and referred to throughout the eighteenth century. In Parliament a frequently quoted speech praised the commissioners as "a set of men, than which this church was never, at any one time, bless'd with either wiser, or better, since it was a church";[35] and nearly a hundred years after the commission's final meeting its efforts were cited as a source and inspiration by the revisers of a Book of Common Prayer for the newly independent church in the United States.

[32] Thomas Babington Macaulay, *History of England*, vol. 3 (Boston: Phillips, Sampson, and Company, 1856), 391.

[33] Norman Sykes, *From Sheldon to Secker: Aspects of English Church History 1660–1768* (Cambridge: Cambridge University Press, 1959), 88.

[34] Gilbert Burnet, *The History of My Own Time*, bk. 5.

[35] *Cobbett's Parliamentary History of England* 6 (London, 1810), col 865. The speech was delivered in 1710 by William Wake, later archbishop of Canterbury.

Nine

The Golden Age

Historians no longer portray Anglicanism in the 1700s as indolent and ineffective. That portrait, once taken for granted, is a caricature. What is none the less true is that the "long eighteenth century" was a comparatively tranquil time for the Church of England. "Extremism was at a discount."[1] Liturgy, in particular, provoked no furious uproars, as it had done in the previous century and would do in the next. If the turbulent seventeenth century gave rise to esteem and even veneration for the Book of Common Prayer, the century that followed was its golden age.[2]

In England there was no change in the text of the Prayer Book, which was used, for the most part, according to its own rubrics. It was used, however, only in churches belonging to the ecclesiastical establishment. Anglicans had at length conceded that Cranmer's ideal of "but one use," which in practice had never been realized, never would be. In 1689, the same year that a royal commission tried and failed to make the statutory liturgy more comprehensive,

---

[1] F. C. Mather, "Georgian Churchmanship Reconsidered: Some Variations in Anglican Public Worship 1714–1830," *Journal of Ecclesiastical History* 36.2 (1985): 255–283 at 282. Among other recent reassessments, see John Walsh and Stephen Taylor, "Introduction: The Church and Anglicanism in the 'Long' Eighteenth Century," *The Church of England c. 1689–c. 1833: From Toleration to Tractarianism*, ed. John Walsh, Colin Haydon, and Stephen Taylor (Cambridge: Cambridge University Press, 1993), 1–64; and Ian Green, "Anglicanism in Stuart and Hanoverian England," in *A History of Religion in Britain: Practice and Belief from Pre-Roman Times to the Present*, ed. Sheridan Gilley and W. J. Sheils (Oxford: Blackwell, 1994), 168–187.

[2] Jeremy Gregory has used the phrase repeatedly, most recently in his introduction to *OHA* 2: *Establishment and Empire*, 1–21 at 5. See also Gregory, "'For All Sorts and Conditions of Men': The Social Life of the Book of Common Prayer during the Long Eighteenth Century," *Social History* 34.1 (2009): 29–54 at 32; and "The Prayer Book and the Parish Church: From the Restoration to the Oxford Movement," *OGBCP*, 93–105 at 93.

The Book of Common Prayer. Charles Hefling, Oxford University Press (2021). © Oxford University Press. DOI: 10.1093/oso/9780190689681.001.0001.

the Toleration Act made it optional. Nonconforming protestants, provided their theology was not unorthodox, were exempted from the penalties to which nonconformity had made them liable. There was now a choice: "church" or "chapel," corporate worship conducted according to the Book of Common Prayer or corporate worship conducted otherwise. Not that the practice of religion entered a free-market economy. Dissenters were still subject to civic exclusions and social disincentives, while the Church of England continued to enjoy enormous advantages. But if the state church was still, in some sense, England's national church, it was not the only legitimate church, and no one was obliged to attend its public prayers.

Anyone who did attend on a Sunday morning would most likely be attending a liturgy such as was described in chapter one. The "long service"—Morning Prayer, Litany, ante-Communion—was normal. From time to time there would be a full Communion service, though how often it took place is a matter of continuing discussion. A quarterly celebration was perhaps the most common practice, but there were certainly churches where communion was administered more frequently, even if not everyone who was eligible to receive the sacrament stayed to receive it.

If eighteenth-century Anglicans did not expect that going to church would ordinarily involve going to communion, they did expect to hear a sermon, and the clergy evidently took this aspect of their calling quite seriously.[3] Sermons were less likely to dwell on divine election and unmerited grace than on practical morals and holy living; Calvinism was on the wane, rational religion on the rise. Another sermon was sometimes preached at Evening

---

[3] William Gibson, "Sermons," *OHA* 2: 270–288 at 270. See also Donald A. Spaeth, *The Church in an Age of Danger: Parsons and Parishioners, 1660–1740* (Cambridge: Cambridge University Press, 2000), 189–190; Jeffrey S. Chamberlain, "Parish Preaching in the Long Eighteenth Century," in *The Oxford Handbook of the British Sermon 1689–1901*, ed. Keith A. Francis, William Gibson, John Morgan-Guy, Bob Tennant, and Robert H. Ellison (Oxford: Oxford University Press, 2012), 47–60.

Prayer, although the Prayer Book rubrics do not require it. They do require catechizing, after the second lesson (OWC 430, 414). Children were expected to learn the Catechism by heart, and their parish priest was expected to instruct and examine them "openly in the church" every Sunday and holyday.[4] Besides fulfilling the stated requirements for Confirmation, and thus for receiving communion, memorizing the Catechism was the primary way in which children—and often their parents too—acquired the rudiments of Christian teaching that sermons could presuppose and build on.

About the statutory liturgy in its official, public role, not much more needs to be said. This chapter will be concerned mainly with its wider employment, its reception, and its influence. The Book of Common Prayer was used not only in church but also in the personal and domestic devotions of families and individuals. There were thoughtful but not hostile proposals for revising it, which, unofficial and largely unsuccessful though they were, remain instructive as indications of what the Prayer Book was expected to be and do. And beyond the limits of the ecclesiastical establishment, the eighteenth century saw the beginning of a development that did win its way to acceptance, in a new version of the Book of Common Prayer in the New World.

The Prayer Book and Personal Religion

The scripts printed in the Book of Common Prayer are by definition directives for public, corporate worship. They presuppose a congregation, a minister, and usually a clerk and a church building.

---

[4] See Ian Green, "Anglicanism in Stuart and Hanoverian England," 182–184; Green, *The Christian's ABC: Catechisms and Catechizing in England c. 1530–1740* (Oxford: Oxford University Press, 1996), esp. 18–24; Green, "'For Children in Yeeres and Children in Understanding': The Emergence of the English Catechism under Elizabeth and the Early Stuarts," *Journal of Ecclesiastical History* 37.3 (1986): 397–425; and James Turrell, "Catechisms," *OGBCP*, 500–508.

But they have always been used in other ways also. Laypeople as well as clergy have said Morning and Evening Prayer privately, and individuals who possessed Prayer Books of their own not only took them to church but made use of them at home in family prayers and private devotions. Instructive commentaries in the tradition of Sparrow's *Rationale*, meant to encourage study of the text, continued to be published throughout the eighteenth century, but there was also an extensive literature of what would now be called spirituality, written to teach people how to pray, and many of these practical, accessible manuals were based on the Book of Common Prayer.[5]

One of the simplest and most popular books of this kind was *The Common-Prayer-Book the Best Companion in the House and Closet, As Well as in the Temple*. First published late in the seventeenth century, it was still going strong when the twenty-first edition appeared in 1758, long after its author, William Howell, had died. With family prayers especially in mind, Howell provides three services, for morning, noon, and night. Prayer at noon consists almost entirely of Prayer Book collects, plus the Lord's Prayer, a prayer slightly adapted from the Baptism office, and the prayer for the whole state of the church from Holy Communion. This last, since it was said every Sunday in Divine Service, would no doubt be familiar, but the holyday collects probably would not. Many of them are small gems of religious prose, which Howell's *Best Companion* brings into regular use. The collect for the feast of St. Simon and St. Jude, for example, is among the best of Cranmer's original compositions. It has no specific connection with the two minor apostles for whose feast it is prescribed, but it is very well suited to the role Howell gives it as a prayer to be said upon entering church.

---

[5] See C. J. Stranks, *Anglican Devotion: Studies in the Spiritual Life of the Church of England between the Reformation and the Oxford Movement* (Greenwich, CT: Seabury Press, 1961), ch. 6, "Devotion Based on the Prayer Book," 149–173.

Collect for the Feast of St. Simon and St. Jude

O Almighty God, who hast built thy Church upon the foundation of the Apostles and Prophets, Jesus Christ himself being the head corner-stone; Grant us so to be joined together in unity of spirit by their doctrine, that we may be made an holy temple acceptable unto thee, through Jesus Christ our Lord. *Amen.*

More formidable, yet evidently just as popular, was Robert Nelson's *Companion for the Festivals and Fasts of the Church of England.*[6] Nelson was a high-church layman who set great store by the authority of the church and its clergy. Throughout his book he is concerned with affirming the separateness and sanctity of all aspects of church life—rites, personnel, buildings, resources—as well as the holiness of days and seasons. He was also a man of his time, convinced that the evidence and embodiment of holiness is to be found in sober, rational morality. His devotional exposition of the Prayer Book holydays displays both these characteristics.

The human mind, Nelson observes, is not capable of uninterrupted contemplation. That being so, it is reasonable that certain appointed times, regular occasions, should be dedicated to working out one's own salvation. Such are holydays. They *are* holy, simply because the church has so designated them; but they must also be *made* holy, not only by resting from ordinary work, but by enlarged devotions as well. That is what *Festivals and Fasts* is for. It represents a sustained, methodical endeavor to "re-inscribe 'holy living' within the offices of [the] established church."[7] Time is sanctified by correlating the sanctity that the Prayer Book distributes over its

---

[6] On Nelson, see Stranks, *Anglican Devotion*, 162–170; on his approach to sanctity, Brent S. Sirota, "Robert Nelson's *Festivals and Fasts* and the Problem of the Sacred in Early Eighteenth-Century England," *Church History* 84.3 (2015): 556–584.

[7] Sirota, "Nelson's *Festivals and Fasts*," 568.

annual round of public services with the sanctity of personal piety and individual conduct.

Nelson treats each of the Prayer Book observances in a series of questions and answers that begin with what is known about the saint or the event to which the day or the occasion is devoted. On the basis of the information expounded in his answers, he goes on to ask what moral precepts can be learned from the exposition, what qualities it brings to light, what ways there are to acquire and exemplify them. Every exercise concludes with prayers; typically, with the collect from the Prayer Book, followed by newly composed prayers that dwell on the aspects of holy living that have been discussed. Dr. Johnson may not have had his facts quite in order when he said in 1776 that Nelson's was the best-selling book after the Bible,[8] but *Festivals and Fasts* was still being sold well into the nineteenth century. By then it had been adapted for use in the United States, where the Protestant Episcopal Church was using its own version of the Book of Common Prayer.

Alternative Prayer Books

Nelson and Howell found in the text of the Book of Common Prayer a source sufficient and more than sufficient for personal religion. Their aim was not to replace the statutory liturgy, but to extend and mediate the meanings and values that infuse its forms of public worship. Nor did they attempt to improve those forms. Others did. The golden age of the Prayer Book saw the publication of dozens of proposals for revising it, and more than a few complete rewrites. Two of these will illustrate two rather different ways in which the enlightened eighteenth century understood the purpose of the liturgy the Church of England had inherited and how that purpose might be better served.

---

[8] James Boswell, *Life of Samuel Johnson* (London: Routlege, 1867), 252.

The Primitive Standard

No document had a more profound effect on eighteenth-century liturgical thought than the so-called *Apostolic Constitutions*.[9] It is now believed to have been written toward the end of the fourth century, but it claims to be an authentic repository of rules, instructions, and teachings delivered by Christ's own apostles. Among those who took the claim at face value was William Whiston, professor of mathematics in the University of Cambridge, who made the first English translation. For Whiston the *Constitutions* were nearly as authoritative as scripture itself, and in one important respect they were more informative. The New Testament says almost nothing about how the earliest Christians conducted baptism or celebrated the Eucharist: the *Apostolic Constitutions* include detailed liturgical texts.

Whiston was sure that the Church of England would do well to acknowledge the unsurpassable authority of those texts by adopting them forthwith, just as they stood, in place of the Prayer Book. If, however, church authorities "dare not yet venture to return entirely and at once to our original Christianity, and the Apostolical Constitutions themselves," he was ready with a less radical alternative: a complete liturgy of his own devising, which modifies the contents of the Book of Common Prayer to make them more consistent with Christian origins.[10]

---

[9] On the impact of the (re)publication of the *Apostolic Constitutions* in 1672 see Leonel L. Mitchell, "The Influence of the Rediscovery of the Liturgy of *Apostolic Constitutions* on the Nonjurors," *Ecclesia Orans* 13.2 (1996): 207–221; Paul F. Bradshaw, *The Search for the Origins of Christian Worship*, 2nd ed. (Oxford: Oxford University Press, 2002), 1–20; and R. C. D. Jasper, *The Search for an Apostolic Liturgy: A Brief Survey of the Work of British Scholars on the Origins of the Eucharistic Liturgy* (Alcuin Club; London: A. R. Mowbray, 1963).

[10] William Whiston, *The Liturgy of the Church of England, Reduc'd nearer to the Primitive Standard* (London, 1713), sig A3 *verso*. The text of the Communion office (only) is printed in W. Jardine Grisbrooke, *Anglican Liturgies of the Seventeenth and Eighteenth Centuries* (London: SPCK, 1958), 249–261.

The existing Prayer Book, viewed in the light of the *Apostolic Constitutions*, was in Whiston's judgment unsound. The *Constitutions* prove, among other things, that liturgies for "churching" women or for "solemnizing" marriage contracts have no apostolic authority. They prove that baptism should be administered only to "such as are of riper years," that it should be administered only after catechesis, not before, and that confirmation should follow at once. And they prove that sacrifice, oblation, and the presence of Christ, all of which were done away with when the office of Holy Communion was revised in 1552, were all genuinely primitive and intrinsic to "our original Christianity." To remedy these and other imperfections Whiston compiled *The Liturgy of the Church of England, Reduc'd nearer to the Primitive Standard*. Like most revisers of the Book of Common Prayer, he kept as much of its familiar phrasing as he could, as long as it agreed with the primitive doctrines that inform the *Apostolic Constitutions*.

Of those doctrines, much the most important had recently been expounded by his friend the redoubtable Samuel Clarke in "the great theological work of the century,"[11] *The Scripture-Doctrine of the Trinity*. Clarke contended that Christianity's original teaching about God was not the teaching of the so-called Athanasian Creed. There are not, that is, three distinct, equally divine persons who are one and the same deity, for neither the Son of God nor the Holy Spirit, as the primitive church conceived them, is on a par with God the Father. To the contrary, their being is derivative and their operations are auxiliary. According to Clarke, therefore, the original, normative doctrine of the Trinity was what theologians would now classify as a species of subordinationism.

To prove his point Clarke examined more than a twelve hundred biblical texts, and went on to present a catalogue of passages from the Book of Common Prayer which showed that his position

---

[11] A. Elliott Peaston, *The Prayer Book Reform Movement in the XVIIIth Century* (Oxford: Basil Blackwell, 1940), 5.

had the support of the church's official language—with certain exceptions. Those exceptions Whiston dealt with in his *Liturgy Reduc'd*, which was published in the following year. Under the guidance of the *Apostolic Constitutions*, he brought the Prayer Book fully into line with Clarke.[12] Among other things, Whiston found it necessary to eliminate the Athanasian Creed entirely, and to bowdlerize the Nicene Creed and the *Gloria Patri*. On the positive side, he composed a remarkable new collect for Trinity Sunday:

> O God, who by thy dear Son Jesus Christ, our Lord, and by thy blessed Spirit, the Comforter, hast united us unto thy holy Church; and who hast appointed Baptism unto the name of the Father, the Son, and the Holy Ghost; Grant that we may live agreeably to our Christian Profession; and that we may pay the highest praises, and humblest Adoration to thy divine Majesty, the most sincere Obedience to the sacred Laws of thy Son, and the most ready compliance with the holy motions of thy good Spirit; till we at length arrive safely at the haven of eternal life: through our Lord and Saviour Jesus Christ. *Amen.*[13]

This stately collect encapsulates what Whiston believed to be authentic, primitive Christian doctrine. It presents God's Son and God's Spirit as divine agencies that make a difference in the world, but no difference in God as such. What is owed to them, accordingly, is obedience and compliance, but not the praise and adoration that belong only to deity. Whiston's Trinity is thus a functional or "economic" Trinity, rather than the "immanent," coequal

---

[12] On Clarke's liturgical views, see Stephen Hampton, *Anti-Arminians: The Anglican Reformed Tradition from Charles II to George I* (Oxford: Oxford Univeristy Press, 2008), ch. 5, esp. 179–183. On Clarke and Whiston, see Bryan Spinks, *Liturgy in the Age of Reason: Worship and Sacraments in England and Scotland, 1662–c. 1800* (Farnham, UK: Ashgate Publishing, 2008), 136–139; and Philip Dixon, *Nice and Hot Disputes: The Doctrine of the Trinity in the Seventeenth Century* (London: T. & T. Clark, 2003), 31, 180–183.

[13] Whiston, *Liturgy Reduc'd*, sig. F4.

Trinity of Athanasian orthodoxy. Today this might be an acceptable way to conceive divine triplicity, but at the time it was not. It was heresy, and for promulgating it Whiston was expelled from his professorship.

Rational Liturgy

Probably the most extensive and influential eighteenth-century argument for revising the Book of Common Prayer was published in 1749 as part of a miscellaneous volume of *Free and Candid Disquisitions Relating to the Church of England*.[14] It takes the form of pragmatic, particular "queries and observations," concerned for the most part with aspects of Divine Service. Is not common prayer on Sunday longer than it needs to be? Would not Morning Prayer be enough? Are not all the necessary modes of prayer represented already, in that one office? Might not some of the more offensive Psalms, 109 for example, be left unsaid? Does not the kalendar's regimented, chapter-by-chapter scheme assign lessons with awkward endings, unintelligible beginnings, and great disparities in length? Could not the Athanasian Creed be left unrecited, not because it is erroneous but because it is incomprehensible? Would not the collects have been "brought to the utmost perfection" if the revisions proposed by the royal commission of 1689 had been adopted? And should not all of the commission's proposals be made public?

Free and Candid Disquisitions provoked lively debate. Soon afterward it was saluted on the first page of a small book entitled *A New Form of Common-Prayer*, which went on to address its queries in the concrete form of an improved liturgy. According to

---

[14] *Free and Candid Disquisitions Relating to the Church of England, and the Means of Advancing Religion therein* (London: A. Millar, 1749). There were evidently several contributors; John Jones, a Welsh Anglican clergyman (1700–1770), is now credited with compiling the book as a whole.

the anonymous author, "a Clergyman of the Church of England," it was high time for the Reformation to be finished and perfected, now that "the sad distinctions of High and Low Church are laid aside" and minds are "calmed and disposed to listen to the Voice of Reason." To that end, he humbly commits his proposals to the patronage of the archbishop of Canterbury for presentation to the king. He may have been laughing up the sleeve of his rochet, since it is fairly certain that *A New Form of Common-Prayer* was the invention of Thomas Herring—the archbishop of Canterbury.[15]

Herring reportedly praised the Book of Common Prayer as "the incomparable liturgy with which the wisdom of our legislature has endowed us."[16] If he did, its incomparability did not keep him from overhauling it. As contrasted with Whiston's deference to primitive precedent, however, Herring declines to rely on any authority, ancient or modern. The criteria of antiquity and universal practice, he says, "are of no force against plain Reasoning."[17] His own reasoning calls for two unified Sunday services, morning and evening. Morning Prayer begins as usual, with sentences, exhortation, and so on. The first change appears in the confession of sin, which omits the acknowledgment that "there is no health in us." "It is confessing too much," Herring's preface explains. "We cannot but be sensible of our own Wickedness and Depravity; but there's no Occasion to say, we are worse than we really are."[18]

With the Psalms, which come next, Herring gets down to work. His ingenious and radical scheme solves all at once the various difficulties that beset the Prayer Book method of recitation. The

---

[15] *A New Form of Common-Prayer, with the Offices thereto belonging; To which are prefixed, Reasons for the Proposed Alterations: Humbly Addressed to His Grace the Lord Archbishop of Canterbury* (London, 1753), 6 (first pagination). The attribution to Herring is widely accepted, but has not gone unchallenged.

[16] Gregory Dix, *The Shape of the Liturgy* (Westminster: Dacre Press, 1945), 695. The quotation, for which Dix gives no source, has proved to be elusive, but "incomparable" was a favorite eulogism for the Prayer Book.

[17] *A New Form of Common-Prayer*, 25.

[18] *New Form of Common-Prayer*, 3 (second pagination).

monthly cycle is abandoned, and everything in the Psalter that could reasonably be objected to is eliminated. From what is left— a few whole Psalms and inoffensive parts of others—Herring assembles twenty-four bricolages. Three of them are to be recited in the morning, the next three in the evening, and so on, day by day; then the series repeats. It takes only four days to recite all of these remodeled "psalms," but in the course of four successive Sundays each set of three will be read just once.

A New Form of Common-Prayer has no Second Service as such. Instead, most of the components of ante-Communion are reassigned. The Collect for Purity, the Ten Commandments, and the Nicene Creed move to Morning Prayer; on Sunday the whole chapter from which the Prayer Book's liturgical gospel is taken becomes the second lesson; similarly, the chapter that includes the epistle is the second lesson in the evening. There is no kalendar, and no need for one, because the Prayer Book table of proper Old Testament lessons covers all the Sundays, and on weekdays there are no lessons at all. Herring says they make the service too long for men of business; besides, people can read their Bibles at home.

What remains in the Lord's Supper, when it is celebrated in full, is the prayer for the whole state of the church, the comfortable words, and a consecration prayer, which Herring, like many revisers before and since, felt compelled to adjust. Whereas the Prayer Book text asks that those who receive the sacrament may be partakers of Christ's body and blood, the prayer in *A New Form* asks that they may be "partakers of his Benefits purchased for us by his offering up of his body upon the Cross." Lest there be any uncertainty about the import of this altered wording, Herring's preface explains that the true doctrine of the Lord's Supper is Zwingli's: "there is nothing but bread and wine that is given and received," and these are symbols or signs only.[19] In keeping with this doctrine, which Herring says is "now generally received by the present members of our church," the

---

[19] *New Form of Common-Prayer*, 91–92, 26.

second half of each administration formula is to be said without the first (see Table 6.1) and addressed to communicants in the plural (*you*, not *thee*).

The premise from which many of Herring's revisions follow comes to light most clearly in his Catechism. A doctrine that is irrational, in the sense of self-contradictory, can have no claim on religious belief enlightened by plain reason. Nor should anyone believe a doctrine or teaching of the church simply because the church teaches it; there must be intelligent reasons for deciding to believe. Thus candidates for Confirmation should be expected to do more than recite a creed by rote: they must be prepared to give rational arguments, grounded in evidence, that establish the coherence—and thus the truth—of doctrinal propositions, beginning with the existence and attributes of God. Judged by the same criteria, Zwinglian eucharistic teaching, which is perfectly clear and reasonable, deserves to be believed, but transubstantiation and consubstantiation, which are both unintelligible, do not. For Herring, it would seem that what rules out belief in Christ's presence is not the word of God so much as the voice of reason.

The Prayer Book Modified

Whiston's reduction and Herring's redaction of the Book of Common Prayer were never much more than paper rites. To use them in public worship was unlawful. Whiston may have used his liturgy in private services, but if *A New Form of Common-Prayer* was ever put into practice there seems to be no record of it. The same is true of other eighteenth-century proposals to remodel the statutory liturgy, with one important exception. On the fringes of the ecclesiastical establishment, the Prayer Book service of Holy Communion did change. It changed little by little, within a community of Anglicans estranged from the state churches of England and Scotland. They were never numerous. In England their separated church faded away. Nevertheless, the liturgical tradition inaugurated and sustained by the nonjurors, as they are known, had lasting effects, first in Scotland, then in America, and later elsewhere.

Nonjurors and Their Liturgy

From their own standpoint, it would be better to call the nonjurors nonperjurers. They declined to take an oath that would falsify the oath they had already sworn to uphold King James II and VII. True, he had taken his leave in the Revolution of 1688; but until such time as he formally abdicated, which he had not done and never did, James was still, by divine right, king of England and Scotland. Nonjurors might not approve of his person or his policies, but it would be a morally reprehensible lie for them to swear allegiance to William of Orange and Mary Stuart as legitimate sovereigns. For refusing to do so, the archbishop of Canterbury, seven other English bishops, the whole Scottish episcopate, and hundreds of priests and deacons were evicted from their ecclesiastical posts.[20]

In England the original nonjurors regarded themselves, not the institution from which they were separated, as the true church. To prove it, they conformed scrupulously to the Book of Common Prayer. From a legal standpoint, however, they were no different from tolerated nonconformists, and as such there was nothing to stop them from changing the Anglican liturgy. Eventually some of them changed it. After the last of the deprived bishops died in 1710,

---

[20] Note that King William disestablished the entire episcopal church in Scotland, and that three of the nonjuring English bishops died before the expulsion. For more nuanced statements of the nonjurors' self-assessment, which varied, see Mark Goldie, "The Nonjurors, Episcopacy, and the Origins of the Convocation Controversy," in *Ideology and Conspiracy: Aspects of Jacobitism, 1689–1759*, ed. Eveline Cruickshanks (Edinburgh: J. Donald; Atlantic Highlands, NJ: Humanities Press, 1982), 15–35, esp. 20–22; and Gerald M. Straka, *Anglican Reaction to the Revolution of 1688* (Madison: The State Historical Society of Wisconsin, 1962), esp. 29–44.

many nonjurors returned to the established church, but others held out, and a number of them became nonconformists in fact as well as law. They had come to regard the Prayer Book's Communion office as woefully inadequate by comparison with ancient liturgies, and to remedy its defects they produced a liturgy of their own.

This subset of nonjurors, known as usagers, centered their criticism on four practices, the "greater usages," which they held to be essential but which had been missing from the English liturgy since 1552. The Communion office had no admixture, no addition of water to the sacramental wine; there were no prayers for the faithful departed; and in what was left of the canon there was no oblation of the bread and wine, and no invocation that asked God to sanctify them with his Spirit. All four of these usages had been prescribed in the original English Communion office, which in that respect was much closer to primitive liturgies than the currently authorized version. In 1717 the office of 1549 was printed on its own in a pamphlet, which was evidently intended for liturgical use, and most likely for the use of nonjuring congregations.[21]

Yet even in its original form, the Prayer Book service did not entirely satisfy the usagers' requirements. The rite prescribed in 1549 had a canon in which there were prayers of invocation and oblation as well as an institution narrative: so far, so good. But these essential prayers were not prescribed in the essential order, which for usagers was the order exhibited in ancient Eastern liturgies. By comparison with such a rite as one in the *Apostolic Constitutions*, the canon in the 1549 Prayer Book was confused and it failed to express adequately what the Christian Eucharist is and means and does.

Usagers conceived the meaning of the Eucharist in terms of sacrifice as well as sacrament. On the analysis of primitive liturgies from which they took their theological bearings, the bread and wine are

---

[21] *The Form and Manner of Consecrating and Administring the Holy Communion, according to the Liturgy of King Edward VI. Called The Book of Common Prayer, And Administration of the Sacraments and Other Rites and Ceremonies of the Church, After The Use of the Church of England* (London: H. Parker, for J. Morphew, 1717).

not only "outward and visible signs" but also an offering, an oblation. The logic implicit in those liturgies is not, however, that bread
and wine are offered to God because—and therefore after—they
have been consecrated as Christ's representative body and blood.
That is a mistake which even the first Book of Common Prayer had
perpetuated. Rightly understood, what happens in the Eucharist
happens almost the other way around. Bread and wine are not
consecrated in order to be offered: offering is what consecrates
them. That is why ancient eucharistic rites place the invocation of
God's Spirit at the culmination of the central prayer or canon, not at
the beginning. For only when a material offering has been (1) *designated* as such, in a narrative of institution, and (2) given over or
presented as an offering, in a prayer oblation—only then, not before, is it appropriate to pray, in (3) an invocation, that the whole act
of offering may be *blessed and sanctified*.

That is the essential order: institution, oblation, invocation. Even
the canon in the 1549 Prayer Book, although it has these three
constituents, mixes them up. An invocation of divine blessing and
sanctification (3) is recited at the outset; but at that point, the institution narrative (1) has not yet identified what God is being asked
to bless. Nor has the offering yet been presented, in the prayer of
oblation (2), for divine blessing.

The details of this analysis are less important, for present
purposes, than its recognition that the formal organization of a
liturgy, its cumulative order or "shape," is as much an exponent
of meaning as are its component expressions. Because usagers
believed that the right order of the sacramental prayer is a matter
of first importance, and because neither the original nor, much
less, the current Book of Common Prayer followed that order, they
devised a rite that did follow it.[22] Much of this rite's wording comes

---

[22] *A Communion Office, Taken Partly from Primitive Liturgies, And Partly from the
First English Reformed Common-Prayer-Book: Together with Offices for Confirmation,
and the Visitation of the Sick* (London: printed for James Bettenham, 1718); text of the
Communion rite (only) in Grisbrooke, *Anglican Liturgies*, 273–296.

from the first Book of Common Prayer. The central eucharistic prayer, however, not only parallels the form and content of ancient rites, but copies its oblation and invocation from the *Apostolic Constitutions.*

The nonjurors' Communion office, published in 1718, did not commend itself to all nonjurors. On the contrary, it widened the rift in their little church between nonusagers, who still regarded the 1662 Prayer Book as adequate to its purpose, and usagers, who did not. Probably because the new office would be divisive in Scotland as well, the Scottish bishops—nonjurors one and all—declined to give it their formal approval, although two of them had collaborated in compiling it. But while Scottish episcopalians may not have made much use of the nonjurors' office as such, the structure of that office did take root in Scotland, and with it the eucharistic theology it expressed.

The Scottish Communion Office

At the time of the nonjuring fracture, episcopalians in Scotland were generally not accustomed to using a scripted liturgy; their services were somewhat more formal than those of Scottish presbyterians, but otherwise much the same. In the years following King William's disestablishment of the episcopal church, the Book of Common Prayer came into use, especially in congregations with "qualified" ministers who had taken the required oaths. Hundreds of Prayer Books were donated by sympathetic English individuals and institutions, among them William's successor Queen Anne, and editions were printed in Scotland.[23]

---

[23] See Tristram Clarke, "Politics and Prayer Books: The Book of Common Prayer in Scotland c. 1705–1714," *Transactions of the Edinburgh Bibliographical Society* 6.2 (1993): 57–70; Griffiths, *Bibliography*, 140–141, entries 1710/7, 1712/6.

As in England, there were nonjuring episcopalians in Scotland who were dissatisfied with the Communion office in the statutory Book of Common Prayer and who would have preferred an alternative. In a sense, they had one already. The Scottish Prayer Book of 1637 had never been formally abolished, and in it, as one bishop pointed out, were two, at least, of the "greater usages," namely the invocation and what its text explicitly refers to as the memorial or prayer of oblation.[24] Some of the bishops allowed their clergy to use this rite, and in 1712 it had been reprinted.

The reprinting was financed by the earl of Winton, who later took up arms in support of King James's son, the Old Pretender, in his campaign to reclaim the throne. The earl's Jacobite sympathies may explain why the Winton Prayer Book does not name the reigning sovereign—whoever that was. Instead, it reproduces, word for word, the text that had been issued in 1637 when Charles I was king. Whose name was actually spoken by ministers who used the Winton edition is not recorded.[25] In any case there were no further reprints, partly, it seems, because after Queen Anne's death in 1714 civil authorities would expect the state prayers to be updated with the name of King George, derided as "the wee wee German lairdie" by Jacobites, who staunchly refused to pray for him. Partly too, and maybe more importantly, the disestablished episcopal church was poor and printing a whole Prayer Book would be costly.

What did appear in print, by itself, was the second part of the Scottish Prayer Book's service of Holy Communion. It appeared in 1722, if not earlier, in the shape of "wee bookies," twenty-four-page pamphlets entitled *The Communion Office For the Use of the*

---

[24] Archibald Campbell, May 27, 1720, quoted from manuscript in John Dowden, *The Scottish Communion Office 1764 with Introduction, History of the Office, Notes and Appendices*, new rev. ed. (Oxford: Oxford University Press, 1922), 61–62. Bishop Campbell was one of the collaborators in the compilation of the 1718 nonjurors' Communion office.

[25] On this reprint, referred to at the time as "Bishop Laud's Common Prayer Book," see Clarke, "Politics and Prayer Books" 66; Dowden, *Scottish Communion Office*, 46–48. The idea that the Winton Prayer Book was merely an antiquarian curiosity seems to be negatived by the fact that 1,500 copies were printed.

Church of Scotland, As far as concerneth the Ministration of that Holy Sacrament. The bookies were cheap; they did not name the king, one way or the other; and they made available that part of the Prayer Book for Scotland which differed most significantly, as chapter seven has discussed, from the version used in England. At a full celebration of Holy Communion, presbyter and people could follow the English Book of Common Prayer as far as the offertory, then switch to their bookies and continue the service according to the Scottish form.

Successive issues of this convenient pamphlet kept the Scottish Communion office in print all through the eighteenth century. The title remained the same, but the text did not: it evolved. Almost from the first, presbyters in Scotland evidently understood their bishops' permission to use the Scottish office as permission to rearrange its parts. They recited the prayers as printed, but not in the printed order. When certain rearrangements became accepted customs, the text in reprinted bookies was rearranged accordingly.

After forty years or so, this largely informal process of experiment and revision arrived at what would be the definitive form of the Communion office, which was published with episcopal endorsement in 1764. Apart from a few phrases, short but important, all of its wording comes from "Laud's Liturgy," the 1637 Prayer Book for Scotland, and thus indirectly from the original Prayer Book of 1549. The structural order, however—and this is the important point—is the same, item for item, as the order in the English nonjurors' office.[26] In its canon, following the institution narrative, it has an emphatic oblation, so named, and then an explicit invocation, likewise so named. In other words, Scottish episcopalians had, if they chose to use it, a prescript liturgy that aligned their celebration of Holy Communion with the "primitive standard" of

---

[26] The most complete *verbatim* genealogy is Philip A. Lempriere, *The Scottish Communion Offices of 1637, 1735, 1755, 1764 and 1889 together with the English Liturgy of 1549 arranged to shew their variations* (Edinburgh: R. Grand & Son, 1909). The parallel with the nonjurors' liturgy is tabulated in *OGBCP*, 173.

ancient Christian liturgies, as known to eighteenth-century liturgical scholarship.

From one point of view the evolution of the Scottish Communion Office is an interesting but minor subplot in the story of the Book of Common Prayer. Unlike most of the liturgies published in the eighteenth century, the wee bookies did see actual use; but the church that used them was small and isolated, and at times it was in danger of vanishing entirely, as its counterpart in England did. From a different point of view, however, the nonjuring Scots can be credited with originating a distinctive offshoot of Anglican liturgy that has grown up alongside the older English branch of Prayer Book tradition. Since 1789, it has flourished in the United States, where it was grafted into the first complete Book of Common Prayer ever used in Anglican public worship without authorization from the English Parliament, the English crown, or the English church.

The American Prayer Book

Although the Book of Common Prayer was originally compiled for the reformed church in England and Wales, it has always been used elsewhere—sporadically in Scotland, here and there in Ireland, in the Channel Islands (translated into French), and in English colonies. In North America it was used more or less widely, depending on the extent of the Church of England's presence, which varied greatly from one colony to another. By the mid-eighteenth century, Sunday services conducted according to the Prayer Book would have resembled the one that was described in chapter one, as far as local circumstances allowed.[27]

Because they were the services of "the king's church," the War of Independence nearly brought them to an end. Some Anglican

---

[27] Marion Hatchett, "A Sunday Service in 1776 or Thereabouts," *Historical Magazine of the Protestant Episcopal Church* 45.4 (1976): 369–385.

clergymen, including many of the missionaries sent from England and supported by the Society for the Propagation of the Gospel, packed up and went home. Some took themselves north, to what is now Canada, along with many loyalist families. Some kept their churches open, adjusting the liturgy to make it politically innocuous. Instead of "O Lord, save the King," one minister was heard to say, "O Lord, save those whom thou hast made it our especial duty to pray for." Where that duty lay, his congregation was left to decide.[28] As many as half the clergy of the king's church may have taken sides with the colonial patriots, among whom were many Anglicans; but even so there was not much of a church left by the end of the war. Whether the remnant would survive, and if it did, how it could best adapt to the new political reality, no one was sure.

Independent American Polity and Prayer

A number of episcopalian congregations, loosely organized within each of the newly independent states, did survive. In order to maintain their institutional identity, their continuity with the Church of England, and their religious and theological difference from other churches, they needed their own liturgy and their own episcopate—properly consecrated bishops and a Book of Common Prayer.

It was obvious that an American Prayer Book would have to be a revision, if only for political reasons, but the revision that was proposed in 1786 went well beyond removing references to the constitution of Great Britain. In its preface, the revisers explain that their intention was to complete the work of "the pious and excellent divines" of the 1689 ecclesiastical commission, "than whom (it hath been truly acknowledged) the Church of England was never,

---

[28] Nancy L. Rhoden, *Revolutionary Anglicanism: The Colonial Church of England Clergy during the American Revolution* (New York: New York University Press, 1999), 108.

at any one time, blessed with either wiser or better, since it was a church."[29] The preface also sets out a catalogue of queries that has been described as an outline of *Free and Candid Disquisitions*.[30] Significant change, not mere adjustment, was clearly what the revisers had in mind.

Queries in the Preface of the American Prayer Book Proposed in 1786

1st. Whether the *public service* on Sunday mornings be not of too *great length*, and tends rather to diminish than encrease devotion, especially among the lukewarm and negligent?

2d. Whether it might not be conveniently *contracted*, by omitting all unnecessary *repetitions* of the same prayers or subject matter; and whether a better adjustment of the necessary parts of the three different services, usually read every Sunday morning in the church, would not render the whole frame of the service more uniform, animated and compleat?

4th. Whether *all the* PSALMS of David are applicable to the state and condition of *christian societies*, and ought to be read *promiscuously*, as they now are; and whether some other method of reading them might not be appointed; including a *choice* of psalms and hymns as well for ordinary use, as for the *festivals* and *fasts*, and other special occasions, of public worship?

5th. Whether the subject matter of our *psalmody* or *singing* psalms should not be extended beyond those of David . . . and whether much excellent matter might not be taken from the

---

[29] *The Book of Common Prayer, And Administration of the Sacraments . . . As revised and proposed to the Use of the Protestant Episcopal Church* (Philadelphia: Hall and Sellers, 1786), sig b3, b2; Paul V. Marshall, *Anglican Liturgy in America: Prayer Book Parallels* (New York: Church Hymnal Corporation, 1989, 1990), I: 67, 63 (corrected).

[30] Marion J. Hatchett, *The Making of the First American Book of Common Prayer* (New York: The Seabury Press, 1982), 76.

New Testament, as well as some parts of the Old Testament, especially the prophets; so as to introduce a greater variety of *anthems* and *hymns* ...?

8th. Whether our epistles and gospels are all of them well selected; and whether after so many other portions of scripture they are necessary ...?

9th. Whether our *collects*, which in the main are excellent, are always suited to the epistles and gospels; ... and whether there is any occasion of using the collect for the day twice in the same service?

10th. Whether the Athanasian creed may not, consistently with *piety, faith* and *charity*, be either wholly omitted, or left indifferent in itself?

11th. Whether our catechism may not require illustration in some points and enlargement in others; so that it may not only be rendered fit for children, but a help to those who become candidates for confirmation? And whether all the other offices, ... and more especially those of baptism, burial and communion, do not call for a review and amendment in sundry particulars?

Their revision, sometimes known as the "southern Prayer Book," met with a cool reception in England. What the bishops who reviewed it had to say, they said in elegant and diplomat terms, but it came down to this: You profess to admire the Book of Common Prayer extravagantly, yet you have performed no little surgery on it, notably by cutting out two of the three creeds and some of the one that remains. If you expect us to consecrate bishops for your church, as you ask us to do, you would do well to reconsider the liturgy you propose to use.[31]

---

[31] On the "southern Prayer Book," which omitted both the Nicene and the Athanasian Creed, see Paul V. Marshall, *One, Catholic, and Apostolic: Samuel Seabury and the Early Episcopal Church* (New York: Church Publishing, 2004), 149–180. The English bishops' recommendations are printed in Marshall, *Parallels*, II: 522–525.

Although four or five thousand copies were printed, this first attempt at revision does not appear to have been used much, except in and around Philadelphia,[32] and in the event the American church did not adopt it as it stood. Three years later, in 1789, a further revision, somewhat less unlike the 1662 Prayer Book, was formally authorized at the General Convention of the newly constituted Protestant Episcopal Church in the United States of America.

Divine Service in America

The representative Sunday service described in chapter one could well have taken place in a colonial church. For anyone who had been present in 1762, Divine Service conducted thirty years later, according to the new American Prayer Book, might have been much the same. Unless it was a Communion Sunday, nearly all the noticeable differences would be abbreviations.

At Morning Prayer, the *Venite* would be shorter. In the American service it switches at the end to verses from another Psalm, which speak of awe and divine judgment, but do so in less forbidding terms than the verses they replace. Next a portion of the "reading Psalms" might be recited, using the traditional Psalter, according to the day of the month, with the *Gloria Patri* after each. After the first lesson, either *Te Deum* or *Benedicite* would be said; after the second lesson, either *Jubilate* or *Benedictus*, as in the English liturgy. The *Benedictus* ends, however, after only four (of twelve) verses, thereby omitting references to particular events. Similarly, the *Benedicite* leaves out the last verse, which names the three holy children who first sang it (see owc 246, 245). In the *Te Deum* the phrase "thou didst not abhor the Virgin's womb" is changed to "thou didst humble thyself to be born of a Virgin."

---

[32] Marshall, *One, Catholic, and Apostolic*, 166–167. An edition of the "southern Prayer Book" was also printed in England (Griffiths 1789/8).

Before the prayers, only two versicles, with their responses, are said; "O Lord, save the King" and two others are omitted. The collect of the day would ordinarily follow, though not if the morning service will include Communion. The prayer for the King's Majesty is turned into a prayer for the President of the United States and all in authority.

In the Litany there are some tiny amendments, but five supplications are gone—for the king, the royal family, the Lords of the Council and all the nobility—while in another supplication Christian rulers are included together with magistrates.[33]

The Second Service, ante-Communion, would be shorter than it was in 1762. The Lord's Prayer, already said at Morning Prayer, is not repeated at the outset. After the Ten Commandments, instead of a collect for the king, there is a new collect that alludes to divine commandments and laws. After the collect for the day, as usual, the epistle and gospel are read. And there, unless it is a Communion Sunday, the service ends with a blessing.

While the noticeable difference between the 1662 Prayer Book and the American version might be fairly small, the important word is *might*, for the rubrics permit a number of variations and give the minister considerable liberty to choose which of them will be used. The *Gloria Patri* need not be said after every Psalm, but just once for all. In that case, the Greater Doxology, *Gloria in excelsis*, may be used instead. The Psalms need not be recited in order according to the day of the month. The alternative is a set of ten "selections," any one of which may replace the portion assigned in the Psalter. Like the twenty-four "psalms" in Herring's *New Form of Common-Prayer*, the "selections of Psalms" in the first American Prayer Book are composites or centos, abridged and stitched together from about thirty of the canonical Psalms, so as to include nothing unsuitable for Christian worship.

---

[33] Marshall, *Parallels*, I: 136 (Morning Prayer); 192, 194 (Litany).

Another of Herring's proposals was to recite the Nicene rather than the Apostles' Creed at Morning Prayer. The American book allows this substitution. Herring objected to the Apostles' Creed partly because it affirms that after his burial Christ "descended into hell." The Prayer Book translation of this clause was widely agreed to be misleading, and there was some question whether it belonged to the original text of the creed. The "southern Prayer Book" had simply cut it out, to the English bishops' consternation. In 1789 it was put back, although a rubric allows it be omitted, or else replaced by an inelegant periphrasis.

Evening Prayer replicates the structure of Morning Prayer, and the same changes to avoid repeating the Lord's Prayer and the *Gloria Patri* are evident. *Magnificat* and *Nunc dimittis* no longer appear, however, even as options; an unvarying Psalm is appointed after each of the lessons. The third collect is different. Since 1549 it had begun with the words "Lighten our darkness, we beseech thee, O Lord," provoking literalists to complain, because Evensong was said before sundown more often than not. Bishop Wren thought God should be asked to "lighten the darkness . . . that the night will bring upon us." The American Prayer Book, as first proposed, resorted to metaphor: "Enlighten our minds . . . with thy truth." The version ratified in 1789 gives up on light and substitutes a prosaic address to God "by whose almighty power we have been preserved this day." (It would later revert to "Lighten our darkness.")

Turning to the occasional offices, the American Prayer Book shortens the ones most often used, notably the Solemnization of Matrimony. The minister's address no longer explains what marriage is for, and everything that follows the benediction in the middle of the 1662 service is omitted. In the Burial office the Psalms are abridged; at the grave, God is thanked, not for delivering the deceased from this sinful world, but instead for the good examples of all who have finished their course in faith and now rest from their labors. At Baptism the minister may leave out either of two prayers before the lesson, as well as the lesson itself and the prayer that follows it, provided that all these are said at least once every month. Instead of rehearsing the Apostles' Creed, godparents are simply asked whether they believe all its articles.[34]

Needless to say, Americans had no use for the three Stuart State Services or the service for the king's accession day, but there were two analogous civic services in the proposed Prayer Book of 1786. The liturgy for Thanksgiving Day follows the pattern of special forms of prayer that went back to Queen Elizabeth, with proper lessons, collect, epistle, and gospel, and an additional prayer in the Litany. In place of the *Venite* there is an abridgment of Psalm 147, which curiously follows the Authorized Version rather than Coverdale, as printed in the Psalter. For Independence Day, July 4, another special service was proposed, but the Book of Common Prayer adopted in 1789 omits it, perhaps wisely. Many Anglicans, now Episcopalians, had been loyalists during the war, while among those who had favored and fought for independence there were some who nevertheless questioned the appropriateness of a liturgy to celebrate it.[35]

As chapter six pointed out, it was a practice as old as the Book of Common Prayer to supplement it by adding to the authorized text either Godly Prayers or "singing Psalms" or both. These unofficial adjuncts have official counterparts in the first American Prayer Book. For domestic use it provides Forms of Prayer to be Used in Families, similar in many ways to household prayers such as those in Howell's *Common-Prayer-Book the Best Companion*. The two services, morning and evening, are brief, simple, and uneffusive. Rubrics in the margin allow the reader to make small substitutions according to circumstance, and to pause in the confession at the

---

[34] Marshall, *Parallels*, I: 440, 442 (Matrimony); 556 (Burial); 242 (Baptism). See also the illustration in *OGBCP*, 181.

[35] For the text of these two services, Marshall, *Parallels* I 222–228; for one of the prayers in the deleted Independence Day service, see Brian Cummings, *The Book of Common Prayer: A Very Short Introduction* (Oxford: Oxford University Press, 2019), 94.

end of the day so that individuals may particularize it with their own silent prayers.

The metrical Psalter in the American Prayer Book is the *New Version of the Psalms of David*, which by 1789 had largely supplanted Sternhold and Hopkins. A preface echoes Queen Elizabeth's injunction about music by allowing any of these paraphrases to be sung before and after Morning Prayer, Evening Prayer, and sermons, at the minister's discretion. All the Psalms are included, together with a collection of twenty-seven "Hymns, Suited to the Feasts and Fasts of the Church, and Other Occasions of Public Worship," which may claim to be the first authorized Anglican hymnal.

The American Communion Office

Holy Communion, celebrated in full, was as infrequent a service in eighteenth-century North America as it was in England. If the revised Prayer Book proposed in 1786 had been adopted, there would have been scarcely any difference. The prayer for the whole state of the church was altered, of course; "Christian rulers" replaced "Christian Kings, Princes, and Governors," and "thy servant George our King" was not named. A questionable editing of the *Gloria in excelsis* was the most conspicuous change.[36] The prayer of consecration was just the same.

It is not the same at all in the Communion service of the Prayer Book that the American church in fact adopted, and the difference is widely regarded as more important than any other departure from the English liturgy. The American consecration prayer is Scottish. Its wording and even its typography follow the later wee bookies, particularly the one published in 1764. In that recension, indented labels designate *The Oblation* and *The Invocation*; and six words, inserted in small capitals, emphasize that the oblation

[36] Marshall, *Parallels,* I: 342, 374.

WHICH WE NOW OFFER UNTO THEE is to be identified with the gifts of bread and wine. The American Prayer Book of 1789 reproduces these details, which can all be seen in Figure 9.1.

How and why this prayer made its way from Scotland to the United States is in some respects an open question. A number of Scottish clergymen ministered in the American colonies; some of them may well have known and used one or another of the wee bookies. Perhaps more directly relevant, though, is an American bookie printed in 1786 with the title *The Communion-Office, or Order for the Administration of the Holy Eucharist . . . Recommended to the Episcopal Congregations in Connecticut, by the Right Reverend Bishop Seabury.*[37]

Samuel Seabury is now reckoned the first bishop of the Episcopal Church. At the time, some Episcopalians questioned whether he was a bishop at all. He had been elected by the clergy of Connecticut and then consecrated, as the Ordinal in the Prayer Book requires, by three bishops; but the bishops were nonjuring Scots. The hope had been that he would be consecrated in England, but the bishops there, although they were not unsympathetic, could not dispense with the oath of the king's supremacy (OWC 646, 629–630); nor could Seabury take it again, now that he was an American citizen. In Scotland, the bishops of the disestablished episcopal church did not act as state officials when they conferred holy orders, and they agreed to confer the episcopate on Seabury.

The day after he was consecrated, the new bishop and his consecrators signed a concordat between his little church in Connecticut and theirs. According to this agreement, Seabury was to review seriously the Communion office which the Scots had adopted; if he found it "agreeable to the genuine standards of antiquity," he was to use "gentle methods of argument and

---

[37] Text in Samuel Hart, *Bishop Seabury's Communion-Office Reprinted in Fac-Simile* (New York: T. Whittaker, 1874) and in Marshall, *Parallels*, II: 489–495; see also Marshall, *One, Catholic, and Apostolic*, 199–202.

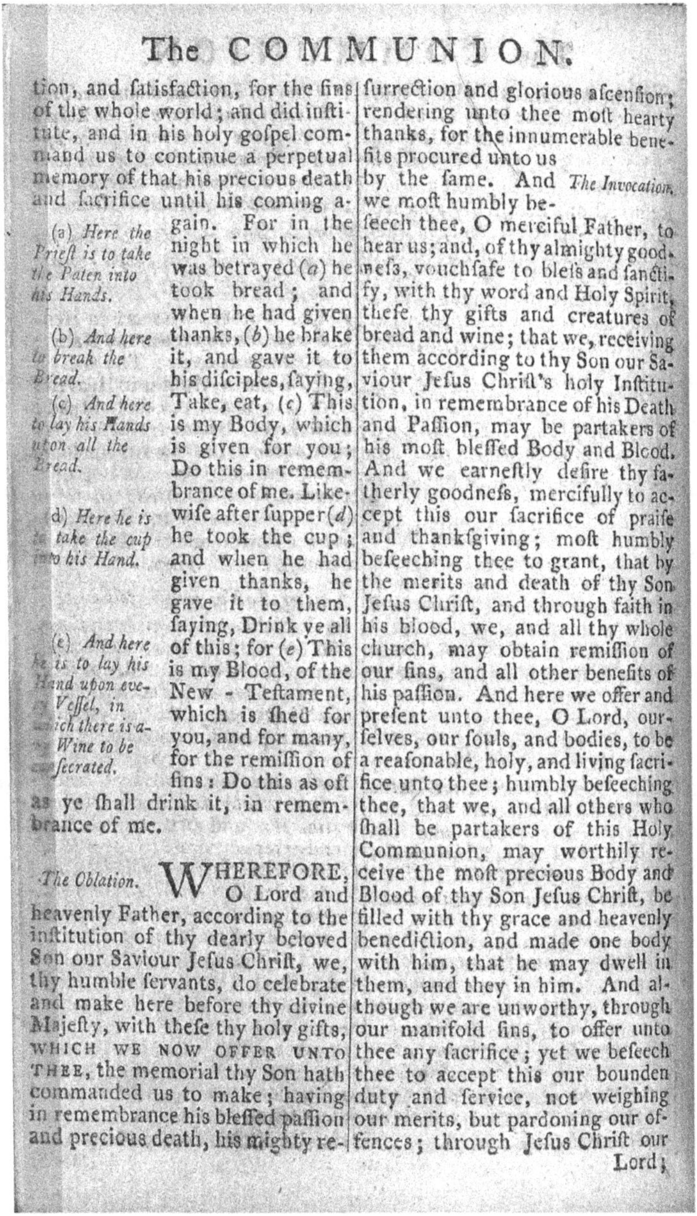

The COMMUNION.

tion, and satisfaction, for the sins of the whole world; and did institute, and in his holy gospel command us to continue a perpetual memory of that his precious death and sacrifice until his coming again. For in the night in which he was betrayed (*a*) he took bread; and when he had given thanks, (*b*) he brake it, and gave it to his disciples, saying, Take, eat, (*c*) This is my Body, which is given for you; Do this in remembrance of me. Likewise after supper(*d*) he took the cup; and when he had given thanks, he gave it to them, saying, Drink ye all of this; for (*e*) This is my Blood, of the New - Testament, which is shed for you, and for many, for the remission of sins: Do this as oft as ye shall drink it, in remembrance of me.

(a) Here the Priest is to take the Paten into his Hands.

(b) And here to break the Bread.

(c) And here to lay his Hands upon all the Bread.

(d) Here he is to take the cup into his Hand.

(e) And here he is to lay his Hand upon every Vessel, in which there is a Wine to be consecrated.

The Oblation. WHEREFORE, O Lord and heavenly Father, according to the institution of thy dearly beloved Son our Saviour Jesus Christ, we, thy humble servants, do celebrate and make here before thy divine Majesty, with these thy holy gifts, WHICH WE NOW OFFER UNTO THEE, the memorial thy Son hath commanded us to make; having in remembrance his blessed passion and precious death, his mighty resurrection and glorious ascension; rendering unto thee most hearty thanks, for the innumerable benefits procured unto us by the same. And *The Invocation.* we most humbly beseech thee, O merciful Father, to hear us; and, of thy almighty goodness, vouchsafe to bless and sanctify, with thy word and Holy Spirit, these thy gifts and creatures of bread and wine; that we, receiving them according to thy Son our Saviour Jesus Christ's holy Institution, in remembrance of his Death and Passion, may be partakers of his most blessed Body and Blood. And we earnestly desire thy fatherly goodness, mercifully to accept this our sacrifice of praise and thanksgiving; most humbly beseeching thee to grant, that by the merits and death of thy Son Jesus Christ, and through faith in his blood, we, and all thy whole church, may obtain remission of our sins, and all other benefits of his passion. And here we offer and present unto thee, O Lord, ourselves, our souls, and bodies, to be a reasonable, holy, and living sacrifice unto thee; humbly beseeching thee, that we, and all others who shall be partakers of this Holy Communion, may worthily receive the most precious Body and Blood of thy Son Jesus Christ, be filled with thy grace and heavenly benediction, and made one body with him, that he may dwell in them, and they in him. And although we are unworthy, through our manifold sins, to offer unto thee any sacrifice; yet we beseech thee to accept this our bounden duty and service, not weighing our merits, but pardoning our offences; through Jesus Christ our Lord;

Figure 9.1 "Scottish" Prayer of Consecration in the First American Prayer Book

Printed at Philadelphia by Hall & Sellers, 1790.

Courtesy of the Beinecke Rare Books Library, Yale University.

persuasion . . . to introduce it by degrees into practice."[38] It was this office, slightly modified, that he brought out in print and recommended to his congregations not long after his return to America.

The first bishop of Connecticut had indeed come to regard the consecration prayer in the Scottish office as fulfilling an essential purpose that the prayer in the 1662 Prayer Book fulfilled imperfectly at best. At the General Convention in 1789, Seabury was asked to consecrate the elements at Holy Communion. Twice he declined. "To confess the truth," he reportedly said, smiling, "I hardly consider the form to be used"—the 1662 form—"as strictly amounting to a consecration."[39] Exactly what happened later in the Convention, when it ratified the American church's Book of Common Prayer, has been interpreted differently by different scholars; but the proposal to adopt the Scottish form of the consecration prayer that was in fact adopted came from the House of Bishops, which is as much as to say it came from Seabury.[40]

As adopted, the American prayer does not match exactly either Seabury's own Communion office or the wee bookie he drew on. The most significant difference concerns the much-debated invocation. Its location within the American prayer is the same as in the Scottish Communion Office—after the institution narrative and the oblation, not before—but its wording follows the classical English Prayer Book: it asks that those who receive the consecrated elements may be partakers of Christ's body and blood (see Table 5.3). The prayer Seabury recommended to his clergy

---

[38] Text of the concordat, Marshall, *Parallels*, II: 485–487.

[39] William White, *Memoirs of the Protestant Episcopal Church in the United States of America*, 2nd ed. (New York: Swords, Stanford, and Co., 1836), 155. Bishop White wrote his memoir long after the fact.

[40] There were two other American bishops in 1789, both consecrated in England. One of them was absent. The other, William White (see previous note), was more or less indifferent, although Paul Marshall points out that he "insisted into his last years that the prayer does not mean what it says" (*One, Catholic, and Apostolic*, 21; also 249–255). For an earlier and somewhat different account see Hatchett, *First American Book of Common Prayer*, 107–115.

had asked that the bread and wine might *become* Christ's body and blood. So strong a word may have been thought, understandably, to verge on transubstantiation.

In the end, the prayer in the first American Book of Common Prayer may not have been all that the first American bishop could have wished. It might not have satisfied the nonjurors in every respect. But it did introduce an authorized liturgical expression of the meaning of Holy Communion that came to be widely admired, accepted, and emulated. In the United States, many Episcopalians have agreed with one of Seabury's successors as bishop of Connecticut, who said of this prayer that "in giving it to us, Scotland gave us a greater boon than when she gave us the Episcopate."[41]

---

[41] The Bishop of Connecticut [John Williams], "The Scottish Communion Office," *American Church Review* 39.138 (July, 1882): 1–18 at 18.

Ten

Recessional

Golden ages never last. The gold gives way to silver, silver to bronze. Some such image of decline could be, and has been, used to describe the fortunes of the Book of Common Prayer since the end of the golden eighteenth century. "By the end of the nineteenth century the Church of England was in liturgical chaos,"[1] and by the end of the twentieth the Prayer Book itself had been cashiered, in England and everywhere else. What was once a sacred text was sacred no longer. The community of faith and worship it had identified chose not to be identified with it.

A narrative constructed on those lines would need a good deal of qualification. Public worship was probably no more chaotic in the Victorian than in the Elizabethan church. Nor has the classical Book of Common Prayer vanished altogether. It is still in print and it is still used, or some of it is, in some places. That being said, it would also be fair to say that what made this text a center of devotional gravity, the measure and expression of a characteristic religious ethos, has largely faded. The Book of Common Prayer remains a venerable book, but it is probably venerated more for what it has been than for what it still is.

Designed as it was on the one-size-fits-all principle—"but one use" for "all the whole realm"—the Prayer Book never fitted everyone exactly. In 1800, however, the consensus in England was that no one but dissenters from the established church would find it so uncomfortable as to require major alterations. An Anglican church

---

[1] Nigel Yates, *Buildings, Faith and Worship: The Liturgical Arrangement of Anglican Churches 1600–1900*, rev. ed. (Oxford: Oxford University Press, 2000), 147.

The Book of Common Prayer. Charles Hefling, Oxford University Press (2021). © Oxford University Press. DOI: 10.1093/oso/9780190689681.001.0001.

used the Book of Common Prayer, with such variations as its rubrics permitted; otherwise it would not be an Anglican church. By maintaining uniformity in its liturgical practice, the church at large was limiting its own comprehensiveness, but without the limits it set, it would lose its identity.

For most of the nineteenth century and much of the twentieth, the pressures which strained those limits did not come, as they had done before the Toleration Act of 1689, from eager protestants who found the Prayer Book insufficiently reformed. "Evangelical" Anglicans, heirs of the puritans, were for the most part content with things as they stood.[2] The pressure came instead from the other end of the ecclesiastical spectrum—from high-church Anglicans who found the Prayer Book insufficiently catholic. When a royal commission famously reported at the beginning of the twentieth century that "the law of public worship in the Church of England is too narrow for the religious life of the present generation," its statement was understood to be an acknowledgment that "Anglo-catholicism" had come to stay, and that something would have to be done to accommodate it. More and more of what was going on in public worship went on in disregard or defiance of the prescriptions of the Book of Common Prayer; and while by no means all the aberration was the result of what came to be called the catholic revival within Anglicanism—evangelicals evaded the rubrics too—Anglo-catholic novelties were the most neuralgic. How to cope with them was a problem that had vexed, and would continue to vex, not only the Church of England but every other Anglican church in so far as it defined itself in part by the Book of Common Prayer.

The aforementioned royal commission issued its report in 1906. In response, measures were taken to address the problem it diagnosed. The upshot of those measures would be such that 1906 dates the dénouement in Bryan Spinks's recent account of *The Rise*

---

[2] See Grayson Carter, *Anglican Evangelicals: Protestant Secessions from the* Via Media, *c. 1800–1850* (Oxford: Oxford University Press, 2001), 14–15.

and Fall of the Incomparable Liturgy.[3] Not that the classical Prayer Book collapsed all of a sudden. Its breakdown went on for most of the twentieth century. How it came about can best be understood by surveying what had happened in the previous hundred years or so.

Anglicans as Catholic

To its adherents, the Anglo-catholic movement was a revival; to its opponents, a recrudescence. At issue was the character and constitution of the form of Christianity to which Anglicanism was committed by its history, its magisterial teachers, and its foundational texts, one of which was the Book of Common Prayer. The interpretation of these authorities that was propagated by the *Tracts for the Times*—the charter of the Oxford Movement, which gave rise to Anglo-catholicism—was not a new interpretation. Or so the writers and their supporters insisted. Tractarians, as adherents of the movement were called, claimed that they were only foregrounding what the previous century had allowed to fade into the background: the genuinely Anglican practice and teaching of the "Caroline" divines of the seventeenth century, which in turn had been the Christianity of the early, undivided, and in that sense catholic church. As it presented itself, in other words, the Oxford Movement took its stand on tradition and continuity. In fact, its achievements brought about "one of the most significant discontinuities in the history of Anglicanism."[4]

Discontinuity was most conspicuous, and for present purposes most important, in the conduct of public worship. First-generation

---

[3] Bryan D. Spinks, *The Rise and Fall of the Incomparable Liturgy: The Book of Common Prayer, 1559–1906* (London: SPCK, 2017).

[4] Peter B. Nockles, "Survivals or New Arrivals? The Oxford Movement and the Nineteenth-Century Historical Construction of Anglicanism," in *Anglicanism and the Western Christian Tradition: Continuity, Change and the Search for Communion*, ed. Stephen Platten (Norwich: Canterbury Press, 2003), 144–191 at 183.

Tractarians valued the Book of Common Prayer for its rein-
forcement of catholic doctrine. Accordingly they insisted, as the
Laudians had done, that its prescriptions should be followed completely and exactly.[5] But it was not long before a second generation,
wryly called subtractarians, began to change the look of the Prayer
Book services, and with it their meaning, by introducing props,
costumes, and ceremonies for which there was no explicit warrant
in the rubrics and no precedent in Anglican tradition.

Whether this "ritualist" phase of the catholic revival was a natural, inevitable development of the original Tractarian impulse is a
disputed question. What seems clear is that many ritualists valued
ritual, not simply as a devotional corollary of religious doctrine accepted on other grounds, but as itself a sort of nonverbal teaching,
addressed to sense, feeling, and imagination more than to understanding and intellectual assent.[6] Affinities to romanticism in
nineteenth-century art and literature have often been pointed out,
with good reason.

Ritualist innovations may or may not have been defensible on
pastoral or psychological or apologetical grounds. They were in any
case perceived as assaults on the protestant character of Anglican
religion. Ritualists brought back "scenic apparatus" that had not
been on show in the Church of England for three hundred years
or more. They put on colored stoles, chasubles, and the whole
pre-Reformation panoply; they set lighted candles on what they
preferred to call the altar while they said what they preferred to
call Mass, and they said it facing east instead of standing "at the
north end" as the Prayer Book directs. They mixed water with

---

[5] On the doctrinal emphases of early Tractarianism, and its connection with the
Book of Common Prayer, see Nockles, "Survivals or New Arrivals?," 149–150; and
R. C. D. Jasper, "The Prayer Book in the Victorian Era," in *The Victorian Crisis of Faith*,
ed. Anthony Symondson (London: SPCK, 1970), 107–121 at 110–111.

[6] See George Herring, "Devotional and Liturgical Renewal: Ritualism and Protestant
Reaction," in *The Oxford Handbook of the Oxford Movement*, ed. Stewart J. Brown, Peter
Nockles, and James Pereiro (Oxford: Oxford University Press, 2017), 398–409, esp. 403–
407; also Herring, *The Oxford Movement in Practice: The Tractarian Parochial World
from the 1830s to the 1870s* (Oxford: Oxford University Press, 2016), 192–194, 208–209.

the sacramental wine, installed credence tables, burned incense, genuflected, blessed persons and things with the sign of the cross, and in general comported themselves as though the Reformation was irrelevant. Their critics, at least, saw them that way. It seemed perfectly obvious that ritualism flouted the provisions of the Book of Common Prayer and that "the law of public worship," civil and ecclesiastical, was being violated.

What seemed perfectly obvious, however, was arguably not perfectly true. A case could be made that the Prayer Book itself, far from ruling out ritualism, ruled it in. The rule was stated in five or six lines of print just before the beginning of Morning Prayer, in the notorious Ornaments Rubric. Ever since it was first included in the Elizabethan Book of Common Prayer, this rubric had required the "ornaments" used in church services to be the ones that Parliament had authorized in the second year of King Edward VI's reign (see Table 6.2). For three centuries no one had worn, on the strength of that requirement, the old eucharistic vestments. But like everything else in the Prayer Book, its rubrics are part of an Act of Parliament, and as such they had to be construed in the same punctilious way any other statutory text would be. Their prescriptions may or may not have been ignored. That was irrelevant. The only relevant question was exactly what the Ornaments Rubric meant. It turned out to be a very intricate question, which there is no need to untangle here. Suffice to say that the Anglo-catholic party insisted they were being loyal to the Prayer Book when they adopted that most symbolically potent "ornament," the chasuble; and that much the same argument would apply to their other practices.[7]

---

[7] Legal arguments are never simple. For two extensive—and irreconcilable—discussions, see the adjacent articles on "Ornaments of the Minister" and "Ornaments Rubric" in *The Prayer Book Dictionary*, 514–523. Both were written when the issue was still very much alive.

Remedial Prayer Books

Claims to the effect that the Book of Common Prayer itself validated ritualist practices met with various responses. One was to retort that the claims were false: Anglo-catholicism could only be read into the Prayer Book, not out of it. But another response was to concede that the claims were—most regrettably—defensible, and that the Prayer Book text does support a more catholic interpretation of Anglican teaching and its liturgical expression than had been supposed. In the United States, the title of an influential tract asked, *Are There Romanizing Germs in the Prayer-Book?* There are, the author admits, and there always have been. They were harmless as long as they lay dormant, but lately "the warm spring-tide brought out the buds of *Tractarianism*. The summer called forth the blossoms of *Ritualism*. The autumnal season will see the full-blown flowers of *Romanism*."[8] The only way to prevent this noxious efflorescence is to disinfect its source. The liturgy must be revised, the sooner the better.

Much the same position was adopted in England by the earnest and energetic Prayer Book Revision Society, which took upon itself the publication of a complete liturgy, intended, as its preface announces, "to cut away the supports, apparent or real, of a Romanizing system, and to deliver the Church of England from the reproach of having in any sense a Popish Prayer Book."[9] The Society's *Book of Common Prayer Revised* is not rebuilt on a different

---

[8] *Are There Romanizing Germs in the Prayer-Book?* (New York and Philadelphia, 1868), 38. The author was known at the time to be Franklin Samuel Rising. On nineteenth-century ritualism in the American church, see David Hein and Gardiner H. Shattuck Jr., *The Episcopalians* (Westport, CT: Praeger Publishers, 2004), 92–94; on the influence and appropriation of the English Tractarians, see Peter B. Nockles, "The Oxford Movement and the United States," in *The Oxford Movement: Europe and the Wider World 1830–1930*, ed. Stewart J. Brown and Peter Nockles (Cambridge: Cambridge University Press, 2012), 133–150.

[9] Preface, *The Book of Common Prayer Revised* (London: Prayer-Book Revision Society, 2nd ed., 1874), 5. See A. Elliott Peaston, *The Prayer Book Revisions of the Victorian Evangelicals* (Dublin: A.P.C.K., 1963), 7; Jasper, "Prayer Book in the Victorian Era," 112.

plan, as was Herring's *New Form of Common-Prayer* for example. On the contrary, only someone quite familiar with the authorized text would be likely to notice the changes, which for the most part delete Romanizing germs. Thus the words "alms and oblations" become "alms and contributions"; priests are termed presbyters, or sometimes pastors. In the Catechism the sacraments are not "generally necessary to salvation" (OWC 429); in Baptism the child is received into the church but is not "regenerate." Before Morning Prayer the Ornaments Rubric states explicitly that at all times of his ministration the minister "shall wear neither Alb, Vestment, nor Cope; but . . . shall have and wear a plain Surplice with Academical Hood and plain black Scarf,"[10] that is, the standard uniform for Anglican clergy, high-church or low, until the Oxford Movement was well under way.

In one sense, there was nothing new about fears that emphasizing the latent catholicism of the Book of Common Prayer could drag Anglicans back into Roman captivity. It was the indictment brought against Laud. Two centuries later, though, the context was rather different. The Laudians, for all their high-church belief and practice, were protestants, though not puritans or Calvinists. The same could probably not be said of the original Tractarians, much less their ritualist successors. The difference is evident in revisions of the Prayer Book from the Anglo-catholic side. Naturally, most of the changes affect Holy Communion, or rather the Mass. Like the nonjurors, Anglo-catholic revisers inserted into the Prayer Book office texts copied from other rites, but they did not turn to the *Apostolic Constitutions* or any other putatively primitive text for the supplementary matter they inserted. Their aim was not to bring the Prayer Book into line with the early church but to bring it into line with western catholicism, or in other words with Rome.

In *Ritual of the Altar*, for instance, which appeared at just the same time as *The Book of Common Prayer Revised*, all the many

---

[10] *The Book of Common Prayer Revised*, 65.

textual and rubrical interpolations are rather wooden translations of the Latin missal. The Prayer Book text is all there, awkwardly shoehorned in at times; but as the candid editor admits, it "cannot be, and is not, maintained" that the resulting combination "is a homogeneous whole."[11] It might better be described as a mongrel. It could scarcely be anything else without abandoning the editor's insistence that because the Prayer Book had not been altered, only supplemented, to use it was not disloyal.[12]

This defense was perhaps less convincing in that *Ritual of the Altar* gives elaborate, illustrated instructions and musical notation for Solemn High Mass, sung in English, but with all the personnel and paraphernalia of the unreformed church. Just this sort of spectacle was what Benjamin Disraeli, then in office as British Prime Minister, had in mind when he condemned "the Mass in Masquerade." He was addressing the House of Commons in support of a bill intended, in his words, "to put down ritualism."[13] By 1874, when the bill became law as the Public Worship Regulation Act, ritualism was no longer an eccentric fringe movement. Its Romanization of Anglicanism, as it was perceived to be, had become enough of a public nuisance to provoke intervention on the part of the state.

Civil prosecutions compelled a number of clergymen to leave the parishes where they had embellished the liturgy with ceremonial practices which secular courts judged to be unlawful. To that extent the Act was successful. But it certainly did not put down ritualism. Far from it. The imprisonment of four ritualist priests made martyrs of them, with predictable consequences. In 1875, according to one tally, there were some two hundred ritualist parishes

---

[11] Orby Shipley, ed., *Ritual of the Altar* (London: Longmans, Green, Reader and Dyer, 2nd ed., 1878), fifth unnumbered page of the preface.

[12] See further Mark Dalby, *Anglican Missals and their Canons* (Cambridge: Grove Books, 1998), esp. 9–11 on *Ritual of the Altar*; Jasper, "Prayer Book in the Victorian Era," 116.

[13] P. T. Marsh, *The Victorian Church in Decline: Archbishop Tait and the Church of England, 1868–1882* (London: Routledge and Kegan Paul, 1969), 186.

in England and Wales; by the beginning of the twentieth century, more than two thousand.[14] The "blossoms of ritualism" burgeoned similarly in the American church, where similar attempts to prune them back similarly failed.

It is not hard to see a certain symmetry between nineteenth-century ritualism and sixteenth-century puritanism. Puritans, obliged by law to use the Book of Common Prayer, took to using it in such a way as to approximate what was done in the "best reformed churches" of Europe. Ritualists, similarly obliged, took to using the Prayer Book so as to approximate what had been done before the Reformation, or else what was currently being done in Roman Catholic churches on the Continent.[15] Puritans saw no reason why a clergyman who dared not wear a surplice should not be allowed to minister in the Church of England. Ritualists saw no reason why a clergyman who dared to wear a chasuble should not be allowed to do the same. After the Restoration, puritans like Baxter pleaded that they ought to be able to remain in the national church as a tolerated minority with a permissible alternative to the Prayer Book. In the nineteenth century, ritualists pleaded for toleration of their own brand of Anglicanism and its expression in permissibly catholic liturgy.

Their plea was somewhat ironic, inasmuch as Anglo-catholic ceremonial could be tolerated only on the basis of the same liberal principles that the early Tractarians had begun by rejecting;[16]

---

[14] Nigel Yates, *Anglican Ritualism in Victorian Britain 1830–1910* (Oxford: Oxford University Press, 1999), 275, 278, and for the details 386–414. It should be pointed out that the four clerical martyrs were jailed for contumacy, not directly for ceremonial extravagance.

[15] The first approach, exemplified by Percy Dearmer's very influential *Parson's Handbook*, was markedly antiquarian; the second took current Roman regulations as normative, usually (but not always) without using Latin.

[16] The point is made by Peter Nockles in *The Oxford Movement in Context: Anglican High Churchmanship 1760–1857* (Cambridge: Cambridge University Press, 1994), 319–320; and Nockles, "Survivals or New Arrivals?," 187. But see also James Bentley, *Ritualism and Politics in Victorian Britain: The Attempt to Legislate for Belief* (Oxford: Oxford University Press, 1978), esp. 122–128.

although it may be that in the long term, intentionally or otherwise, the ritualists' refusal to relinquish practices they believed were right and proper helped to promote a culture of toleration. In the short term, however, "by the end of the nineteenth century the Church of England could more accurately be described as an alliance of separate sects" than as a church. All that held it together was the machinery of the establishment, since the unity which the texts and rubrics of the Book of Common Prayer had once enabled and supported was "destroyed forever by the ritualist innovations." They had not been stopped in time.[17]

There was one more attempt to stop them. In 1904 a new royal commission was constituted, with a remit specifically limited to investigating irregularities in the conduct of Divine Service and recommending what to do about them. The first conclusion in the commission's report was quoted at the beginning of this chapter: the law of public worship is too narrow. Having conceded that much, however, the report goes on to recommend that a number of illegal practices of "special gravity and significance" should promptly be made to cease.[18] At the head of the list is "the interpolation of the prayers and ceremonies belonging to the Canon of the Mass"—exactly the strategy of liturgical hybrids such as *Ritual of the Altar*. Nine further items were likewise hallmarks of *fin de siècle* Anglo-catholicism. The commission's positive recommendations include instructing the Convocations to prepare a new Ornaments Rubric and new, more elastic, more comprehensive regulations with regard to the conduct of Anglican worship. As in 1662, Convocation would then offer its proposals to Parliament for enactment.

---

[17] Yates, *Anglican Ritualism*, 379, 378.
[18] See R. C. D. Jasper, *The Development of the Anglican Liturgy 1662–1980* (London: SPCK, 1989), 75–79.

The Twentieth Century

More than twenty years later, the proposals that had been arrived at were finally put to a parliamentary vote. They failed. They failed twice, in fact, both times in the Commons, first in 1927 and again, after some adjustments, the next year. Absent Parliament's endorsement, they could not officially supplant the 1662 Book of Common Prayer, and officially they never did. The bishops, however, in despite of Parliament, announced that during the "present emergency" they would regard as lawful any liturgical practice consistent with the rejected proposals in the Deposited Book, as it was called. By what authority they would be licensing this nonconformity was not evident, but no one tried to stop them.

Episcopal defiance not only started to unravel the fabric of establishment with regard to public worship; it also ushered in an unexampled liturgical pluralism. If the voting in the House of Commons had gone the other way, there would still have been but one Prayer Book, in the sense of a single volume. The volume, however, which the bishops were determined to permit, was in effect two Prayer Books. It had two complete liturgies for Morning and Evening Prayer, Holy Communion, Public Baptism, Confirmation, Matrimony, and Visitation. In each case, one of the two was the received text; the other incorporated the proposed revisions. Taking all the permitted options into account, one eminent liturgist calculated that there could be 384 varieties of Morning Prayer, if not more.[19] It was the end of "but one use."

There is no need here to catalogue the innovations in the proposed texts, but one of them should be mentioned. The alternative order for Holy Communion prescribes an enlarged eucharistic canon that bears a strong resemblance to the one that had been adopted by the American church in 1789. Thus did the

[19] F. E. Brightman, "The New Prayer Book Examined," *Church Quarterly Review* 104 (1927): 219–252 at 221.

"Eastern" form of consecration that evolved in Scotland through the wee bookies make its way into the Church of England. As might be expected, this prayer was regarded in some quarters as alarmingly catholic. Together with new rubrics that permitted eucharistic vestments and reservation of the sacrament, both of which were meant to be congenial to moderate Anglo-catholics, the alternative canon seems to have fueled much of the opposition to the Deposited Book as a whole. Antipathy toward Roman Catholicism was not the only force that defeated the revisions, but it was perhaps the strongest. "The flame which burned the martyrs," as one member of Parliament put it, "has never quite died down in the horrified eyes of the British people."[20]

The 1927–1928 proposals were not unique. Self-governing Anglican churches in former British colonies were and had been making changes on similar lines. Early in the twentieth century the international gathering of Anglican bishops known as the Lambeth Conference (see Appendix 2) had discussed liturgical adaptation and enrichment, and had reported a list of principles for future revision. Presently some of the churches in which the 1662 Prayer Book was used revised it, and the American church revised its own version. Compared with what came later, these revisions were fairly conservative. Thus, when the Lambeth Conference that met in 1930 emphasized the importance of the Book of Common Prayer as "the Anglican standard of doctrine and practice," it was referring to a text that was recognizably if not precisely the same everywhere. As such it was both a marker of worldwide Anglican identity and a bond of unity between the offshoots of the Church of England.

The next Lambeth Conference reiterated the assumption that there were "features of the Book of Common Prayer which

[20] John G. Maiden, *National Religion and the Prayer Book Controversy, 1927–28* (Woodbridge, UK: Boydell Press, 2009), 149–150, 170. See also Maiden, "The Prayer Book Controversy," in *Oxford Handbook of the Oxford Movement*, ed. Brown et al., 530–541; and Donald Gray, *The 1927–28 Prayer Book Crisis* (2 parts; Norwich, UK: SCM-Canterbury Press, 2006).

are essential to the safeguarding of the unity of the Anglican Communion," although it also said the time had come for examining what those features might be.[21] The Conference of 1958 took a notably different position. Obliquely but unmistakably it announced that so far as the Anglican Communion was concerned there was no longer any such thing as *the* Book of Common Prayer, chiefly because liturgical revision was going forward in many and various ways and its progress could not be halted. The Conference's lengthy report adds that Anglicans "are not the only branch of Christendom to have set about this task"; liturgical renewal "has already begun to draw Christians closer to one another in thought and ways of worship," and "we cannot wish that our own Communion should stand aside."[22]

Accordingly the 1958 report abandons the idea of "essential features" and goes on to make very specific recommendations that would propel existing Prayer Books a long way beyond where they were. The stated rationale is that a common approach to revision, rather than a common liturgy, will in some way preserve the "distinct ecclesiastical culture" which, until then, the Prayer Book had fostered among Anglicans. In other words, the bond of unity would not be agreement on a shared, inherited text: it would be agreement on how to get rid of it.

The Prayer Book Superseded

Twenty years later, the results of this program were becoming evident. In 1978 *An Australian Prayer Book* was published; in 1979 the Episcopal Church in the United States gave final approval to

---

[21] *The Lambeth Conference 1948: The Encyclical Letter from the Bishops; together with Resolutions and Reports* (London: SPCK, 1948), 86, quoting resolution 37 of Lambeth Conference 1920.

[22] *The Lambeth Conference 1958: The Encyclical Letter from the Bishops together with the Resolutions and Reports* (London: SPCK, 1958), 2.93–2.94.

a heavily revised Book of Common Prayer; in England the "present emergency" declared after the débâcle of 1928 came to an end with the fully legal *Alternative Service Book 1980: Services authorized for use in the Church of England in conjunction with the Book of Common Prayer.*

Like the new Australian and American Prayer Books, the *ASB* had been prepared for by issuing a series of temporary, paper-covered, trial-use texts. The chairman of the commission that produced these experimental liturgies would later insist that they had not been designed on purpose to kill the 1662 Prayer Book. "If it were to die," he wrote, "it must die a natural death, simply because people did not want it any longer." Once the commission's alternatives were placed beside it, public worship would find its own level. "Whatever survived" would have won its way on its own merits.[23]

In due time, survival of the fittest brought forth in the *ASB* a new species, an alternative to the Book of Common Prayer that could be described as an aggregate of options. The 1928 Deposited Book had permitted more variety than any Anglican liturgy had previously done, but the *ASB* was a kaleidoscope. Sections of each service were numbered according to an elaborate two-color scheme, which may or may not have made for easier navigation. At one point there was a kind of flow-chart, meant to help users sort out the possible configurations and find the items that could but need not be included. In 1549 Cranmer had complained about "the number and hardness of the rules called the pie," the medieval manual of liturgical instructions. They made turning the book, he wrote, "so hard and intricate a matter that many times there was more business to find out what should be read than to read it when it was found out" (owc 5). In 1980, inevitably, there were complaints about the number and hardness of the rules in the *ASB*.

---

[23] Jasper, *Development of Anglican Liturgy*, 241. Jasper was the chairman.

The new Australian and American Prayer Books were somewhat less intricate, but they shared with the *ASB* what was undoubtedly its most controversial feature: a language. For many though not all of the services, the scripts are written in what is usually called contemporary English, instead of the early modern English of the classical Book of Common Prayer and the Authorized Version of the Bible. The difference, which is most obvious in pronouns and verbs, will have been noticed by anyone who has read the excerpts and quotations in earlier chapters of this book.

Some of the contemporary English in the late twentieth-century revisions "translates" sixteenth-century texts by substituting newer forms of the same words. Prayers, however, which make use of second-person inflections, are not always amenable to this sort of updating, and the formal structure of the Prayer Book collects compounds the difficulty. Typically a collect addresses God as characterized in a relative clause. The collect for All Saints Day, for example, begins: "Almighty God, who hast knit together thine elect." It would be quite correct, in grammar, to contemporize this as "Almighty God, who have knit," but it would hardly be idiomatic. A change to "who has knit" would preserve the relative clause, but not the second-person address.

One strategy used in recent liturgies, here and often elsewhere, is to forego the relative clause as such and turn its characterization of God into a statement: "Almighty God, you have knit." The disadvantage is obvious. Instead of being a single complex sentence centered on a petition, the "translated" collect consists of two sentences, grammatically independent, the first of which provides God with information about himself. Another strategy, used in one version of the Lord's Prayer, avoids this difficulty by eliminating the second-person verb entirely, so that the relative clause becomes a qualifying phrase: "Our Father in heaven" instead of "Our Father, which art in heaven" (or "Our Father, you are in heaven").

None of the new books completely abandoned texts written in the older English idiom. The 1979 American Prayer Book, for example, provides both "traditional" and "contemporary" rites for Morning and Evening Prayer, the Holy Eucharist, and the Burial of the Dead, with two sets of collects, though only one (contemporary) Psalter. There were similar provisions in *An Australian Prayer Book* and the *ASB*—both of which have been replaced by still further revisions—as there are also in the Anglican Church of Canada's *Book of Alternative Services* (1985). It remains that few books, as the preface of the *ASB* remarks, "can have had their origin in so much, and such detailed, public debate"—to which might be added, "so rancorous."

Despite the survivals of older usage, the debate was largely concerned with language. Without reviewing the controversies, which have not yet subsided, it can be said here that they brought to light, perhaps more clearly than ever before, aspects of what had made the classical Book of Common Prayer a sacred text. Although liturgists are wont to emphasize that liturgy is something *done*, it is arguable that the services of the Prayer Book have for the most part taken effect because they were *uttered*, "sung or said." Performing these scripts brings into being a worded religion; meaning, verbally expressed, is at once its vehicle and the substance of what is conveyed. That the wording must be intelligible was a Reformation principle, honored in every version of the Book of Common Prayer; but until the middle of the twentieth century it was not self-evident to anyone that the pedestrian style of everyday discourse is the best idiom for enabling common prayer, let alone the only idiom that is intelligible. Nor, of course, is there any reason to think that "Jacobethan" English alone can do what the words of the Prayer Book have in fact done. Still, no poets came forward to commend the English of the "contemporary" services, and more than one poet assailed it.

From time to time it is said that the Book of Common Prayer has died, and that its official obituary was written in 1988. The report of that year's Lambeth Conference declined to dwell, as previous reports had done, on the strengths of the classical Prayer Book. To do so would be a needless distraction because, as the report put it, that once-peerless liturgy was "slipping irretrievably into the past."[24] Campaigns to retrieve it have been mounted. They have met with limited success. But since the Book of Common Prayer was never intended to be an end in itself, perhaps the sacred ends it could and did serve are now being served by other means.

[24] *The Truth Shall Make You Free: The Lambeth Conference 1988: The Reports, Resolutions & Pastoral Letters from the Bishops* (London: Church House Publishing, 1994), 68–69.

PART III
CONTEXTS

Eleven
The Prayer Book Printed

The text of the Book of Common Prayer has always been a printed text. There are other ways to communicate its words—sounds, pixels, braille dots—but for the most part the technology of printing is what has made it possible for the meaning of those words to become common prayer. They have been apprehended and appropriated by different people at different times and places because the Prayer Book has coincided with Prayer Books—a prescriptive text, with material objects made of paper and ink.

As books in that sense, Prayer Books have varied in all the ways books can vary. The text they embody, considered as a verbal sequence, may not be affected by their physical characteristics, but its visible presentation on bound and printed pages does affect, and is affected by, its reception, its status as a sacred text, its stability in space and time, and its relation to other texts. A few aspects of this complex reciprocity will be sampled in the present chapter.

Regulating the Text

Both of the volumes required for the conduct of public worship in the Church of England, the authorized Bible and the Book of Common Prayer, have been deemed to belong to the sovereign as the church's supreme governor. As such, they have always been printed by His or Her Majesty's Printers for the time being, and both remain under Crown copyright. In the seventeenth century permission to print the Prayer Book was extended to the university

The Book of Common Prayer. Charles Hefling, Oxford University Press (2021). © Oxford University Press.
DOI: 10.1093/oso/9780190689681.001.0001.

presses at Cambridge and Oxford. From then on, it has been law-fully issued in England only by these three "Privileged Presses."[1]

In return for their privilege, printers of the Book of Common Prayer have been expected to print it correctly. What counts as cor-rectness, however, has not always been the same, and over time the line separating unacceptable errors from insignificant vari-ations has shifted. In the mid-sixteenth century, when the Prayer Book was first printed, consistent spelling was not a high priority and punctuation was unruly. Compositors who set texts in type for printing were wont to spell and punctuate them according to their own lights. Of perhaps a dozen issues of the first Prayer Book in 1549, no two are exactly alike. Not all of the many discrepancies are trivial, but for the most part they make no difference in the meaning of the text, and might not have been regarded at the time as culpable blunders.[2] Not so when the second, revised Book of Common Prayer was printed in 1552. The "faults escaped in the printing" were serious enough for Archbishop Cranmer to inter-vene, and both of the printers who allowed them to escape had to issue lists of *corrigenda* that were tipped into finished copies.[3] One of these is illustrated in Figure 11.1.

When the Book of Common Prayer was revived in 1559, Queen Elizabeth appointed a new royal printer, who seems to have been fairly meticulous, although there were a few mistakes at first. The Declaration on Kneeling, which ought to have been omitted, still appears in two quarto editions, and there was some confusion about which prayers, in what order, were to be included at the end of the

---

[1] On the history of the office of King's or Queen's Printer in England and Scotland as it bears on the Book of Common Prayer, and the involvement of the two university presses, see Bret Ince, "Printers and Printed Editions of the Prayer Book," in W. K. Lowther Clarke, *Liturgy and Worship* (New York: Macmillan, 1932), 798–805; and Griffiths, *Bibliography*, 7–14. The Privileged Presses are now two; in 1990 the dignity of Printers to the Queen was invested in the university press at Cambridge.

[2] There are, however, significant differences: copies exist that do not have all of the canticles, and some copies put them in a kind of appendix. Possibly these were trial runs.

[3] For Cranmer's letter to the king's privy council, October 7, 1552, see Henry Gee, *The Elizabethan Prayer-Book and Ornaments* (London: Macmillan, 1902), 224–227 at 225.

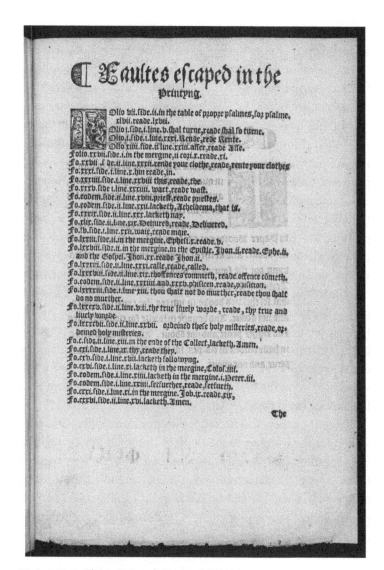

❡ Faultes escaped in the Printyng.

Olio vii.side.ii.in the table of propre psalmes,for psalme. xlvii.reade.lxvii.
Olio i.side.i.line.v.shal turne,reade shal so turne.
Olio.i.side.i.line.xxxi.Rende,rede Rente.
Olio xiiii.side.ii.line.xxiii.asser,reade Asse.
Folio.xxvii.side.i.in the mergine,ii cori.x.reade.xi.
Fo.xxvii .s de.ii.line.xxxii.rende your clothe,reade,rente your clothes
Fo.xxxi.side.i.line.x.hii reade.in.
Fo.xxxiiii.side.i.line.xxviii this,reade,the
Fo.xxxv.side i.line.xxxiiii. wart,reade wast.
Fo.eodem.side.ii.line.xviii.priest,reade priestes.
Fo.eodem.side.ii.line.xxii.lacketh,Acheldema,that is.
Fo.xxxix.side.ii.line.xxx.lacketh nap.
Fo.xlix.side.ii.line.xix.Deliured,reade,Deliuered.
Fo.lv.side.i.line.xxii.waie,reade maie.
Fo.lxriii.side.ii.in the mergine,Ephest.x.reade.b.
Fo.lxxviii.side.ii.in the mergine.in the Epistle.Jhon.ii.reade.Ephe.ii, and the Gospel.Jhon.xx.reade.Jhon.ii.
Fo.lxxxii.side.ii.line.xxxi.calle,reade,called.
Fo.lxxxviii.side.ii.line.xix.thoffences commeth, reade.offence cometh.
Fo.eodem.side.ii.line.xxxiiii.and.xxxv.phisicen,reade,phisicion.
Fo.lxxxiii.side.i.line·xiii. thou shalt not do murther,reade thou shalt do no murther.
Fo.lxxxv.side.ii.line.viii.the true liuely worde , reade, thy true and liuely worde.
Fo.lxxxxbii.side.ii.line.xxvii. ordeined these holy misteries,reade,or deined holy misteries.
Fo.x.side.ii.line.xiii.in the ende of the Collect,lacketh,Amen.
Fo.xxi.side.i.line.ix. thy,reade they.
Fo.xxv.side.i.line.vii.lacketh followyng.
Fo.xxvi.side.i.line.xi.lacketh in the mergine,Colos.iiii.
Fo.eodem.side.i.line.xiiii.lacketh in the mergine.i.Peter.iii.
Fo.eodem.side.i.line.xxiii.setfurther,reade,setfurth.
Fo.xxxi.side.i.line.xi.in the mergine. Job.ix.reade.xix,
Fo.xxxvi.side.ii.line.xvi.lacketh.Amen.

The

Litany. Aside from these initial hitches, there were no significant textual anomalies until the Barker family began their long tenure— three generations, 132 years—as royal printers in 1577. Published the next year, perhaps not by coincidence, was the pared-down and redacted "puritan Prayer Book" that was discussed in chapter six.

As a rule, however, the Barkers' folio Prayer Books print the authorized text completely and accurately. They have much the same layout from one edition to the next, presumably because a previous print was used as the copy-text when type had to be (re)set. One unfortunate side-effect was that inconspicuous but consequential misprints could be passed on, uncorrected, from printing to printing. An example was mentioned in chapter eight: at some point two letters dropped out of the word *unrighteous* in one of the Psalms, and one edition after another printed the distressing statement that "the righteous shall be punished." This was not so egregious a mistake as the one in the "Wicked Bible," a Barker edition that left the third word out of "Thou shalt not commit adultery"; but it was regrettable. Numbers too, especially roman numerals, could easily go awry. For years the fortieth chapter of Isaiah was wrongly listed as the first lesson on Epiphany. It should have been the sixtieth, but *lx* had been inadvertently switched to *xl*.

Before 1662 there was no single benchmark for determining exactly what the wording of the Book of Common Prayer ought to be. Allegations of deliberate tampering with the text were made at times, especially against Laudians. A small alteration in the wording of one collect was blamed on Archbishop Laud himself, and his protégé John Cosin appears to have made a number of alterations, on his own authority, in the 1627 Prayer Book that chapter seven has discussed. It was to prevent future disagreement about the correct wording that in 1662 the Act of Uniformity specified one document, the manuscript "annexed and joined" to the Act itself, as the exemplar for all printed copies of the Prayer Book it authorized.

In spite of this provision, there is reason to think that when the King's Printers (one of them still a Barker) printed the first edition, they may also used as a copy-text an existing Book of Common Prayer, perhaps one they had themselves printed recently to meet the need for new editions of the old version. All the Prayer Books published in 1662 place the tables and rules for feasts after the twelve kalendar pages, as earlier editions had commonly done, despite the fact that in the Book Annexed those items come before the kalendar and are so listed in the manuscript list of contents. The Psalter too is printed just as it had always been. The compositors used one size and style of type throughout, disregarding the manuscript, in which the copyists had carefully transcribed the Great Bible's differentiation of words added to the translation to clarify its meaning.

But time was short, and the King's Printers had a lot to do. Twenty thousand copies of the new Book of Common Prayer were needed, according to one report, to supply all the parishes in England. Two folio editions were printed. The first edition is more impressive; the second, by using slightly smaller type and cutting back on big decorative initials, reduces the number of pages by about a hundred. The Act of Uniformity stipulated that a number of printed copies were to be examined, compared with the manuscript, corrected as necessary, certified under the Great Seal, and deposited for future reference at cathedral churches and the courts of law. Thereafter, these so-called Sealed Books would be legally equivalent to the Book Annexed. The Prayer Books used for this purpose, most of which survive, are printed on extra-large pages; otherwise they are no different from copies of the first edition that were made available to the public at six shillings apiece. And they did need correction.[4]

The appointed examiners made corrections by hand in each of the Sealed Books. They also removed the three leaves on which

---

[4] On the two folio editions of 1662, see Griffiths, *Bibliography*, 115. The remarkable figure of twenty thousand, far greater than an ordinary print-run, is mentioned by Gilbert Burnet (1643–1715) in his *History of My Own Time* (Oxford: Oxford University Press, 1897), 328. The price of the first edition is stated in an announcement of availability in [Giles Drury,] *Mercurius Publicus* 31 (July 31 to August 7, 1662), 514.

the misplaced tables were printed, reinserted them in front of the kalendar, and substituted a new table of contents that matches the Book Annexed.[5] The printers never moved the tables, however, and they were slow to make some of the handwritten corrections. For several years the first rubric after Holy Communion, as printed, referred to the general prayer "for the good estate of the Catholic Church of Christ" when it ought to have read "for the whole state of Christ's Church militant here in earth" (owc 406).

On the other hand, the examiners did not see fit to alter the typography of the Psalter. Nor did they strike out a new-fangled punctuation-mark, never before seen in a Book of Common Prayer and evidently put there by the printers—the apostrophe. In the Book Annexed the possessive form of *Christ* is either *Christs* or *Christes*, as it had always been. The Sealed Books, however, have *Christ's* in one place, and a little later they print *turn'd* where the manuscript has *turned*.[6] The next folio edition banished these intruders, but it was not long before they found their way back.

Changes, Authorized and Not

There are certain textual changes that printers are not only authorized but obliged to make. The Act of Uniformity permits no deviation from the official wording, with the stated exception of prayers that refer specifically to the sovereign or the royal family. In those places the text is to be "altered and changed from time to

---

[5] Another new page was printed to correct the order of two prayers later in the book. On the repositioned pages see Archibald John Stephens, *The Book of Common Prayer. . . with Notes, Legal and Historical* (3 vols.; London: Ecclesiastical History Society, 1850), I: 184, 304, and cxcvii–cxcviii; for the corrected table of contents, see the unnumbered pages preceding p. 1: "8. Tables and Rules . . . 9. The Kalendar . . . ." The Oxford World Classics edition follows the uncorrected, unofficial order ("8. The Kalendar . . . 9. Tables and Rules . . . "; owc 185). Present-day editions do the same.

[6] See owc 615, 620 and the editor's notes. The Book Annexed does use one apostrophe, to contract *writest* to *writ'st* for the sake of the meter in the Ordinal's somewhat improved version of the *Veni Creator* (owc 640).

time, and fitted to the present occasion, according to the directions of lawful authority" (OWC 204). The most important prayers that come under this proviso are the "state prayers" at the end of Mattins and Evensong (OWC 248, 256), certain clauses in the Litany, each of the alternative collects for the sovereign at the beginning of Holy Communion, and the prayer for the whole state of the church.[7] On the occasion of a birth, a death, or a marriage that comes within the meaning of the Act, lawful authority, usually in the shape of a royal order in council, has prescribed a new form of words to be used and printed thereafter.

Because the appropriate names and titles must be spoken in public worship as soon as they are announced, a minister who did not trust his memory might resort to writing them in the margin of his Prayer Book, as many a minister did, sometimes more than once, and not always very neatly. Eventually updated editions would be published; meanwhile, for Prayer Books already printed, the necessary revisions were sometimes issued on slips that could be pasted on the appropriate pages.[8] A more costly alternative was to print "cancels," amended pages to replace the ones that were out of date. Mismatches are not unknown. In one folio Prayer Book, which according to its title page was issued in 1687 while James II was king, not only are there prayers that name William and Mary, who succeeded him in 1689; in another section there are also prayers for his brother Charles II, who died in 1685.[9]

From time to time the almanack, which lists the dates of moveable holydays for forty years or so, has been updated. The Privileged

---

[7] There are also nominal prayers, less frequently used, in the Ordinal, the Sea Prayers, and the State Services. A catalogue of official changes, down to the marriage of (then) Princess Elizabeth, is given in Frank Streatfeild, *The State Prayers and Other Variations in the Book of Common Prayer* (London: A.R. Mowbray, 1950), 18–26.

[8] For the bibliographical complexities, see B. J. McMullin, "The Book of Common Prayer and the Monarchy from the Restoration to the Reign of George I: Some Bibliographical Observations," *Bulletin of the Bibliographical Society of Australia and New Zealand* 5 (1981): 81–92.

[9] Griffiths 1687/1. Since the title-page also has James's royal cipher, the date is presumably not a misprint.

Presses have also taken it upon themselves to alter other parts of the text in keeping with currently acceptable spelling, punctuation, or style. *Moneth, murther,* and *Jury,* for example, became *month, murder,* and *Jewry.* At some time in the mid-eighteenth century, Prayer Books began to print *impatient* and *imperfect* instead of *unpatient* and *unperfect.* Oxford opted for the new forms; Cambridge kept the old ones (and still does).[10] Over the years, there have been many adjustments of stops and numerals. Commas and semicolons were added and subtracted; most brackets, which are frequent in early editions, were removed; roman numerals became rarer and arabic numerals more common; and so on. The apostrophe was permitted to punctuate possessives, though where to put it has not always been clear. *Wits end* and *troubles sake,* so printed in the Sealed Books, might be *wit's* and *troubles',* as Oxford decided to print them, or *wits'* and *trouble's,* as in Cambridge editions.[11]

In some respects the authorized printers were simply keeping abreast of the times, as they did when they stopped using antiquated typefaces, or adopted the modern distinctions between the letters *i* and *j* and between *u* and *v*, or retired *ſ*, the long *s*. Removing the column of Roman dates from the kalendar could be defended on the ground that even people who knew how to use it never did, but other unauthorized edits, such as dropping or rewriting the rubrics, were less defensible. In 1849 a fastidious barrister went to the trouble of noting all the places where recent editions of the Book of Common Prayer differed from the authoritative standard of the Sealed Books. Extrapolating from the number of deviations he counted in Morning Prayer, he arrived at an estimate of the total for one Prayer Book then in print—twelve thousand, all of them illegal. The Privileged Presses were all guilty, and by rights they

---

[10] In the Everyman edition (1999) and the Penguin edition (2012). The words occur in Psalm 99:1 and Psalm 139:15 respectively; see owc 560, 603. See also Streatfeild, *State Prayers and Other Variations,* 53.

[11] Psalm 12:5 and Psalm 108:27.

deserved to forfeit their patents and privileges.[12] This verdict was not well received. It did however raise a question touched on at the beginning of this chapter—exactly what marks on paper do and do not constitute a Book of Common Prayer.

The question came up again when the Book Annexed, which had been mislaid for a time, was rediscovered and later published in a full-sized photographic replica that anyone could compare with currently available Prayer Books.[13] Presently a conference of representatives from the three presses met to discuss whether anything should be done about differences. In their report, as delivered to Parliament,[14] they made no apology for trivial variations—S. or St. for *Saint*, roman or arabic numerals—but they did present a list of thirty-some recommendations that all parties had agreed to adopt. Most of these have not much bearing on the meaning of the text, but two are worth mentioning.

The punctuation of the Lord's Prayer was one point of consensus. There are nineteen places in the Book Annexed where the whole prayer is written out, but it is written in eighteen slightly different ways. One variation appears in the petition "Thy will be done in earth as it is in heaven," which sometimes has a comma after *earth*, sometimes not. The three presses agreed that the text should be regularized and that there should be a comma, but that it should be placed not after *earth* but after *done*. This punctuation probably brings the English wording closer to the meaning of the original Greek, but it is certainly a change.

Another possibly relevant comma affects the Catechism's definition of a sacrament as "an outward and visible sign of an inward and

---

[12] Stephens, *Common Prayer with Notes*, II: vi–vii, xxxvi–xxxvii. Stephens had done the counting himself.

[13] The (re)discovery was made in 1867, shortly after the appointment of a Royal Commission on Ritual, which prompted a new search. The facsimile was published in 1891, when ritualism was again a contentious issue.

[14] "Alterations in the Book of Common Prayer," March 1903; *Accounts and Papers*, vol. 50 (1903) 551–557. The publication of the facsimile of the Book Annexed is specifically mentioned. See also Frederic F. Grensted, "Punctuation of the P[rayer] B[ook]," *Prayer Book Dictionary*, 580–583.

spiritual grace given unto us." There could be some question as to which word, *sign* or *grace*, the word *given* modifies. Is a sacrament a sign that is given, or is grace that is given the thing that a sacrament signifies? With a comma after *grace*, the meaning seems to be that what is given in a sacrament is a sign (only), in which case the grace of which it is a sign is, or might be, given independently. Without this comma, it would seem that what is given in a sacrament is the grace of which it is the sign. In quite a few Prayer Books published after the definition was added to the Catechism at Hampton Court, the text has no comma. The Book Annexed has one, plainly written, but the presses agreed to omit it, without prejudice as to the theological implications of the omission.

As contrasted with the Church of England's Prayer Book, the American Book of Common Prayer was for many years a work in progress. After the first two printings, an edition published in 1793 was designated as the standard. It printed the text more attractively, but often incorrectly, and did not remain the standard for long. In the next hundred years there were six further standard editions, each incorporating changes approved by the Episcopal Church's General Convention. Individual bishops took responsibility for inspecting, usually by deputy, any Prayer Books printed within their dioceses, and a statement of episcopal approbation will often be found on the back of the title-page. One of the early standard editions added the ordination services, which had been issued separately. Also added were the Thirty-nine Articles, slightly modified, and rites for consecrating a church or chapel and for instituting a minister.[15]

In 1892, the whole American liturgy was carefully revised, and the General Convention that authorized it also established the

---

[15] Frederick Gibson, "The Standard Editions of the American Book of Common Prayer," in William McGarvey, *Liturgiae Americanae; or, The Book of Common Prayer as Used in the United States of America* (Philadelphia: Philadelphia Church Publishing Company, 1907), lv–lxxiii at lxii, lxvi; Marion J. Hatchett, *The Making of the First American Book of Common Prayer* (New York: Seabury Press, 1982), 136–141.

office of Custodian of the Standard Book of Common Prayer. It was intended that the revision, which had been painstakingly and accurately printed, would be as it were the Episcopal Church's Sealed Book. It was not copyrighted, however. No American Prayer Book has ever been protected by copyright. Anyone may print all or part of the current version, but only copies certified by the Custodian as conforming with the current standard, including its pagination, are authorized for use in Episcopal churches.

The Red and the Black

For a century and a half, editions of the Book of Common Prayer meant for ministers' use in church were printed using a gothic or "old English" typeface known as *blackletter*, which can be seen in several of the illustrations in this book (Figures 5.2, 5.3, 7.1, 11.1, 12.1). Reading early blackletter print takes a little practice; it made use of ligatures or joined letters, marks of abbreviation, an odd kind of ampersand, two forms of *r* and two of *s*, and sometimes the old letter *thorn*, usually in abbreviated combinations such as $þ^t$ for *that* and $þ^e$ for *the*.[16] Printers began to use roman type (which you are reading) for smaller-format Prayer Books around 1586, and by 1600 about half of all Bibles published in England were set in roman, especially the Geneva version. Blackletter held on, however, perhaps because of its ecclesiastical overtones. The King James Bible used it in 1611 for the first edition; Archbishop Laud insisted on it for the Scottish Book of Common Prayer in 1637; and blackletter Prayer Books were printed for churches until the end of the seventeenth century.[17]

---

[16] In Figure 5.2, the "bowed" *r*, something like the numeral 2, is used after *b, d, h, o, p*, and *y*. In line 18, *whē* is an abbreviation for *when*. Both forms of *s* appear in *sinnes* (line 5); the short form, now the normal one, is used only at the end of a word. The "Tironian *&*" resembles the numeral 7; it can be seen in Figure 7.1, line 7. Notice also the rubrics on the page illustrated; by 1627 they were routinely printed in roman type.

[17] Griffiths records a blackletter Prayer Book as late as 1706; see *Bibliography*, 121, 136.

Blackletter print need not be black. Not all of it was, as a rule, in folio Prayer Books. Beginning with the original version, the kalendar pages were regularly printed in two colors, red being used for the names of the major feasts, as in Figure 2.1. Besides these "red-letter days," other parts of the same page may be printed in red; headings, for instance. There may also be red on the conjugate page, meaning the page that was *printed* next to a kalendar page on the same side of the same sheet of paper, although it may not *face* that page, and usually does not, once all the sheets have been folded, assembled in gatherings, and bound as a codex. In some printings of the 1549 Prayer Book, for example, each of the four pages before the kalendar has red print. There is no particular reason for its being there, as there is in the kalendar, but there is an explanation. These four pages happen to be, respectively, the conjugate pages of the December, November, October, and September kalendar pages. In other words, they came from the press on sheets that would have had two colors anyway. None of the pages that precede these four has any red; nor does any page after the kalendar for December.

Two-color printing was not uncommon, but it was a finicky process that added to the cost of a book, because each sheet had to be "pulled" twice, in exact alignment. That may be why red print appears in early Prayer Books, if it appears at all, only on the kalendar pages, where it has a purpose, and nowhere else, except (incidentally) on neighboring pages. In any case, once the services begin with Morning Prayer, the letterpress is uniformly black.[18] Straight red *lines* that frame and divide columns of printed text, as in Figure 7.1, are another matter; they were ruled by hand, not printed.

It follows that unspoken instructions in the Prayer Book services are called rubrics only by courtesy: despite the name, they are

---

[18] Every rule has exceptions. Some early *title*-pages are partly printed in red, in which case the conjugate page usually has some red too. The 1637 Prayer Book for Scotland is comparatively lavish (twenty pages) in its use of red ink, but all of it appears in the preliminaries—none in the services, which is the point at present.

almost never literally red. Using red to differentiate these words was an old custom, used in medieval manuscripts and adopted in printed liturgical books. The authorized printers of the Book of Common Prayer might have followed it, but before the eighteenth century they never did.[19] From this a further conclusion follows: there is nothing anomalous about the fact that in 1552 the Black Rubric was black.

The Blackness of the Black Rubric

When the Declaration on Kneeling, *alias* the Black Rubric, was first printed, the print was certainly black, as chapter five pointed out. But reputable scholars have been known to repeat the tale that it was black because the text was a last-minute addition; had there been more time, the Declaration would have been red. That is very doubtful. It is also said to have been *because* the ink was black that the Declaration acquired its now-familiar nickname. And it is said to have been in the nineteenth century that the name began to be used. Those statements are both doubtful too.

It is true that the Declaration on Kneeling was put into the second version of the Book of Common Prayer only after printing had begun. In some copies, it stands by itself on an inserted page. In other copies, presumably later ones, it appears among the rubrics after the Communion office, in different positions. Figure 5.3 shows an example. All these rubrics are black—as usual. If there exists a 1552 Prayer Book in which the Communion rubrics are red, it has not been reported.[20] So much for the tale. As for the name Black

[19] John Booty's edition of the Elizabethan Prayer Book (Washington: Folger Shakespeare Library, 1976) is misleading. It is printed, attractively but anachronistically, in two colors throughout, using red for the rubrics which in Elizabethan folios were, as usual, black.

[20] Isabel Davis, who has examined multiple copies of the 1552 Prayer Book, is rightly skeptical of red anywhere except around the kalendar; see "Prosthesis and Reformation: The Black Rubric and the Reinvention of Kneeling," *Textual Practice* 30.7 (2016): 1209–1231 at 1216 and 1229 note 31. For other placements of the added text, see

Rubric, it was evidently not a nineteenth-century invention, and at least to begin with it seems to have had nothing to do with the fact that the paragraph it is popularly attached to was not printed in red.

The Declaration on Kneeling was omitted from the Elizabethan Prayer Book. No one ever thought it was a rubric in the sense of a liturgical instruction, and when it reappeared in 1662, printers consistently distinguished it, one way or another, from ordinary rubrics, and continued to do so until the twentieth century. In blackletter editions, for example, the rubrics are regularly printed in roman type but the Declaration is printed in italics. When the main text is set in roman, rubrics are italicized but the Declaration is not. Toward the end of the seventeenth century, some folio Prayer Books in which roman type was used for the main text italicize the rubrics, in the customary way, but print the Declaration—nothing else—in blackletter type, as in Figure 11.2. Later it was sometimes printed with a vertical array of quotation-marks in the margin.

Yet another way of distinguishing the Declaration appeared in 1716, when Prayer Books began to be printed in two colors throughout.[21] There are (a few) editions with red rubrics in which the Declaration is black. That, however, cannot be the origin of the name, because the name had already been used in print, and to judge by the context in which it was used, it did not refer to what the words of the Declaration looked like on the page: it referred to what they meant. The "Black" Rubric was not the other-than-red rubric: it was the blackguardly rubric.

The name appears in that sense in a long satirical poem which portrays Queen Elizabeth's ecclesiastical advisers discussing what

OGBCP, 27; Ratcliff, Eighty Illustrations, plates 47 and 48; and Davis, "Prosthesis and Reformation," 1210.

[21] For the date, which has been verified, see J. F. Gerrard, Notable Editions of the Prayer Book (Wigan: J. Starr & Sons, 1949), 19; and Griffiths, Bibliography, 144, entry 1716/4. Griffiths's statement elsewhere that "the first modern BCP to have rubrics in red" was published in 1826 (Bibliography, 29, 258) appears to be a slip.

Figure 11.2 The "Black Rubric" in Blackletter Type

An edition of the 1662 Prayer Book published in 1693.

should be included in the Book of Common Prayer when it is restored. What they really care about is how to keep themselves in Elizabeth's good graces:

> *We'll therefore now put-out, or in,*
> *What may, or may not please the Queen.*

But the queen, one of the speakers points out, believes that Christ is present in the sacrament of Holy Communion. That being so,

> *. . . she'll hate our Book of Prayer,*
> *If that black Rubrick be left there. . . .*
> *This Rubrick Cranmer did invent,*
> *'Gainst Worshipping the Sacrament.*
> *But pray-ye let us throw't away,*

> *That People, if it please 'em, may*
> *Adore our Lord as present there . . .* [22]

The writer, who died in 1708, several years before his poem was published—and before the first two-color Prayer Book—was a Roman Catholic convert and controversialist. He may have invented the epithet he used, but it could have been borrowed from an anonymous co-religionist who had written, much earlier, that among the "cunning demands" of the puritans at the Savoy Conference was "the restoring of the *Black Rubrick* into favour."[23]

It is not surprising that both of these polemicists would disparage the Declaration on Kneeling, since it rules out one of their church's most important teachings. For them, the rubric was black in the metaphorical sense of sinister. The metaphor could have been suggested by the appearance of the printed text as a block of thick, dark letters in Prayer Books like the one shown in Figure 11.2. That is chronologically possible. What is not possible is that the name was suggested by the exceptional color of the ink itself, because there was nothing exceptional about it. Rubrics had always been black. No Prayer Book had yet been printed in which they were not.

A more plausible guess would be that it was the other way around—that the printed color, when it was different, was suggested by the name. By the time Prayer Book rubrics were first printed partly in red, the name Black Rubric, whatever its origins, may already have been a commonplace. If it was the printers—Oxford, as it happens—who decided to turn a familiar expression into a visible fact, they need not have intended it to mean what the derogatory metaphor had meant. Since the Declaration had always been printed distinctively, printing it in a distinctive color could simply

---

[22] Thomas Ward (1652–1708), *England's Reformation . . . A Poem in Four Cantos* (London: John Baker, 1715), 270, 272.

[23] R. H., *A Compendious Discourse on the Eucharist. With Two Appendixes* (Oxford, 1688), 157. The author was certainly a Roman Catholic and almost certainly Abraham Woodhead (1609–1678), who used these initials in anonymous publications.

have been another way to indicate that it is not a true rubric. And though the new way of marking the difference did not give rise to the name, it must surely have reinforced it. In any case, it was the printers who had the last word. One of the recommendations of the Privileged Presses' conference mentioned earlier was that typographical differentiation of any kind at all should be discontinued: the Declaration on Kneeling should be "printed uniformly with the preceding rubrics." It is so printed in currently available editions, usually in black, occasionally in red, but in the same color and style as ordinary rubrics either way.

Prayer Books and Pictures

There is no reason for illustrations in the Book of Common Prayer, and none were printed in early editions. The big initials that some-times include representational images were standard print shop equipment, and the picture of the Virgin Mary in one 1552 Prayer Book can only have got there by a fluke and was certainly never repeated. It would have been quite possible to include pictures of some sort, just as it was possible to use (more) red ink. The Bishops' Bible was illustrated;[24] so too were Roman Catholic books of devo-tion, as well as their protestant counterpart, *A Booke of Christian Prayers.* This little book, first printed by John Day in 1578, includes the Litany and other texts from the official Book of Common Prayer, and the elaborate borders, which resemble those in contem-porary Books of Hours, feature vignettes that show Prayer Book services.[25]

---

[24] Some of the illustrations had to be censored, however. See Margaret Aston, "The *Bishops' Bible* Illustrations," in *The Church and the Arts*, Studies in Church History 28, ed. Diana Wood and Robert Swanson (Oxford: Blackwell Publishers, 1992), 267–285.

[25] The vignettes of Prayer Book services, which include Baptism and the Lord's Supper, are illustrated in Judith Maltby, *Prayer Book and People in Elizabethan and Early Stuart England* (Cambridge: Cambridge University Press, 1998), 48, 51, 56; and in *OGBCP,*

If Day had been licensed to print the whole Prayer Book, there might have been editions with similar embellishments. But more likely not. For one thing, the price had to be kept down, since every parish was required to purchase a copy. For another, the religious climate in some sectors of the reformed English church was inhospitable, violently inhospitable at times, to visual mediations of the sacred. The association of images with idolatry and with the Roman church was probably enough to keep pictures out of the official liturgy.

Pictures could be added, however, and before long they were, usually in the form of engravings. Day's images were woodcuts, printed with blocks that could be combined with moveable type and used at the same time on the same press to print words and pictures together on the same page. Engravings, on the other hand, had to be printed by themselves. The metal plates on which they were cut required a different process and different equipment, which ruled out any adjoining words set in type. Instead, the separate pages on which engraved images were printed were either bound into books, interleaved with the letterpress pages, or pasted in afterward. Seventeenth- and eighteenth-century printmakers produced sets of engraved pictures, uniform in size, which booksellers or their customers could add to suitable volumes. Bibles were often "extra-illustrated" with such engravings, and so were copies of the Book of Common Prayer.

One high-end example is a group of twenty-seven large images that can be dated to the 1650s, shortly after the civil wars, in which William Faithorne, who engraved most if not all of them, had fought on the royalist side. Among the images are a number of portraits, which were Faithorne's specialty. In this case they are imagined portraits of biblical figures—the four evangelists, Christ's

82–84, 86. Two of them are shown in color, each on its own full page, in Eamon Duffy, *Marking the Hours: English People and Their Prayers 1240–1570* (New Haven, CT: Yale University Press, 2011), 172.

apostles, St. Paul, the Virgin Mary, and Christ himself. The same set also has several illustrations of events in the gospel narratives. Prayer Books that have been extra-illustrated with these engravings distribute them among the collects, epistles, and gospels for Holy Communion. Christ, portrayed as *Salvator Mundi* (Figure 11.3), comes first, at the beginning of Advent. The saints' portraits are inserted next to their feast days, the narrative pictures near the corresponding gospel readings.[26]

In so far as their subject-matter is biblical, there is nothing incongruent with the Book of Common Prayer in what engravings such as these depict. But they do depict. They are images, not words; their meaning is apprehended and mediated by sight, not hearing; and their effect is not, or not only, decorative. They interact with the printed text, which was meant in the first instance to be read aloud, so that the words could address the ear and edify the mind. It would be hard to say what influence a quasi-icon might have on an individual's observance of a saint's feast day, or how an illustration might inform the way a gospel story was understood, but there would be a difference. In this case there are engraved inscriptions as well, drawn from the Creed and from scripture; but the texts are mostly in Latin, and in two cases—the portraits of Christ and the Virgin Mary—the words were sung as antiphons in Roman Catholic liturgy.[27] To Laudians, perhaps, there would be nothing objectionable in any of this, but not everyone would have agreed.

Nevertheless, a similar repertoire of images—portraits of saints and pictures of episodes in the gospel narratives—was adopted by

---

[26] These images, which were still being used in 1661 if not later, have been studied in a folio Prayer Book of 1636 by Posey Krakowsky in "The Ecclesiology of Prayer Book Illustrations," *Anglican and Episcopal History* 83.3 (2014): 243–291 at 244–257. Another portrait is illustrated in *But One Use*, 101. Some of the engravings that are certainly Faithorne's work were evidently not made in the first place for the Book of Common Prayer; see Louis Fagan, *A Descriptive Catalogue of the Engraved Works of William Faithorne* (London: Bernard Quaritch, 1888), 71–73.

[27] In Figure 11.3, the verse from Psalm 44 (Latin Bible numbering) is Psalm 45:3 in the numbering of the Prayer Book, where it reads: "Thou are fairer than the children of men: full of grace are thy lips, because God hath blessed thee for ever."

SPECIOSVS FORMA PRÆ FILIIS HOMINVM, DIFFVSA EST GRATIA
IN LABIIS TVIS: PROPTEREA BENEDIXIT TE DEVS IN ÆTERNVM.
Psl. 44.

Figure 11.3 Christ as *Salvator Mundi*

Engraving, about 1650, inserted into a 1636 Prayer Book.
Christopher Keller, Jr. Library, The General Theological Seminary.
Image courtesy of Toby McAfee Photography.

other seventeenth-century printmakers who offered sets of smaller illustrations, less accomplished and less costly, made specifically for personal-use Prayer Books. Typically, as in Figure 11.4, each image comes with a title and a quotation from the (English) Bible. In this example the main subject is Christ, asleep in the storm-tossed boat; in the background is a preview of the next episode in the gospel, which shows the pigs that plunged into the sea, possessed—and on a close look, pursued—by the demons called Legion that Christ is driving out of the man who writhes on the ground.

Events reported in scripture were not the only ones pictured in these engravings. The 1662 Prayer Book enlarged sacred history to include the frustration of the Papists' Conspiracy, the martyrdom of Charles I, and the restoration of Charles II at the end of the Great Rebellion. The services for the "solemn days" that commemorate these episodes were regularly provided with illustrations, which usually include biblical passages that invite and support an interpretation of the illustrated events as special dispensations of divine providence.

So familiar was the image for November 5, Powder Plot Day, that the author of *Tom Jones* could count on readers to know exactly what one of the characters had in his mind's eye when he shouted, "Look, look, madam! the very picture of the man in the end of the common prayer-book, before the gunpowder-treason service." One very common version of this image, Figure 11.5, shows Guy Fawkes, the would-be assassin, stealthily arriving at the old House of Lords, where fellow-conspirators had piled gunpowder in the cellar, ready to blow up the protestant regime of James I at the opening of Parliament.[28] But there is no hiding from the all-seeing eye of God. Dispelled by heavenly aid, *cælitus discussa*, the

---

[28] The Fawkes image is discussed in Alexandra Walsham, *Providence in Early Modern England* (Oxford: Oxford University Press, 1999), 264–266. See also Whitney Anne Trettien, *The Collation* (Washington, DC: Folger Shakespeare Library), April 19, 2013. There is another version of the image in Streatfeild, *State Prayers and Other Variations*, plate 2, opposite 31. The line from Henry Fielding's novel (1749) is in book 16, ch. 5.

Figure 11.4 Christ Rebukes the Winds

Anonymous engraving, inserted into a 1681 Prayer Book.

Christopher Keller, Jr. Library, The General Theological Seminary.

Image courtesy of Toby McAfee Photography.

Figure 11.5 Guy Fawkes: A Conspiracy Exposed
Anonymous engraving, about 1662, to illustrate the Gunpowder Treason service.

conspiracy will fail, while the king will escape "as a bird out of the snare of the fowlers."

Extra-illustrated Prayer Books were not uncommon in the later seventeenth century. In the eighteenth century they began to be marketed as such. One of the first engravers to collaborate in the publication of an illustrated edition was John Sturt, who produced engravings for several issues of what the extra title-page he provided called *The Liturgy of the Church of England Adorn'd with 55 Historical Cuts*. Calligraphic engraving was Sturt's forte, and the lettering of the titles and quotations that accompany his pictures is impressive in its own right. More impressive still is Sturt's complete Book of Common Prayer, every word of which he engraved, reportedly on silver, in tiny italic script. The words of the services are perfectly legible, although it may take a magnifying glass to read the sixty-some lines of Prayer Book texts that Sturt wove into his frontispiece, a portrait of King George II all of three inches tall.[29] Just after this extraordinary page comes the mobile table of the ecclesiastical year that was discussed in chapter two (Figure 2.2).

Sturt engraved a picture for every Sunday and holyday gospel, and for most of the major offices as well. It is instructive to compare the way he illustrated the service for the Public Baptism of Infants in 1717 with an illustration made for the same service a hundred years later. Sturt's engravings are biblical; they point the viewer toward sacred events in the past. On the page shown in Figure 11.6, the image links the Prayer Book office with Christ's own baptism, which the first prayer alludes to. By contrast, the nineteenth-century stipple engraving shown in Figure 11.7 portrays baptism as a rite of passage taking place in the present. It belongs to a set of twelve images that show three generations of a devout Regency family as they attend Divine Service and take part in the occasional offices, moving through the human life-cycle from birth, growing up, and marriage to sickness and death.[30]

Baptism is depicted taking place in church, as it should, but though the Prayer Book rite gives parents nothing to say or do, the

---

[29] The portrait is illustrated in *OGBCP*, 122 and Griffiths, *Bibliography*, 146. Sturt managed to include the Lord's Prayer, the Creed, the Commandments, prayers for the king and the royal family, and Psalm 21.

[30] Griffiths 1813/5; Cambridge: J. Smith; published, London: James Carpenter, Sharpe and Hailes, Scatcherd and Letterman, Taylor and Hessey, and John Carr. See Krakowsky, "Prayer Book Illustrations," 276–291.

Figure 11.6 The Ministration of Baptism, Engraved and Illustrated
An edition entirely engraved by John Sturt, 1717
Courtesy of the Beinecke Rare Books Library, Yale University.

Figure 11.7 Infant Baptism, Early Nineteenth Century
Stipple engraving, one of twelve illustrations made for an 1813 Prayer Book
Christopher Keller, Jr. Library, The General Theological Seminary.
Image courtesy of Toby McAfee Photography.

most prominent person in the illustration is the child's mother.
Since the woman on the right is the grandmother, the figures behind her may be the baby's godparents; if so, they are very much in
the background. At this baptism, the primary community would

seem to be the family rather than the church. All this might be the artist's imagination; it might show how christenings were typically conducted at the time; either way, it was felt to be an appropriate image for a domestic Prayer Book. In this edition and a number of others with similar sets of images, the events illustrated as sacred are events that the text itself prescribes.[31]

The Prayer Book as Art

Before the nineteenth century, there was usually nothing remarkable about the typography and printing of the Book of Common Prayer. Apart from Sturt's extraordinary edition, which was not set in type at all, there was probably only one occasion when, as one survey puts it, "typographical history was made." In 1760 John Baskerville, who gave his name to a typeface still in use, "raised the Book of Common Prayer to its highest level of presentation and made it superior in that respect to any Continental production."[32] Unfortunately, the paper and types that Baskerville used were unusable for large printings, and his editions, excellent though they were, had little influence on the usual run of Prayer Books.

When Prayer Books admirable in themselves began to appear, their appearance, in both senses of the word, owed something to nineteenth-century advances in the technology of printing, something to the intertwined revivals of gothic art and medieval ritual, and something to economic prosperity that made upscale Prayer Books marketable. This confluence could yield strikingly different results, as shown by two equally striking Prayer Books published almost at the same time. Owen Jones, best known for

---

[31] For another example of baptism in a Prayer Book illustration of about the same time, see Streatfeild, *State Prayers and Other Variations*, plate 6, opposite 48.

[32] Stanley Morison, *English Prayer Books: An Introduction to the Literature of Christian Public Worship* (Cambridge: Cambridge University Press, 1949), 143. See also Griffiths, *Bibliography*, 11 and for an illustration 177.

his encyclopedic *Grammar of Ornament*, put all the resources of chromolithography to work in his Book of Common Prayer, a bumptious, eclectic romp illustrated with drawings copied from the works of great painters and illuminated by Jones himself. His embellishments range from quasi-gothic borders of vegetation on ordinary pages to visual extravaganzas on the divisional title-pages, printed in several colors plus metallic gold.[33] Compared with the decorations, the typography is lackluster. Perhaps Jones did not care, or perhaps the printed words were meant to be drab, the better to show off his own artistry.

Entirely different in that respect, though published at just the same time, is the set of seven Prayer Books printed by the firm of Pickering in 1844. Each version of the English liturgy from 1549 to 1662, including "Laud's Liturgy," is reprinted *verbatim* in a separate folio. For good measure there is also a matching volume, updated for Queen Victoria. Whereas in Jones's edition ornament is paramount and typography negligible, it is the other way around in the Pickering Prayer Books. A suggestion of medievalism appears in their blackletter typeface, but the only adornments are printer's flowers and subdued initials, all of them variations on the same design. Although these elegant books are not page-for-page facsimiles, they are careful reprints. The 1552 volume includes the original printers' errors as well as their list of "faults escaped," similar to the one illustrated at the beginning of this chapter.[34]

Different yet again, but just as striking, is another hefty folio, *The Prayer Book of King Edward VII*, published at the turn of the century. On its pages words and images, illustration and typography,

---

[33] Griffiths 1845/24; illustrated in Griffiths, *Bibliography*, twelfth unnumbered page of color plates, and in *But One Use*, color plate for Item 61. Another page is illustrated in *OGBCP*, 124. A replica of the whole volume, as lavish as the original, has been published (Norwalk, CT: Easton Press, 2013).

[34] On these reprints, see Griffiths, *Bibliography*, 304 and the eleventh unnumbered page of color plates. There are also illustrations in *OGBCP*, 126, 127 and *But One Use*, 118.

contribute equally to a design remarkable for its overall unity. The designer was the Arts and Crafts polymath Charles Robert Ashbee, who created the typeface, drew the woodcut illustrations, and planned the layout of every page. As in many earlier editions, the frontispiece is a royal portrait, which in this case shows the eponymous king enthroned within a frame that includes smaller images of the first six Edwards. Many of the large initials are "historiated," inhabited by figures related to the text. Like all the other illustrations and decorations, they are linear, stylized, sometimes austere, and thoroughly congruent with the rounded letters of the text.

Probably the most memorable feature of Ashbee's Prayer Book comes at the front. Along the top of its eight-page table of contents a parade of ecclesiastical worthies marches in historical order, beginning with St. Alban and St. Patrick. George Washington and Bishop Seabury represent the Americans, Thomas Tallis the church musicians, Christopher Wren the architects. Not all the marchers were Anglicans; Queen Mary I and John Bunyan both appear, though neither of them thought much of the Book of Common Prayer. Ashbee, a socialist and a modernist, was at the same time deeply appreciative of the Prayer Book and the history it embodies. The procession he marshalled at the beginning of his edition is an eloquent expression of that sense of continuity.[35] *The Prayer Book of King Edward VII* may not have seen much liturgical use, but it was not only a treasure book, valued for its artistry and craftsmanship. It was also, and it remains, a kind of shrine, a testament of religious and cultural meaning, an outward and visible sign of reverence for the words its pages carry and for the religious tradition those words helped to form. Here, it announces visibly, is a sacred text.

[35] *The Prayer Book of King Edward VII* is discussed in Alan Crawford, *C.R. Ashbee: Architect, Designer & Romantic Socialist* (New Haven, CT: Yale University Press, 1985), 390–395, with illustrations, among them the last two contents pages. The frontispiece is reproduced (with hand coloring) on the back cover of *But One Use* and in Griffiths, *Bibliography*, facing 469.

A separate printing of Ashbee's Prayer Book was made available in the United States, where the Episcopal Church had recently issued an impressive printing of its own Book of Common Prayer. A revision had been authorized in 1892, as was said earlier, and a limited, deluxe edition of the new standard text was planned. There could be no change in the somewhat uninspiring typography, but a young book designer, Daniel Berkeley Updike, was called upon to improve the appearance of the pages. He had little choice but to add borders, which he added. The result was not wholly successful. Thanks to the generosity of J. Pierpont Morgan, the financier, who served on the printing committee, the binding of the limited edition is resplendent—gilt on vellum, with brass clasps—but inside there is a disconcerting mismatch between the exuberant borders, drawn in the William Morris manner, and the letterpress they surround. Public reception was enthusiastic, but Updike's own opinion was that the best things about the book were its cover and its endpapers. They have no typesetting.[36]

Two outstanding Prayer Books printed in the early twentieth century share the unusual distinction of being books that books have been written about. One of them, described in full as the Fell Double Pica Imperial Quarto Book of Common Prayer, belongs to an ensemble of ecclesiastical volumes that the Oxford University Press began to publish in connection with the coronation of King George V in 1911. Traditional private-press methods were deliberately chosen for the printing, which made use of types purchased by John Fell, a seventeenth-century dean and bishop of Oxford, to whose zeal the press was indebted for its right to print the Book of Common Prayer in the first place. A medium-sized Prayer Book was printed with Fell types before war broke out in 1914, but only

---

[36] A page is illustrated in *OGBCP*, 129. The artist was Bertram Grosvenor Goodhue. See Daniel Berkeley Updike, *The Well-Made Book: Essays & Lectures*, ed. William S. Peterson (West New York, NJ: Mark Batty, 2002), 283–287 and 221–276 at 226–227; also George Parker Winship, *Daniel Berkeley Updike and the Merrymount Press* (Rochester, NY: Leo Hart, 1947), 12–14.

part of the large "imperial quarto" edition was finished. The sheets that had been printed languished in storage until 1989, when they were rescued, together with the types, which were used to print the remaining pages. Seventy-five years after it began, "perhaps one of the most monumental pieces of liturgical printing of all time" was brought to completion.[37]

With their ornate initials and antique typography, the Fell Prayer Books belong to the apogee of the Arts and Crafts movement. Ten years after the Great War ended, an equally monumental but aesthetically quite different Prayer Book was published in the United States. Once again the Episcopal Church had revised its liturgy; once again, as in 1892, there was to be a limited edition of the newly authorized standard; once again the book was designed by Daniel Berkeley Updike. This time there was no incongruity.[38] Updike knew as much as anyone, probably more, about the peculiar requirements of liturgical typography and how they applied to Anglican texts in particular. Other designs were considered, but afterward even Updike's rivals agreed that his was the best. There are large initials, but no decorations except a modest fleuron, printed once on the title page and very sparingly elsewhere. The visual impact of the book depends entirely on its typography, on proportion, arrangement, balance, and spacing. According to the letter sent to potential printers, the hope was that the projected Book of Common Prayer would be "historical in the development of printing."[39] And so it was. Updike's 1928 Prayer Book has been

---

[37] Peter Foden, *The Fell Imperial Quarto Book of Common Prayer: An Account of its Production* (Rishbury, UK: Whittington Press, 1998), 42. The smaller, two-column Prayer Book printed with Fell types is illustrated in color in Updike, *Well-Made Book*, 102.

[38] The evolution and production of the book have been studied in detail; see Ray Nash, "Types for the Standard Prayer Book of 1928, *The Library* 29 (1974) 61–79; Martin Hutner, *The Making of The Book of Common Prayer of 1928* (Southbury, CT: Chiswick Book Shop, 1990), with illustrations; Winship, *Daniel Berkeley Updike*, 123–126.

[39] Letter on behalf of the younger J.P. Morgan, who underwrote the project, to the four competitors, quoted in Nash, "Types for the Standard Prayer Book," 63.

called the pinnacle of American printing and the best work of the best printer of the twentieth century.

Fifty years later there was yet another revision of the American Book of Common Prayer, and for a third time a limited edition of the standard volume was planned. A printer was chosen, sample pages were handsomely printed in black and red, pledges of financial backing were invited, and orders were taken, at two thousand dollars apiece, for copies additional to the ones that would be sent, as canon law required, to the church's dioceses and seminaries. But the project was canceled. There was not enough money, and maybe not enough interest. The Episcopal Church had many other priorities and commitments; and to its members it may have seemed that the 1979 Prayer Book, with its contemporary-language services, did not call for the same reverential treatment as its predecessors.

Indeed, it would not be long before the Prayer Book as any sort of permanent material object, let alone an *objet d'art*, began to give way to multiple sources of interchangeable texts that could be retrieved electronically, supplemented, rearranged, projected on a screen, and photocopied in disposable pamphlets.[40] Whether there will much longer be such a thing as a *Book* of Common Prayer is at least a question; but the likelihood of another edition like Ashbee's or Updike's is small.

---

[40] See Donald Kraus, "The Book of Common Prayer and Technology," *OGBCP*, 541–544, and Clayton L. Morris, "The Prayer Book in Cyberspace," *OGBCP*, 545–550

Twelve
The Prayer Book Sung

Until they have been uttered, the words of the Prayer Book are only potentially common prayer. They are meant to be realized, to become actual in the sound of human voices. They can be spoken, enunciated in the form of ordinary speech. That is how they have been heard most frequently. But they can also be made audible by singing them. The rubrics make provision for certain words to the "said or sung," and the practice of singing these and other parts of the Prayer Book text is as old as the text itself. Not only has that practice been a performative acknowledgment that the text it brings to expression is a sacred text: it has also done much to make it so.

Had it not been for Queen Elizabeth, the tradition of singing the English liturgy might have been stifled at birth. At first it had seemed that the reformed services could and would be performed in much the same way as the Latin offices had been: Mattins, Mass, and Evensong would be sung when that was possible, and the priest who sang them would be assisted by as many clerks, choirmen, and choristers as his church could support. But the militant reforming impulse that tore down altars and demolished images as irredeemably superstitious was equally hostile to music of the kind that had long been normal in Christian worship. By the end of King Edward VI's reign, many choral foundations had been dissolved, many pipe organs were dismantled, and a new, austere Book of Common Prayer had closed off much of the original version's openness to maintaining the musical traditions of the past.

It was this more uncompromisingly protestant Prayer Book that Elizabeth's first Parliament reinstated, following her predecessor's counter-Reformation. The legislation that reinstated it, however,

The Book of Common Prayer. Charles Hefling, Oxford University Press (2021). © Oxford University Press.
DOI: 10.1093/oso/9780190689681.001.0001.

expressly reserved to the queen the right to adjust and augment the statutory pattern of worship—which she did, almost at once, in a set of injunctions, one of which could be said to have rescued English church music and set it on the course it would follow for three hundred years and more.

"Modest and Distinct Song"

The queen's injunction is vividly ambivalent. It disavows any practice by which "the common prayer should be the worse understanded of the hearers." So far, so protestant. At the same time, there should be no decay of the "laudable science of music" that depended on endowments "appointed to the use of singing or music in the church." The disbanding of choral foundations must cease. The injunction famously continues:

> And that there be a modest and distinct song so used in all parts of the common prayers in the church, that the same may be as plainly understanded, as if it were read without singing; and yet nevertheless for the comforting of such that delight in music, it may be permitted, that in the beginning, or in the end of common prayers, either at morning or evening, there may be sung an hymn, or such-like song to the praise of Almighty God, in the best sort of melody and music that may be conveniently devised, having respect that the sentence of the hymn may be understanded and perceived.[1]

The queen's orders could be taken in two directions. Musicians in cathedral and collegiate churches, large parishes, and above all the

---

[1] Cardwell, *Annals*, 1: 228–229. See Nicholas Temperley, *The Music of the English Parish Church* (2 vols.; Cambridge: Cambridge University Press, 1979), I: 39–42; Peter le Huray, *Music and the Reformation in England 1549-1660* (London: Herbert Jenkins, 1967), 31–35.

chapel royal could pick up where things had left off, and they did so. The Prayer Book services were sung, and appropriate music was composed for them. William Harrison, in the "Description of England" that chapter six discussed, makes a point of saying that the trained choirs in great churches sang "in so plain, I say, and distinct manner that each one present may understand what they sing, ... though the whole harmony consist of many parts, and those very cunningly set."[2] That on the one hand. On the other, the queen's permission of "an hymn, or such-like song" before and after Divine Service was construed as authorizing whole congregations to sing rhymed, stanzaic translations of the biblical Psalter—the "singing Psalms." Harrison mentions those too. In smaller churches, which is to say most parish churches, "Psalms in meter" were almost the only music that anyone ever heard.

So it was that with the approbation of one royal injunction two musical traditions went forward in the Church of England. One of them, "cathedral music," relied on formal training, specialized ability, and competence in the laudable science of music. The other, "parochial music," did not. It called for simple skills, "attainable by the ear," which almost anyone could learn through informal custom and rote. Cathedral music enhanced the statutory liturgy; parochial music supplemented it. The two were never completely disparate or entirely independent, but there was a difference, which was recognized and accepted until well into the eighteenth century.[3] A "cathedral" service, wherever it took place, was largely though not entirely sung by an officiating minister and a choir. A parochial service, which was far more common, was spoken, but it began and ended with congregational singing, usually led by the parish clerk.

---

[2] William Harrison, *The Description of England* (Ithaca, NY: Cornell University Press, 1968), 34.

[3] See esp. Jonathan Willis, *Church Music and Protestantism in Post-Reformation England: Discourses, Sites and Identities* (Farnham, UK: Ashgate Publishing, 2010), 138–139, 155–159; and Temperley, *Music of the English Parish Church*, I: 76.

The Psalms in Meter

The rhymed versions of the biblical Psalms that framed public prayers in most churches were introduced in chapter six. They were commonly thought to be as much a part of the Book of Common Prayer as the prose Psalter, and were certainly used as if they were. When the Protestant Episcopal Church in the United States included a set of them in its first authorized Book of Common Prayer, it was only regularizing a custom that had been all but universal for two centuries.

The "singing Psalms" in the American Prayer Book followed the *New Version of the Psalms of David*, first published in 1689. This collection had gradually replaced the "Old Version," known as Sternhold and Hopkins from the names of its compilers. The Old Version, parts of which were older than the Prayer Book itself, had been extraordinarily popular—perhaps as many as a million copies were printed[4]—and it established a genre which the New Version made no attempt to alter. A singing Psalm, old or new, was a poem in several stanzas, one for every verse of the biblical text. By way of example, Table 12.1 compares the first five verses of Psalm 24, the first Psalm at the service described in chapter one, with the metrical rendering in Sternhold and Hopkins.

Like nearly all the singing Psalms, this one exemplifies the pattern of stressed and unstressed syllables known to hymnologists as "common meter": fourteen iambic feet in four lines, 4 + 3, 4 + 3. The great advantage of repeating the same metrical pattern in

---

[4] Ian Green, *Print and Protestantism in Early Modern England* (Oxford: Oxford University Press, 2000), 503. There is a large literature. See esp. the critical edition of text and tunes by Beth Quitslund and Nicholas Temperley, *The Whole Book of Psalms*, 2 vols. (Tempe: Arizona Center for Medieval and Renaissance Studies, 2018); Hannibal Hamlin, *Psalm Culture and Early Modern English Culture* (Cambridge: Cambridge University Press, 2004); and Rivkah Zim, *English Metrical Psalms: Poetry as Praise and Prayer* (Cambridge: Cambridge University Press, 1987).

Table 12.1   Psalm 24, *Domini est terra*
(first five verses)

The Prayer Book Psalter	*Sternhold and Hopkins*
1 The earth is the Lord's, and all that therein is:	The earth is all the Lord's, with all her store and furniture:
the compass of the world, and they that dwell therein.	Yea his is all the world, and all that therein do endure.
2 For he hath founded it upon the seas:	For he hath fastly founded it, above the sea to stand:
and prepared it upon the floods.	And laid alow the liquid floods, to flow beneath the land.
3 Who shall ascend into the hill of the Lord:	For who is he (O Lord) that shall ascend into thy hill:
or who shall rise up in his holy place?	Or pass into thy holy place, there to continue still?
4 Even he, that hath clean hands, and a pure heart:	Whose hands are harmless, and whose heart no spot there doth defile:
and that hath not lift up his mind unto vanity, nor sworn to deceive his neighbor.	His soul not set on vanity, who hath not sworn no guile.
5 He shall receive the blessing from the Lord:	Him that is such a one, the Lord shall place in blissful plight:
and righteousness from the God of his salvation.	And God, his God and Savior shall yield to him his right.

every stanza is that they can all be sung to the same tune. Each
paraphrased Psalm-verse has twenty-eight syllables, whereas the
verses in Coverdale's prose translation vary. Metrical regularity
comes at a price, however, especially if the fourth line must rhyme
with the second, as it always does in Sternhold and Hopkins. In
order to make the words fit, it is often necessary to pinch or pad
the original sense, or contort the syntax, or both. The Old Version
was notorious for its infelicities in that regard; poems made fun of

its poetry.[5] But to fault the metrical Psalms on literary grounds is in some sense to miss the point. Singing them was not an aesthetic or a didactic exercise so much as a ritual. It was acting, doing something, as contrasted with passive listening; and the activity was both corporeal and corporate, embodied and social, an event of self-identification with others. For some people it was also a confessional act. "Geneva jigs," as scorners called them, could express and reinforce loyalty to Swiss-style protestantism. But they were sung in cathedrals too, and during the civil wars Royalists as well as Roundheads sang them. They were Psalms, after all; not in the first instance, if at all, doctrinal manifestoes.[6]

With very few exceptions—notably "All people that on earth do dwell," set to the tune "Old Hundredth"[7]—the verses in the metrical Psalters have ceased to be sung, but the ubiquitous practice of singing them has had a lasting effect on the part that music plays in Prayer Book liturgy. Sternhold and Hopkins gave rise to a settled expectation that Divine Service will begin and end with congregational singing, and that what is sung will be verse, written in several rhymed stanzas. The expectation remains as strong as ever, but it is now met by hymns rather than versified Psalms.[8] It was only a short step from the rhyming paraphrase of the *Te Deum* in the Old Version to hymnody in the modern sense. The New Version took that step in a supplement which includes, among others,

---

[5] For the Earl of Rochester's poem, which rhymes *Psalms* with *qualms*, see Ian Green, "'All People that on Earth Do Dwell, Sing to the Lord with Cheerful Voice': Protestantism and Music in Early Modern England," in *Christianity and Community in the West: Essays for John Bossy*, ed. Simon Ditchfield (London: Routledge, 2001), 148–164 at 157.

[6] "Jigs" was perhaps ironic, since metrical Psalms were evidently sung very, very slowly. See in particular Nicholas Temperley, "'All Skillful Praises Sing': How Congregations Sang the Psalms in Early Modern England," *Renaissance Studies* 29.4 (2015): 531–553. Beth Quitslund, *The Reformation in Rhyme: Sternhold, Hopkins and the English Metrical Psalter 1547-1603* (Aldershot, UK: Ashgate Publishing, 2008) emphasizes metrical psalmody as ideology, while recognizing important qualifications; see 111–113, 194–195, 225, 230–231. See also Temperley, *Music of the English Parish Church*, I: 86–87.

[7] As it happens, this well-known paraphrase of Psalm 100 does not conform to the typical Sternhold and Hopkins meter.

[8] Temperley makes the point in "All Skillful Praises," 553.

the Christmas hymn "While shepherds watched their flocks by night." Once it was determined, early in the nineteenth century, that singing hymns was as lawful for Anglicans as singing versified Psalms, hymn texts and hymn tunes proliferated and Prayer Books, once routinely bound with metrical Psalters, began to be bound with hymnals.

Anglican Chant

The name "singing Psalms" suggests that the official Psalter, Coverdale's prose translation, was not sung but only said. In most places, most of the time, that has no doubt been the case. The Psalms in meter are easy to sing and were devised to be so. The Prayer Book Psalms cannot be sung in the same way, because none of them fits into a melody that can be repeated, verse after verse. Nevertheless, they have always been sung. In order to sing them without changing the words, a distinctive musical form evolved, which more than any other has come to be identified with the Book of Common Prayer. This "unique and distinguishing feature of the English liturgy" has "its own highly specialized genre of chant with an official name, Anglican Chant."[9]

A written description of this or any other musical form can only be informative up to a point. One good audio recording is worth a thousand words. But words may give some indication of what there is to be heard. An Anglican chant tune, then, can be described as a short hymn in two lines or phrases, which is generally sung in four-part harmony, often though not necessarily with organ accompaniment. There are hundreds of these tunes.[10] In each of them, as a rule, the first melodic phrase has four notes, and thus a progression

---

[9] Ruth M. Wilson, *Anglican Chant and Chanting in England, Scotland, and America 1660–1820* (Oxford: Oxford University Press, 1996), 59.
[10] It should be said at the outset that most of them are "double chants"—spliced pairs with four lines. The doubling does not affect the basic principles discussed here.

of four chords; the second phrase has six. Both phrases—and this is the important point—are elastic. They can be extended or telescoped to accommodate more or fewer syllables, depending on the wording of the text that is to be sung.

To continue the example in Table 12.1, the words of the first two verses of Psalm 24 in the Prayer Book translation are arranged here so that the syllables represent the structure of a typical Anglican chant. Each verse of the Psalm, as usual, is divided in two at the colon. The first half of each verse is sung to the notes of the first phrase of the chant, the second half-verse to the second phrase.

1 The earth is the Lord's, and all that ‖ thére- in | ís :
    the compass of the world, and ‖ théy   that | dwéll there- | ín.

2 For he hath founded it up- ‖ ón   the | séas :
    and prepared ‖ ít   up- | ón   the | flóods.

In each of the chant's two musical phrases, the adjustable part is its first note, the "reciting note." On this note the beginning of each half-verse is sung. The same pitch is repeated as many times as there are syllables before the double vertical stroke; that is, before the last three syllables in the first half-verse, or the last five syllables in the second half-verse. Thus in the first verse of Psalm 24, the three-note close or cadence of the first musical phrase begins at *therein is*. Similarly, the five syllables of *they that dwell therein*, to the right of the double stroke, are sung on the last five notes of the second musical phrase; everything *before* those five syllables is sung on the reciting note. The syllables of the second verse of the Psalm are distributed in exactly the same way.

The accents and the single vertical strokes are meant to suggest the exigences of the harmony, but the main point is the distribution of words. Any suitable sentence can be sung this way, including the one that you are reading now.

Any suitable sentence can be ‖ súng   this | wáy :
including the one that ‖ yóu   are | réad-   ing | nów.

When the full title of the Book of Common Prayer announces that
the Psalms of David are "pointed as they are to be sung or said in
churches," it means only that the dividing-point between the two
halves of each verse is marked by a colon or, in some editions, a
more obvious asterisk. Given this minimal punctuation or pointing,
a singer need only apply the "rule of three and five": three syllables
back from the printed colon, the three-note ending of the first
phrase of the chant tune begins; five syllables back from the end
of the verse, the full cadence of the whole tune begins.[11] In principle, any pointed Psalm can be sung to any chant tune; and since
the canticles at Morning and Evening Prayer are similarly pointed,
the same simple method can be used to sing them as well.

The three-and-five rule is only a rule of thumb. It happens to
work fairly well on the first two verses of Psalm 24. But not as well as
it might. In the second half of the second verse, for musical reasons,
there would be a stress on the word *it* which in ordinary speech
would fall on the second syllable of *prepared*. To avoid such ungain-
liness, adjustments can be made, the better to match locutionary
emphasis with harmonic emphasis. Even with these refinements,
Anglican chanting may fail to satisfy some musicians,[12] but its
conventions do allow an ensemble of singers to sing, in understandable English, the words of the prose Psalms and the canticles
in the Prayer Book, which is practically the whole point.

---

[11] See Wilson, *Anglican Chant*, 93 for the rule.

[12] For example, Charles William Pearce, "The Futility of the Anglican Chant," *The
Musical Quarterly* 6.1 (1920): 118–126. The poet and composer Robert Bridges gives an
instructive and constructive account of the problems in his article on "Chanting" in the
Prayer Book Dictionary, 176–181. The previous article, "Chant, Anglican," by the same
author (171–176) discusses origins and evolution. Both articles use musical notation.

The Prayer Book "Noted"

The Psalms and canticles invite singing. If anything in the Book of Common Prayer has been sung, it has been those texts. But nearly everything else has been sung too. Queen Elizabeth's injunction refers to "modest and distinct song ... in *all parts* of the common prayers in the church," and a rubric in the 1559 Prayer Book orders, in particular, that "in such places where they do sing, there shall the lessons be sung in a plain tune after the manner of distinct reading; and likewise the epistle and gospel" (owc 106). In practice, the minister who declaimed those passages of scripture was presumably meant to chant them, reciting the words in a sustained singing voice, perhaps on just one musical pitch throughout. If the text of the Bible was sung in some fashion, other parts of the liturgy could equally well be chanted "after the manner of distinct reading," and no doubt they were.

Both the injunction and the rubric emphasize audibility and understandability. The words must be heard *as* words, not just as sounds pleasingly voiced. That indispensable requirement could not be met by many of the traditional melodies used to chant parts of the Latin liturgy. Some of them had become so elaborate that the texts they set to music were not "understanded of the hearers" even if the hearers understood Latin. In a reformed church, that would not be acceptable at all. In anticipation of the reformed English liturgy, Archbishop Cranmer wrote to Henry VIII that what would be needed was music which

> would not be full of notes, but, as near as may be, for every syllable a note; so that it may be sung distinctly and devoutly, as be in Mattins and Evensong *Venite*, the hymns *Te Deum, Benedictus, Magnificat, Nunc dimittis*, and all the Psalms and versicles; and in the Mass *Gloria in excelsis, Gloria Patri*, the Creed, the Preface, the *Pater noster* and some of the *Sanctus* and *Agnus*.[13]

---

[13] Cranmer to Henry VIII, October 7 [1544], in Cranmer, *Works* 2: *Miscellaneous Writings* (Parker Society, Cambridge University Press, 1846), 412. See le Huray, *Music and the Reformation*, 5–7; Temperley, *Music of the English Parish Church*, I: 12–13.

Cranmer assumes that the Psalms, as well as the constant texts in the principal daily offices and in the Mass, would continue to be sung, as by custom they had been. The customary music, however, would have to be revised or replaced, if it stretched a single syllable over a series of many notes, as the old chants very often did. Cranmer himself may have had a hand in "noting" or setting to music the text of the litany that would later be included in the Prayer Book. The music, which was issued in 1544, the same year as his letter to King Henry, is a little more complex than "distinct reading," but very little, and it never assigns more than one note to any syllable.

Many musicians may well have taken on the task of noting the other liturgical items that Cranmer mentions, setting them to the sort of music he had in mind. If they did, not much of what they wrote still exists, perhaps because it was left in manuscript.[14] At least one such project was printed, however, and a few copies have survived. In 1550 John Merbecke or Marbeck published *The booke of Common praier noted.*[15]

Marbeck's book can best be understood as one of several semi-official adjuncts to the official Book of Common Prayer, all of them designed to make it more usable in practice. Cranmer had said in his original preface that besides a Bible and the new English liturgy, "the curates shall need none other books for their public service." That was true in one sense: between them, the Bible and the Prayer Book did print all the required words. But the Prayer Book itself presumes that in public service not all the required words will be heard in the minister's voice. If anyone else made the responses, as the parish clerk might be expected to do, he would have to read them from another copy of the Prayer Book; but a whole Prayer Book was both

---

[14] For evidence that does survive, see John Milsom, "English-texted Chant before Merbecke," *Plainsong and Medieval Music* 1.1 (1992): 77–92.

[15] There are two fine facsimile editions printed, as was the original, in two colors: Nottingham Court Press (1979) and Sutton Courtenay Press (1980). The latter has an introduction and detailed commentary by Robin A. Leaver.

more and less than what a clerk needed. On the one hand, a great part of the text consists of the epistles and gospels. Only the priest read those. On the other hand, there was no Psalter. Only if the clerk read the Psalms from a Bible could they be read antiphonally.[16]

In short, Cranmer's preface notwithstanding, other books besides the Prayer Book were practically if not absolutely necessary. Even before the Prayer Book had been officially issued, it must have been evident that a separate Psalter would be very convenient for clerks, as well as for choirs and perhaps ministers also, because at least one pointed Psalter was printed on its own in 1548.[17] Shortly afterward, another pointed Psalter appeared, with user-friendly additions that have been retained ever since: running headlines and labels that make finding the daily portions easier and show where each of them begins. But this Psalter was more than a Psalter. Included together with the Psalms are the texts of Mattins, Evensong, the Litany, and "all that shall appertain to the clerks to say or sing" at the Lord's Supper and several of the occasional offices. The more apt name of *The Clerk's Book* is often used for this handy compilation.[18] Marbeck's book complements it.

The booke of Common praier noted contains "so much of the order of common prayer as is to be sung in the church," either by the priest or by the clerks or both.[19] The priest's music is quite simple. He is to chant almost everything on a single pitch, one note to each

---

[16] The 1549 Prayer Book does include (most of) the Psalms, but they are parceled out individually in the occasional services, and as introductory introits at Holy Communion, which are printed together with the collects, epistles, and gospels—not all together in the biblical order that Mattins and Evensong presuppose. In 1552 the introits were deleted.

[17] *The Psalter or Psalmes of David after the translacion of the great Bible, poincted as it shalbe song in Churches* (STC 2375.5; London: Richard Grafton, November 27, 1548).

[18] *The Psalter or Psalmes of David, corrected and poynted, as thei shalbe song in Churches after the translacion of the greate Bible* (STC 2377; London: Richard Grafton, August 1549). The cover page and the list of contents are shown in Ratcliff, *Eighty Illustrations*, plates 32 and 33. The book is reprinted with extensive commentary by J. Wickham Legg as *The Clerk's Book of 1549*, Henry Bradshaw Society 25 (London, 1903).

[19] Marbeck does not give music for the Litany. Since that text had already been "noted," he may have assumed that copies with musical notation would be available.

syllable, very much in "the manner of distinct reading." The clerks are given somewhat more elaborate music, which echoes but does not replicate medieval chants. Figure 12.1 gives a brief example, the first of the offertory sentences at Holy Communion (OWC 25).

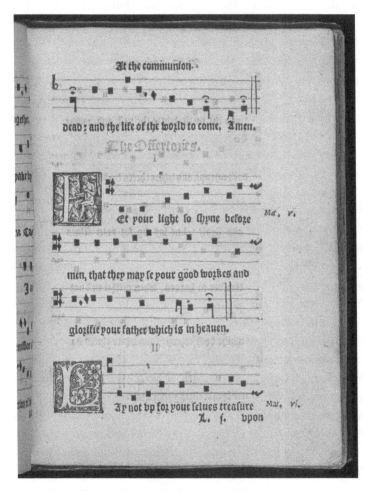

Figure 12.1 The First Prayer Book, Set to Music
John Merbecke, *The booke of Common praier noted*, 1550
Courtesy of the Beinecke Rare Books Library, Yale University.

This text begins with *Let your light* beneath the second four-line staff, which is printed in red. From there through the words *good works and*, every syllable is assigned a square note, indicating that all these syllables, as sung, have the same duration. In the third line of text, the word *glorify* is sung on one pitch—the three notes on the staff above are on the same red line—but the first syllable is lengthened and the second is shortened. The dot or "prick" after the first note prolongs it; the diamond-shaped note over the second syllable is shorter than the regular pulse of the square notes. The notes for the words *is* and *heaven* (one syllable, *heav'n*) indicate that these syllables will be sustained. There is rhythmic as well as melodic variety in this brief chant, but neither here nor anywhere else is Marbeck's music "full of notes."

In the Psalms, of which there are five in *Common praier noted*, Marbeck notes only the first verse. He evidently assumed that the clerks could sing the remaining verses from a complete Psalter, something like the *Clerk's Book* perhaps. This would not be difficult, because the same music would be repeated. The melody that Marbeck assigns is one of the ancient Psalm "tones" or tunes, slightly adapted. Every clerk was familiar with these eight tones, and knew how to match them with texts. The method was not unlike the method that would later be used in Anglican chanting, which is in fact descended in part from the Psalm tones. Toward the beginning of each tone there is an adjustable reciting note, followed by a constant melodic cadence, on which the last few syllables are sung. As a species of plainsong, the tones for the Psalms were sung without harmony or accompaniment, whether by one voice or by many in unison. Marbeck's notation, as it stands, likewise calls for unison (or solo) singing; but if clerks were to add improvised harmony, as clerks had often done with the traditional Psalm tones,[20] the result would be a sort of proto-Anglican chant.

---

[20] Interested readers should consult a reference work on music, under *faburden*.

Service Music

Although Marbeck's music was not meant for congregations to sing, it would have been within the competence of many parish clerks. By contrast, the "cathedral music" that flourished in Elizabeth's reign and afterward demanded trained choirs. Its two main forms, anthems and "services" or service settings, have made choral performance of the daily Prayer Book offices "unique in the world of modern music; nothing quite like them exists on the continent of Europe."[21]

An anthem, in the relevant sense, is a fairly brief extra-liturgical composition for which musicologists today might use the term *motet*. There are hundreds of "cathedral anthems," written to be sung "in quires and places where they sing" after the third collect at Morning or Evening Prayer. They are usually intended for performance by a choir, sometimes with passages for solo voices; accompaniment, if any, is played on the organ, though occasionally other instruments are called for. The grandest anthems, such as Handel's *Zadok the Priest*, employ a whole orchestra.

A service, in the musical sense, could be thought of as a set of anthems, each of them a setting of one of the constant texts in Divine Service. Listed here are the texts included in what many would regard as the *ne plus ultra* of the service-music genre, the so-called *Great Service* composed toward the end of Queen Elizabeth's reign by William Byrd.[22]

for Morning Prayer:
Venite
Te Deum
Benedictus

[21] Edmund H. Fellowes, *English Cathedral Music*, 5th ed., rev. by J. A. Westrup (London: Methuen, 1969), 2.

[22] Byrd (c. 1540–1623) composed several Anglican services. Neither the date of his *Great Service* nor the occasion for which he wrote it is known.

for the Communion Service:
   responses to the Commandments (misleadingly called *Kyrie*)
   the Nicene Creed
for Evening Prayer:
   Magnificat
   Nunc dimittis

This list was and would be fairly standard. Composers of service music have almost always set the same two Evening Prayer canticles that Byrd did. For the alternatives, both of which are Psalms, there are no settings to speak of. They were evidently added to assuage the scruples of puritans who objected to using *Magnificat* and *Nunc dimittis*, but since puritans objected to choral music too, musicians have seldom taken their concerns into account. All four Morning Prayer canticles, on the other hand, have been set to music. There are fewer settings for *Benedicite*, the alternative to *Te Deum*, but Henry Purcell, among others, wrote music for it. Many sixteenth-century composers set the *Benedictus*, as Byrd did, but later the alternative Psalm *Jubilate* (which is much shorter) came to be preferred. The *Venite*, however, gradually dropped out of service settings and was sung instead to an Anglican chant as the first of the Psalms, so that what is meant by a Morning Service is most often a paired *Te Deum* and *Jubilate*.

The two items that Byrd set for Communion need some explanation. In the original Prayer Book, the service for the Lord's Supper, "commonly called the Mass," had the same texts, in English, that were most commonly included in musical settings of the Latin Mass (owc 20, 22, 29, 34). These were:[23]

---

[23] Note that *Benedictus* is used to name two quite different texts, both of which begin with the Latin word for *blessed*. In the context of the Eucharist, liturgists and musicians use *Benedictus* (more fully *Benedictus qui venit*) for part two, as it were, of the *Sanctus* hymn. In the Prayer Book, *Benedictus* (more fully *Benedictus Dominus Deus Israel*; see owc 11) always refers to the canticle after the second lesson at Morning Prayer, as it does in Cranmer's letter to King Henry.

Kyrie	Lord, have mercy upon us
Gloria in excelsis	Glory be to God on high
Credo	I believe in one God (the Nicene Creed)
Sanctus	Holy, holy, holy, Lord God of hosts, *followed by*
Benedictus (*qui venit*)	Blessed is he that cometh in the name of the Lord
Agnus Dei	O Lamb of God

All of these except the first are mentioned or implied in Cranmer's letter, quoted earlier, and Marbeck noted all of them. In 1552, however, the second version of the Book of Common Prayer drastically curtailed and rearranged Holy Communion, and with it this traditional ensemble of texts. There is no *Kyrie*, no *Benedictus qui venit* after the *Sanctus*, no *Agnus Dei*. The *Gloria in excelsis* comes at the end of the service, not the beginning. Only the Nicene Creed and the *Sanctus* itself remain where they had been.

Early Elizabethan composers set the *Sanctus* and the *Gloria* to music; there are examples in in John Day's *Mornyng and Euenyng prayer and Communion, set forthe in foure partes, to be song in churches*, published in 1565.[24] But when Communion took the abbreviated form of "table prayers," as it most often did, the *Sanctus* and the *Gloria*, which belong to the part of the service that was left out, would not be said or sung. That may explain why Byrd did not set them in his *Great Service*. He did set the *Credo* or Nicene Creed, which occurs in ante-Communion and was always used. He also set a text that is neither in the Latin Mass nor in the original Prayer Book: the responses to the Ten Commandments, which were added in 1552. These responses are not really an English *Kyrie;* some of the words are the same, but their liturgical function is quite different.

---

[24] There was an earlier version with a different title, *Certaine notes set forth in foure and three parts* . . .; see John Aplin, "The Origins of John Day's 'Certaine Notes,'" *Music and Letters* 62.3 (1981): 295–299.

As time went on, choral responses to the Commandments and settings of the Creed fell into the background, perhaps because the Prayer Book certainly assigns the former and almost certainly the latter to the congregation at large. Even a full celebration of Holy Communion was apt to be spoken, mainly if not entirely, rather than sung; and a suite of service music came to consist of four canticles: for Mattins, *Te Deum* and *Jubilate* (or perhaps *Benedictus*); for Evensong, *Magnificat* and *Nunc dimittis*.

Besides the Psalms and canticles, both Morning and Evening Prayer, sung in the cathedral manner, have as a rule included harmonized settings of the preces (the versicles "O Lord, open thou our lips," and so on), the Lesser Litany, the suffrages, and sometimes the (second) Lord's Prayer. The Apostles' Creed may be chanted on a single pitch; the three collects may be sung by the minister "after the manner of distinct reading," often with harmonized choral *Amen*s; and usually, "in quires and places where they sing, here followeth the anthem." What the anthem that follows will be, the Prayer Book does not determine in any way. Anthems are independent, optional extras, and no generalizations about them will be attempted here.

Toward the Present

Choral Mattins or Evensong, with Psalms sung in Anglican chant, canticles sung to a service setting, and an anthem added in the appointed place, has always been a comparatively rare form of common prayer. But as more and more parish churches did their best to emulate their "mothers," the cathedrals, there was less and less of an artistic and liturgical gap between cathedral music and parochial music. Antipathy on the part of some Anglicans toward any church music other than Psalm-singing faded; organs, choirs, and chanting of some sort came to be regarded almost everywhere as not just permissible but desirable; anthems and services were composed with amateur singers in mind.

These developments took different directions in practice. According to one school of thought, the highest achievement that any church could aspire to was a fully choral liturgy. To the objection that such a performance deprives the congregation of any opportunity to participate, the answer was that people in general must not expect to have a vocal role in Divine Service, any more than they ought to preach the sermon or read the prayers. Besides, even if musical excellence invites outward passivity on the part of those who only listen, it stimulates and enhances their inward devotion.

From quite another point of view, the Psalms and canticles should certainly be sung, and they should be sung as they are printed in the Prayer Book, not in metrical paraphrases; but they should be sung by everyone, not just the choir. Anglican chanting might be too difficult for most people, but plainsong would not be; led by a competent choir, ordinary congregations could learn to sing their part of the service to simple "Gregorian" music—Marbeck, for example, whose *Common praier noted* was reprinted in the nineteenth century, adapted for use with the words of the classical Book of Common Prayer.

These differing conceptions of how music could best inform Prayer Book worship shared at least one assumption, namely that Prayer Book worship on Sunday would be, as ever, Morning Prayer, followed by the Litany and the beginning of Holy Communion. As the nineteenth century went on, that assumption began to lose ground. Largely owing to Tractarian influence, the full Communion service was celebrated more and more frequently, and it was celebrated more often on its own, rather than as a coda to Morning Prayer. One way to promote its status as the main liturgical event on Sundays and feasts was to make it a sung service in its own right, like cathedral Mattins. But while there was a long tradition of choral music written for Morning and Evening Prayer, very little was available for the Communion office—even less, if liturgical items that had been dropped in 1552, such as the *Benedictus qui venit* and the *Agnus Dei*, were reintroduced, as Anglo-catholics insisted they should be. In contrast with sung Mattins and Evensong, the choral celebration of Holy Communion was "a Victorian creation: an amalgam of authorised, revived, and newly interpolated elements."[25]

The shift away from Morning Prayer toward Holy Communion continued throughout the twentieth century, which also witnessed a movement away from liturgy as something like a pageant, enacted by professionals before a silent audience, toward liturgy as a collaborative event of prayer in which congregation, choir, and clergy all take active, vocal, complementary roles. "Full, conscious participation" was the watchword of what came to be known as the Liturgical Movement, which began in Roman Catholic circles but took on an ecumenical dimension in which Anglicans were prominent. Many of the contemporary-language texts that were proposed and adopted as replacements for the "Jacobethan" prose of the classical Prayer Book were products of consultations and committees in which Anglicans and Roman Catholics collaborated with members of other liturgical churches.

Inevitably, the migration of Holy Communion from the margins to the center of Anglican worship, combined with the retirement of traditional versions of the Book of Common Prayer, brought about an eclipse of the musical forms that had been Anglican hallmarks— service music and Anglican chant. Neither of these has had much to contribute to what might be called post-Vatican II Anglicanism, for which the Eucharist—solemnly sung Mass or informal parish Communion or something in between—has come to be regarded more and more as "the principal act of worship on the Lord's Day."[26]

One tradition of cathedral music, however, is not extinct. There are still places where choral Evensong is sung in the customary way, with Coverdale's Psalms and the *Magnificat* and *Nunc dimittis*

[25] Temperley, *Music of the English Parish Church*, I: 295.
[26] The Book of Common Prayer of the American Episcopal Church (1979), 13.

worded as they were in 1549. This service, as Thomas Cranmer's biographer has remarked, is probably the most widespread use of the original Prayer Book texts in pure form. Evening Prayer is not a rite that makes overt demands. It raises few if any of the theological issues that have made the Book of Common Prayer a contentious text. It is unconducive to heart-pounding fervor. But "this Anglican performance of patterned liturgical beauty may provide a window on seriousness" and its "understated presentation of the sacred" may be "the solace of those who find other, more demonstrative, expressions of Christianity beyond their powers of assent."[27] Evensong can be an occasion for aesthetic enjoyment, for otherworldly contemplation, or both.

As such it would still be likely to have the approval of the first Queen Elizabeth, to whose stubbornness the survival of any sort of choral service owes so much. Her notion of common prayer, it will be recalled, was "to hear and read the Scriptures, to pray to almighty God by daily use of the Psalter of David, and of the ancient prayers, anthems and collects of the church, even the same which the universal church hath used, and doth yet use."[28] There is nothing other than that in Evensong. And nothing less.

[27] Diarmaid MacCulloch, introduction to the Everyman edition of the 1662 Book of Common Prayer (1999) xxiii; see also MacCulloch, *Thomas Cranmer: A Life* (New Haven, CT: Yale University Press, 1996), 629.

[28] Elizabeth to Francis Walsingham, May 1571, in Dudley Digges, *The Compleat Ambassador: or Two Treatises of the Intended Marriage of Queen Elizabeth* (London: Bedell and Collins, 1655), 99.

APPENDIX 1

Vesture

Described here are all and only those ecclesiastical garments which are or have been mentioned (or in once case implied) in the Book of Common Prayer: *alb, cope, hood, rochet, surplice, tunicle, vestment* (and *chasuble*).

Strictly speaking, the 1662 Prayer Book never refers to *liturgical* clothing at all. It does mention the **rochet**, an ankle-length tunic made of white linen, with full sleeves gathered at the wrist. Only bishops wore the rochet, but they did not wear it in church only. It was part of their dress uniform. As such it is worn by the seven bishops portrayed as "compilers of the English liturgy" in Figure 5.1. The final version of the Prayer Book orders a new bishop to wear a rochet at his consecration (OWC 646); following the examination, he is to put on "the rest of the episcopal habit" (OWC 649), which is not specified, but which probably included the *chimere*, a sleeveless coat, usually black, open in the front. The bishops in Figure 5.1 wear chimeres over their rochets.

The two Prayer Books of Edward VI refer to several other garments, all of which were at least somewhat objectionable to godly, puritan, or nonconformist protestants. Roughly speaking, there were three degrees of disapprobation. Some critics insisted that the clergy of a reformed church ought not to wear distinctive clothing of any sort. Others held that ministers ought not to wear anything that had been worn for the services of the church before its Reformation, but that it was permissible to wear the simple black gown that is worn by the six compilers in Figure 5.1 who were clergymen but not bishops. And there were also those who would rule out the costume that had been specifically prescribed for the celebration of the Mass, but not other liturgical garments, such as the surplice and perhaps the cope.

The **surplice**, like the rochet, was a long, white smock, full and loose, but with wide, open sleeves. The minister in Figure 11.7 wears a surplice with very wide sleeves indeed.[1] Before the Reformation, the surplice was worn at church services, included the Mass, but was not limited to ministers in holy orders; anyone who had a liturgical function to fulfill might wear it. In connection with the surplice, the earliest Prayer Books mention the **hood**, a cowl with a

---

[1] Over his shoulders he is presumably wearing the black scarf that was sometimes called a *tippet*. The Prayer Book never mentions this vestment, although the Canons adopted in 1604 do. The rectangular "bands" that he and all the clergymen in Figure 5.1 wear under their chins never had any specifically ecclesiastical significance.

short cape, which had become a conventional, nonfunctional badge of academic (but not ecclesiastical) rank. As such, a hood was to be worn by church dignitaries and by preachers, provided they were graduates (owc 98).

Both the rochet and the surplice seem to have evolved from the **alb**, another ankle-length white garment, which was less ample than the surplice and had narrower, ungathered sleeves. In the medieval church the alb, like the surplice, might be worn by various liturgical functionaries. It was always worn, however, by the celebrating priest at Mass and by the assisting clergy, if any. Unlike the surplice, it was tied at the waist with a narrow sash or cincture, and worn with a kind of neckerchief.

Over their albs, each of the (usually two) ministers who assisted the celebrant at a solemn Mass wore what the original Prayer Book calls a **tunicle** (owc 19), a little tunic, which was something like a tabard or an oversized t-shirt with short, wide sleeves. It was commonly made of colored silk and sometimes richly decorated. The same was true of the garment reserved for the celebrant and worn over his alb at every Mass—the **chasuble**. The shape of the chasuble varied, but it was something like a poncho or a rain cloak with an opening in the middle so that it could be put on over the wearer's head. In the Book of Common Prayer the chasuble is never named as such. By process of elimination, however, it was almost certainly the article of clothing referred to under the name of **vestment** (see Table 6.2). Today that name is used in a generic sense for any item of liturgical attire, but it is reasonable to think that in the sixteenth-century rubrics what is meant by a *vestment* is a specific ensemble, a suit of what would now be called vestments, which included a chasuble together with certain accessories. In any case, the first Prayer Book departs from medieval custom in permitting the priest at Holy Communion to wear a **cope** instead of a chasuble. Like the other items mentioned in this paragraph, the cope was often made of silk and usually decorated; in form it was a long cloak or cape, open at the front, sometimes with an ornamental hood. Like the surplice, it could be, and sometimes was, worn by persons who were neither deacons, priests, nor bishops.

Notice that from these descriptions it follows that a minister who wore a surplice and a cope for the Prayer Book's Communion office would not be wearing anything specifically associated with the Mass, or even specifically clerical.

The Anglican Communion

The name *Anglican Communion* is used for and by an international association of Christian churches, most of them entirely self-governing and independent of the others. Because its largely unwritten constitution continues to evolve, the sense in which the Communion is a unity is not easy to define. It is not itself a church, however; nor does it claim to be *the* church.

In the nineteenth century, when the English word *Anglican* came into general use,[1] its meaning was more restricted. At the time, besides the Church of England (then united with the Church of Ireland), there were protestant, episcopal churches in the United States and in Scotland, each of them related in its origins to *ecclesia Anglicana*, the English church. But neither Scottish nor American episcopalians would have called themselves Anglicans; it would have implied that they belonged to England's established church. The Church of England acknowledged these other churches as family; it had a sister in Scotland and a daughter in America; but only gradually did *Anglican* become a family name.

The Church of England also had outposts, branch offices, extensions, and offshore chaplaincies throughout the British Empire, planted there either for colonists or by missionaries or both. All these satellites were dependent in various ways on the "home church" in England. Over time, outlying congregations were organized into local dioceses, and bishops, usually English, were appointed to oversee them. In 1867 the archbishop of Canterbury invited bishops from these various ecclesiastical constituencies to meet for consultation at Lambeth Palace, his official residence in London. This gathering, which also included American bishops, was the first of what came to be known as the Lambeth Conferences. It is commonly said to have inaugurated the Anglican Communion as an institution, although no formal action was taken. The name did however begin to be used not long afterward.

For nearly a hundred years, membership in the Communion was entirely a matter of being invited by the archbishop of Canterbury to send bishops to take part in the Lambeth Conference, which was held at roughly ten-year intervals. From the first, it was stated in very definite terms that the Conference was

---

[1] See J. Robert Wright, "Anglicanism, *Ecclesia Anglicana*, and Anglican: An Essay on Terminology," in *The Study of Anglicanism*, rev. ed., ed. John E. Booty, Jonathan Knight, and Stephen Sykes (London: SPCK, 1998) 477–483.

neither an ecclesiastical synod nor a legislature. It did however issue reports and encyclical letters. Over the years, British colonies, protectorates, and dominions began to govern themselves, and as they became increasingly and then entirely independent, so too did the Anglican churches within their geographical boundaries. Today these autonomous national (in a few cases, multinational) churches are called *provinces* of the Anglican Communion; at the moment there are about forty of them.[2] Internal constitution and polity differ from province to province, as does the role of the bishop or archbishop at the head of the ecclesiastical hierarchy, who is referred to in that capacity as the primate. Some provinces have *Anglican* in their official name; others eschew it in favor of *Episcopal*; a few make no use of either term. Counting heads is difficult, but none of the other provinces is as populous as the Church of England, and some are very small by comparison.

With self-governance came the possibility of revising liturgical standards, as the Scottish church had done with its Communion office and as the American church did in 1789 when it authorized a revision of the whole Book of Common Prayer. Not long after the Church of Ireland was disestablished in 1869 it took the opportunity to adopt its own Prayer Book, which differed only a little from the Church of England's. Slowly at first, other provinces did likewise. In some parts of the world, a distinctive variant of the Book of Common Prayer has been regarded almost as a sacrament of independence, an outward and visible sign of provincial autonomy. Until the later twentieth century, however, Anglican Prayer Books were enough alike to constitute a de facto bond of unity among the churches of the Communion.

Beginning in 1958, there have been a number of structural developments—officers, organizations, networks, committees—intended to provide continuity in the intervals between meetings of the Lambeth Conference, and to promote cooperation among the Anglican churches. One of these institutions is the International Anglican Liturgical Consultation. Four "instruments of communion" are now recognized: the Conference itself, the archbishop of Canterbury, an elected Consultative Council, and a separate meeting of the primates. Whether the fissures that have threatened the unity of the Communion in the twenty-first century will dismantle it remains to be seen.

---

[2] There are also a few small "extra-provincial" churches, which belong to the Communion under the aegis of the archbishop of Canterbury, but are not part of the Church of England. A number of groups that have removed themselves from provinces of the Communion continue to regard themselves as authentically Anglican churches.

Index

engravings, printing of, 270
Epiphany, proper collect and
    readings, 47–49
epistle (liturgical epistle), 27
Eucharist, names for, 99
evangelical Anglicans, 235
Evening Prayer (Evensong), 30–32,
    60, 154, 227, 304–305
exhortation
    in the Middleburg Prayer
        Book, 151
    in *The Order of the Communion,*
        102–104
    in the Visitation office, 70
exorcism at Baptism (1549), 125

Faithorne, William, 270
fast books, 139
Fawkes, Guy, 273
feasts, moveable and
    immoveable, 46, 49
Fell, John, 282
Forms of Prayer to be Used at
    Sea, 188
Free and Candid Disquisitions,
    211, 223

Geddes, Janet (Jenny), 171
General Confession, 16, 32
General Supplication. *See* Litany
General Thanksgiving, 192–193
Geneva Bible, 142, 158, 263
Gloria in excelsis, 116, 226, 229,
    294, 301
Gloria Patri, 17, 226
Godly Prayers, 136–138, 183, 228
godparents, 65–66, 68
Golden Numbers, 55–58
gospel (liturgical gospel), 27
Great Bible, 140, 185, 257
Gregorian ("new style") calendar, 58
Gunpowder Treason,
    commemoration of, 189, 273

Hammond, Henry, 175
Hampton Court conference, 156–
    158, 181, 262
Hardy, Thomas, 34
Harrison, William, 144–146, 287
Henrietta Maria, Queen, 166
Henry VIII, King, 99, 294
Herring, Thomas, 212–214,
    226–227, 240
Holinshed, Raphael, 144
Holy Communion (the Lord's
    Supper), 12, 38, 60, 65, 74
    in the American Prayer Book,
        229–233
    ante-Communion, 25–29
    explained in Catechism, 158
    in the 1549 Prayer Book,
        104–113
    nonjurors' critique, 216–218
    revisions in 1552, 116–124
    revisions in 1662, 193–195
    Scottish Communion office,
        218–221
    in the Scottish Prayer Book, 168–170
    at the Visitation of the Sick,
        71–72, 127
holy orders (diaconate, priesthood,
    episcopate), 60–63
holydays
    feasts and days of fasting and
        abstinence, 37
    moveable, 49–53
Homilies. *See* Books of Homilies
Howell, William, 205, 228
humble access, prayer of, 102,
    117–118, 121
hymnal, 229

incipit, 17
Independence Day, American
    service for, 228
institution, words (narrative) of,
    97–98, 101, 217, 220